DAKOTA

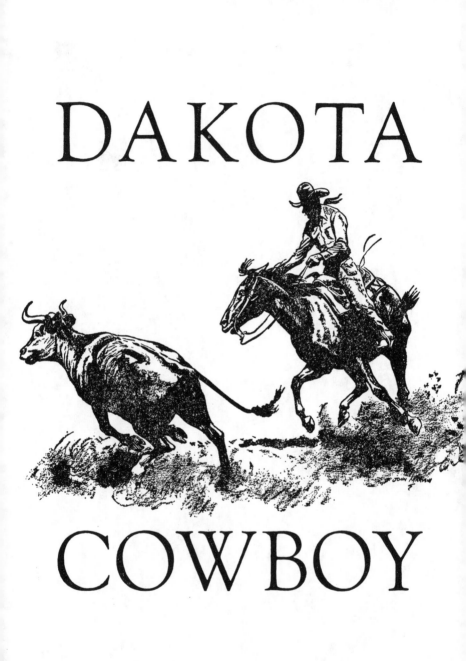

COWBOY

MY LIFE IN THE

OLD DAYS

by Ike Blasingame

ILLUSTRATED BY John Mariani

UNIVERSITY OF NEBRASKA PRESS
Lincoln and London

Copyright 1958 by Ike Blasingame
Library of Congress catalog card number 58-11667
International Standard Book Number 0-8032-0906-1
International Standard Book Number 0-8032-5015-0 pa

First Bison Book printing: 1964

*Bison Book edition reprinted from the G. P. Putnam's Sons
1958 edition by arrangement with Mrs. Ike Blasingame.*

Manufactured in the United States of America
∞

DEDICATED
TO THE CATTLEMEN AND THE COWBOYS
WITH WHOM I WORKED
—AND TO MY TIRELESS WIFE,
WHO WROTE THIS WHILE I TALKED

Preface

When the Bureau of Indian Affairs—the United States Indian Department—decided in 1903 to lease the vast domain west of the Missouri River for the Indian ward owners, it was made known that bids on individual tracts would be accepted at Washington, D.C. This chance to obtain virgin grassland at a time when many stockmen with large herds were being crowded out of pastures by the ever-increasing homesteader and small rancher was something like a glimpse into Utopia. The Matador Land and Cattle Company, a Scots syndicate guided by the canny wisdom of Murdo Mac-Kenzie, was immediately interested.

The over-all size of the Cheyenne River Sioux Indian Reservation was almost three million acres. Its northeast corner was also the southeast corner of the Standing Rock Sioux Indian Reservation, west of the Missouri. Standing Rock wasn't as large as its neighbor to the south, but its natives were also bands of Sioux, and most of their reservation was leased to white cattlemen about the same time as the Cheyenne River reserve. Here, clustered around the Cheyenne

Agency, lived most of the Indians, although families of French-Indian blood had moved back farther, where they had more room and grass and water for their livestock. There were, reportedly, three thousand heads of families throughout the reservation then.

The Milwaukee Railroad, looking forward to big business from the new land of cattle and cowboys, was keen to help the Indian Department in its campaign to bring large herds to Evarts, at the end of the rails. The transportation out and back was free of charge.

The Milwaukee held a lease on the whole north tier of townships of the Cheyenne River reservation. A six-mile-wide lane was fenced on both sides to provide a driveway for herds coming to Evarts to ship, and was known as the Strip or Trail. It was eighty miles long. The watering places on the Strip were spaced about twelve miles apart—a day's drive for a beef herd. Some of them were natural water—lakes, creeks or water holes—but the railroad built several big dams, too, so there was plenty of water even in dry times. Thousands of cattle were taken down this trail, going in or coming out to grass, and big cattle operators from far west of the reservation, too, regularly used the Strip. The thirty thousand acres bordering the Matador could be grazed by them during the several months when there were no herds occupying the Strip, which was considerable free grass.

The Milwaukee Railroad showed a sharp eye for business when they arranged for the Strip and extended the rails out to it from Selby. This spur road passed through Evarts, hugged the Missouri shore to a point just opposite Blue Blanket Island, and ended with its feet in the stockyards on the east side, connected with the ferryboat landing and pontoon bridge.

The Milwaukee was not only interested in the reservation stockmen; they sought herds for their rails from ranges as far west as the Black Hills, and the Strip was no small attraction. Freight rates were far cheaper from the east shore of the Missouri, so stockgrowers chose to come down the Strip to Evarts.

Some of the large cattle operators west of the reservation line that ran ten thousand to fifty thousand head, included the H A T outfit, owned by A. D. Marriott, using this brand in three shapes—square, round, and pointed tops. Cowboys referred to them simply as the "Hats."

The Three V's, owned by Western Ranches, Ltd., was a Clay-Robinson Company outfit managed by John Clay.

The vast Sheidley Company, of the Flying V brand, was one of the oldest cattle companies in the West.

The reservation outfits were not slighted either. The Strip touched the ranges of the Matador, the H O's to the west, and the 73. To the south of these ranges, and still a part of the reservation, were the Turkey Track, the Sword & Dagger, the Mississippi Cattle Company, and numerous large operators among the Indians, whose stock ranged in white-man leases. Some of these Indians ran a roundup wagon of their own—the Benoists, La Plants, the Narcelles, Herbert (French pronunciation *Ayebear*), the Le Beau's, and Claymore, Rouseau, Traversie, Du Pris, and many more having reservation rights. All were adjacent to the Strip and would ship from Evarts, as well as dozens of smaller owners who let the big outfits ship their stock for them.

On the north, the Standing Rock reservation, the L7's would pour thousands onto the strip; later shippers from far to the northwest would come to the Milwaukee Trail.

All of these big cattle spreads were thriving concerns. Those of the reservation all came in and stocked their leases at about the same time—an empire of cattle and cowboys in almost unbelievable proportions.

Contents

DAKOTA COWBOY

1. Spring 1904

The vanguard of the Matador left Texas and began arriving at Evarts, South Dakota, in May of 1904—and I was with them.

The Matador Land and Cattle Company—with the famous Drag V brand—operated vast Texas ranches. Our top boss, Murdo MacKenzie, leased over a half-million acres of Cheyenne River Indian reservation in South Dakota and started stocking it that year. Earlier in the spring the Matador assembled a complete range outfit—saddle horses, cowboys, roundup wagons, and the thousands of cattle that left the shipping corrals at Murdo, on the Los Alamocitas Ranch. Our immediate boss, Con McMurry, entrained with us at Murdo when we set out with the first loads of cattle. A tall, dark-eyed cowman wearing a heavy moustache, Con gave his orders in his soft-spoken way. Like the rest of us, he wore a gray Stetson hat with wide brim, good pants and boots, a vest with all its little pockets for tobacco, a pencil and a small book for jotting down things—all of it a part of our garb, topped off with a silk scarf, jacket, and leather chaps.

When I first met Con he was wagon boss at Los Alamocitas. He was one of the best cowmen I ever knew, and I
learned from him about handling cattle in a big way, about
working in a roundup and handling a beef herd.

Roy Vivian, Dan Busby, Ott Cassidy and the cook were
among the hands on the first trains, besides Con and me. For
some time I had been the bronc rider at Alamocitas, and I
went to South Dakota—in charge of the horses and mules—as
"rough-string" rider for the new setup. Frank Mitchell was
to follow us by fast train and overtake us before we reached
Dakota. He was to be manager of the Dakota spread, under
Murdo MacKenzie.

We were going to a great new range and all of us were as
keen to get on to the north as wild geese. Spring was in the
air. New grass would be rising and winter fading out as we
landed on the east Missouri shore at Evarts. Young, and with
a big, new adventure just ahead of us, we were eager for the
different life among the northern Indians who still lived on
their own domain—the San Arc, Minneconjou, Blackfeet, and
Two Kettle bands. We would still work with cattle as we always had, yet we would find life on the range west of the
Missouri strange indeed.

When the first trains of the Matador outfit pulled into the
Evarts stockyards, we unloaded them and separated the weak
or crippled cattle from the main bunch. Then we drove the
big herd to the surrounding hills where grass was good and
Con set up a guard on them. They didn't need much guarding for they were hungry, thirsty, and glad to get onto the
ground. It had been a long haul.

I was with the horses and mules and it was late afternoon.
At dark, the "night hawk," a cowboy who watches over the
remuda of saddle horses during the night, took over. His
duty was to pen the horses into a rope corral in the morning
so cowboys could rope a fresh mount for the day's work.

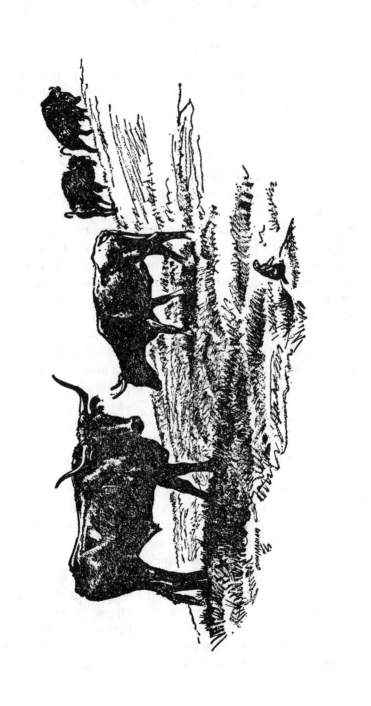

After that he ate breakfast, helped break camp, hitched the teams to the bedwagon and drove it to the next campground. After turning his teams loose at the next camp, he was free to "hit the sack" and sleep or do whatever he wanted to until he went on night hawk again.

Con put some cowboys on the cattle night guard and the rest of us returned to unload the trains of more than a thousand weary cattle still coming in. The night guards worked through the day, too; night duty was cut up into shifts, the men taking turns of two hours each during the night.

Matador cowboys usually numbered at least ten steady men, besides the night hawk, horse wrangler, and cook, and each cowboy rode a string of ten or more horses. Later on, "reps" from neighboring ranges worked with us, gathering stray stock in their outfit's brand. A "rep" was a cowboy representing other outfits, gathering cattle wearing his boss' brand and returning them to home range. These men were good brand men, could spot earmarks as well, and could be relied upon to attend to business when away from their own outfit.

Cattle mostly strayed away while "going along" with winter storms, tail to the wind, walking to keep warm. Surrounding cattlemen often had to cross Matador country with stock to reach their own pastures in those first years, or when going in to ship, so there were always cattle escaping and remaining in the Matador range. The reps gathered this stock from our roundups and drove them back to their owners. Such a drive was known as a "throw-back."

The cowboy box on the chuck wagon usually held our guns, ammunition, razors, soap, and perhaps a can of talcum powder and a comb, although some of us kept these in the little canvas "war-bag" in our bedroll, too. Each man was required to care for his own bed, roll it neat and tight, and tie it securely. It was supposed to be left close to the bedwagon so the men could throw it aboard when they got ready to load up, helping the cook move camp. A man who left his bed rolled and tied in a sloppy way was reprimanded, and if he didn't heed, he would likely find his bed left behind.

The cookstove was hauled along behind the chuck wagon in a little cart—"stove cart," we called it. It was mounted on two wheels, had a short tongue anchored to the wagon reach by a stout chain. The chain, with a big hook in one end, went around the stove, cart and all, and when pulled tight and bolted to the wagon there was no chance to lose it. The stove was the first thing unloaded at the new camp and the cart pushed out of the way. A steel ring set in the front of the cooktent fitted over a heavy rod bolted to the back of the grub box on the wagon. When this was in place and the rest of the tent set up with ridgepole and tent pegs, the cook's department was protected from the weather. The grub box, built across the back of the wagon, was a large affair. Its door dropped forward when unhooked, providing a stout table for the cook to work on.

A flat-sided coffee grinder was bolted to the side of the wagon, handy to reach, for in those days our coffee was made from freshly ground coffee beans. Most all outfits used the famous Arbuckle brand. It came in huge burlap bags holding one hundred one-pound packages of whole beans which were ground in the mill as needed. I remember the stick of candy in each package, as well as a coupon, good for dozens of premiums—handkerchiefs, lace curtains, shears, Torrey razors, and jewelry of all descriptions, including wedding rings.

We had arrived in Evarts short of men, so Con hired several. Charley Root, whom Con had known in Texas; Clem Decker, who had been in Dakota working for the Benoists (a French name pronounced *Ben-Way*); a Russian fellow to wrangle horses—we called him "Wrang." Some months later, Bill Rickles—later sheriff of Dewey County—Charley Berry, and a man named Perkins—known as "Perk"—came to Dakota as Matador cowboys.

Perk was a noisy guy who couldn't keep his mouth closed for long at a time, and he gave us many a laugh. Once, when Murdo MacKenzie came to our wagon, he had a new rifle which he was eager to try out. We had been making a roundup and out on the hill not far from the wagon the cowboys were holding the day herd. Unthinkingly, Murdo got his rifle, cut down on a target out in the opposite direction from the herd and banged away. The rifle sounded like a cannon and the herd jumped and ran, although it wasn't bad and they were soon halted. But not before the ever-sharp Perk roared: *"What goddam fool did that?"* When Perk found it was Murdo who had fired the shot, he faded from the cooktent, mortified over his blunder. Most of us present had sudden business with our horses or saddles, or anything else which would give us a chance to laugh unseen by MacKenzie, who was also embarrassed by his mistake. Perk never lived down that remark.

The first few days before we got organized, we guarded the stock, and ate our meals in the little two-story hotel in Evarts run by Joe Green, a former Hash Knife cowboy from Texas. He had married a widow with two young daughters, Rose and Violet Darling. We cowpunchers spotted these little darlings the first thing and lost little time horning each other for their smiles.

Con didn't waste much time on the east side of the Missouri. He loaded us on board the ferryboat—the roundup wagons, the mules, our cook, Walker Krump, a few of us cowboys with our bedrolls—and we landed on the Strip, west of the Missouri.

Krump always drove the mules. Although he was a short-order cook from Amarillo, Texas, he had never cooked out in the open, never driven a team—much less two spans of mules to a chuck wagon in rough country. But he picked it up quick, and his grub was excellent—one thing which will keep hard-riding cowboys contented. Walker could move camp, set up his stove and tent and handle thirty hungry men easily. He would ask how you liked your eggs when you came in to wash up, and you would have them that way. His five-gallon cans of doughnuts, his pies (made ten or twelve at a time), sour-dough bread, and biscuits were delicious. He wasn't cranky or stingy with them, either. If a man wanted an extra wedge of pie or a few more biscuits, there was no holler from Krump.

Not only did the cowboys like Krump's cooking, but the old "camp rustlers" and the mules did, too. If they were close, they sniffed the breeze every time a pan of bread came out of the oven, and they gathered round Krump like a flock of loot-hunting magpies. The cowboys themselves spoiled these horses—old pets, night horses, or favorite roping horses —by saving bits of piecrust or a biscuit for them, and soon the horses learned where these prizes came from. They vied with one another for what favors they might garner from the cook, but of all these robbers, the mules were the worst. Once they ambled up, following the fresh pie smell drifting down breeze, and while Krump was sleeping they located the goodies and proceeded to eat them. Krump awoke in time to save a hunk out of each pie, but what he said to the mules and any person owning them is unprintable. He lambasted them out of camp with everything he could lay hands on but made few direct hits. They all ran, excepting old Pete. When we cowboys rode up, Pete was out a little ways from the tent, dodging everything thrown his way, but kicking up as high as he could, angry that he had things thrown at him.

The mules and the horses weren't the only things that gave Krump trouble. He was naturally a clean man, kept dish towels and the face towels the men used washed up. He'd spread his "wash" out on the grass and low bushes to dry in the sun. Con had an old bird dog, Jack, that he thought the world of. He stayed with the wagon and went along to the different campgrounds. Old Jack had a great liking to lay on Krump's clean wash, and Krump knew that Con wouldn't stand for anyone to fight his old pet. As the days passed, the cowboys noted that Jack ceased to bed down on the towels; in fact, he didn't flop on anything but Con's bed or the ground. No one ever knew what system Krump used to convince Jack that towels were entirely unsafe. He didn't beat the old dog, or use other visible means of punishment. Krump outsmarted Jack some other way. There was a lot of speculation, and although Krump kept his own council, it was suspected that a few drops of water, just hot enough to sting Jack's hide, judiciously flipped from a distance and landing on his tail end just after he had nicely settled himself on a towel, tipped off the dog to stay away from them.

Besides the chuck wagon, there was the bedwagon, pulled by Bull and Baldy. In case of wet weather and heavy mud underfoot, another team was hooked on to lighten the load.

Bull was a temperamental cuss and often displayed anger. He would sit down on his hunkers like a dog, refusing to get up or to work. He had been bought from a man named Bull —perhaps that is where he got his name. But because he sat down and refused to be driven, the cowboys called him Ol' Sitting Bull. After a temper fit, Bull would go along for quite a while before having another one.

Our bedwagon hauled two tents made of extra-heavy canvas. The extra-large seams were threaded with heavy rope which extended continuously from tent pegs to side wall, then up and over the ridge and down the opposite roof to the side wall, and thence out to the pegs on that side—the whole of it an almost indestructible 250-pound tent. The cook's tent was always with us, but in mild weather the sleeping tent was left at the ranch. Our bedding was rolled in heavy tarpaulins which withstood considerable rainy weather before wetting through. Rolled tight and buckled securely with the straps, it shed water like a duck, and when spread out for sleeping on the ground with the tarp tucked in all around, leaving a generous length for a flap over the head, a cowboy was well protected through a night storm. Most of us selected a place to sleep which was on rather high ground, even ditching around our bed a little if a dark, stormy night loomed ahead and we had to put out our bed before going on night guard. All cowboys got a share of that unpleasant duty, but our only real discomfort was in having to get out of a warm bed to help hold a herd with big notions of stampeding, and often enough they did run on a black night when lightning and crashing thunder of a rain- or hailstorm was beating down on us.

With Walker Krump and the wagons camped out on the west side of the Missouri, we gradually moved all of our livestock over as they came in. The thousands of cattle crossing over this wide stream, coming in from the south to graze, thin and weak, had to cross by ferry when the river was rolling high from spring rains and melting snow.

The ferry was a barge built like a floating stockyards, each pen holding from twenty to forty cattle, depending on age and condition. Each pen had a gate to close off the stock from those in the next one. This kept them from crowding and pushing all to one side, possibly capsizing the boat. A ferry could handle up to five hundred head. The captain's tower was penned off, too.

These river men knew every current and sandbar in the river and could be depended on to pilot the ferry safely across even when the Indians' rain god took charge of the skies and the river rolled high, muddy, and debris-laden.

What a sight the fabled Missouri river was to us—this longest and unruliest river of the nation, already muddy and rushing along on its 2465-mile journey to empty into the

Mississippi ten miles above St. Louis. It begins its long run four thousand feet above sea level in a beautiful Montana valley. Three sparkling-clear rivers, the Madison, Gallatin, and Jefferson, flowing down from the Continental Divide northwest of Yellowstone National Park, come together at Three Forks to form it. After it tumbles, foamy and white-capped, through "Gates of the Mountains," the Missouri starts gathering the waters of the Teton, Marias, the Mussel-shell, and the Milk River, with three prongs heading in Canada.

It is not until it nears the North Dakota line that the Missouri becomes the Big Muddy. Here, the Yellowstone and its tributaries and the Tongue, Greybull, Shoshone, the Big and Little Big Horn, and Powder rivers dump their great loads of silt into it. Most of it is gathered from the brown Wyoming plains, but as the big stream sweeps on, it picks up the Little Missouri, Knife, Heart, Cannonball, and Grand rivers, each with its contribution of soil—until it rolls past Evarts, above its South Dakota tributaries, the Moreau and Cheyenne, the Bad and the White rivers in turbulent, mighty anxiety which swept away whatever dared to challenge its course.

The great river was a part of our lives in western Dakota. It divides the state almost exactly in half. Out in the west-of-the-river country was cowboy land—Indians, cattle, wolves, coyotes, wildcats, beaver, and rattlesnakes—wild and some-what desolate, but country a cowboy loves. And for a few more years it was to resound to cowboy shouts and bawling cattle.

2. Filling the Range

The three thousand head of cattle that had arrived in South Dakota with us were the first herd we drove out through the Strip to turn loose in the west end of the new pasture—though we didn't move them all at one time.

Con McMurry used a map to scout out the unfamiliar terrain ahead of us, for none of us knew where we were. Every road and trail was strange. The creeks, landmarks and divides, the rivers, watering places, hills and prominent buttes had to be located and made known to us cowboys. The buttes, tall hills or little mountains rearing up suddenly out of the prairie, made a strange contrast in this level country.

Most of the streams flowed into the Moreau and were easier identified because they were usually named for the Indian or Frenchman living at the mouth of them. Twin Butte creek was named for the double buttes where it headed; Dog Buttes, from an Indian legend. Patched Skin Buttes had a "patched" look and character when seen from a distance. Gray Buttes was hidden in a grayish haze. Eagle Butte was where the Indians trapped eagles. Coffee Buttes

was named for an old campground. Virgin Creek, named for the three famous virgins who camped there. The highest buttes, such as Twin and Dog Buttes, had great tall rock towers atop them, built by the Indians to mark the springs found at their bases. These "water monuments" could be seen for miles, a welcome sight to those in search of water.

There were no bridges across the creeks, so we had to find suitable places and dig out passable roads for the roundup wagons to cross. These places would be permanent, for range work would require using them often.

We turned the first herds loose on the Little Moreau, near the west end of Matador range. Here the beaver had dammed the stream, holding the water in check. Grass was good, and there was a heavy stand of timber—cottonwood, ash, elm, and many plum, chokecherry, and Juneberry thickets lined the river. The air was heavy with the fragrance of the fruit blossoms and millions of wild-rose blooms just bursting out. The Little Moreau joined the Moreau about nine miles downstream near the Indian subagency of White Horse, a trading post that got its name from Chief White Horse, whose band was located near there. Years before, the Indian Department had built four two-story frame houses, one for each chief in that end of the reserve. Chief White Horse got one, but it was cold and drafty and seldom used; he preferred his tepee. But the building was there, still in good repair.

It was while we were bringing the yearlings out to the Little Moreau that an amusing incident occurred. We were having considerable difficulty with these tired, car-sore yearlings to keep them going. They would move as long as a man was right behind them, but when left alone for any time, they slowed to a stop to eat or to lie down. Once down, they would not get up without a lot of prodding. We would ride to them, scare them along, but the whole drive had slowed

almost to a standstill, which even the plentiful cowboy cuss-
words couldn't budge.

We knew Con wouldn't stand for any rough treatment of
the yearlings. He was an excellent cowman and he knew that
patience and steady attention to our business would eventually get these little critters where he wanted them—they
would "locate" and remain in that region until mature and
ready to fatten in the shipping pasture. So no matter how
we were irked, we didn't chouse the stock unless Con was
out of sight.

Everything was as strange to the yearlings as it was to us.
For one thing, in Texas these cattle had always watered out
of steel tanks at tall windmills, and the long blue water holes
of Dakota looked just like shallow little Texas lakes after a
rain. Accordingly, they stepped confidently into them, expecting to wade across, but instead, they dropped out of
sight. This amused the cowboys and before long we were
heading some of them toward every water hole we passed,
just to see them duck themselves. But range boss McMurry
soon caught onto this, after he saw a few wet ones, and he
strictly ordered us not to do it, and not to "yell or spook the
yearlings in any way."

"Handle them easy. Don't stampede them into the water
or scare them at all," Con said. Then he rode on again in the
lead, to explore, leaving us with a herd that was growing
harder to move by the minute.

With Con out of sight, we resorted to yelling, but it did no
good. So we hunted up any sort of "spooker" we could find.
As we crossed over an old campground, some of us found old
cans which we filled with little rocks, but Dave Carpenter
came across a real find. It was an old coffeepot. When filled
with rocks and rattled, it made more noise than all the others
put together.

Dave was riding a big, snorty gray horse raised in Colorado
and branded a Drag Y. I never knew why Dave called him

San Diego. If this horse ever saw anything in the distance, perhaps only a rider coming along alone or an antelope bounding off a ridge, he would stop in his tracks, throw up his head, stare wildly, and snort like a wild mustang.

Dave kept rattling his worn-out coffeepot full of rocks, ably assisted by the rest of us, and it certainly put life into the herd. They were afraid of the racket and San Diego didn't like it any more than the yearlings did. Time and again he rolled an eye back to watch it—and then we spotted Con riding out of a little clump of ash, coming our way.

All of us who saw Con dropped our spookers right then, but Dave didn't see him in time to drop his coffeepot. So he held it down on the "off" side of his leg, waiting for Con to look in the opposite direction so he could drop it in the tall grass. It had been Dave who had agreed loudly and emphatically with Con that morning that spooking the yearlings was very bad business indeed, so he had to rid himself of his rattle without being caught.

Dave watched Con, and San Diego watched the coffeepot dangling from Dave's hand. When Con finally moved on, Dave leaned over to easy-drop his noisemaker into the heavy forage. *Bang!* Before the pot could touch grass, San Diego caught it in mid-air with a hind foot, kicked it thirty feet high and snorted to high heaven. Dave stood convicted of his deed, which tickled all of us immensely. Even Con looked back and grinned faintly.

As we lingered on the Little Moreau, it was inevitable that we should come across another landmark as well known as the old beaver dam. It was a badland butte which stuck up out of a gumbo flat—not tall, as compared to the nearby Twin Buttes, but steep and straight up on three sides. The fourth side had slope enough to allow a horse to climb it to the heap of boulders on the summit. Known to all the natives as Rattlesnake Butte, it was home to thousands of the dangerous reptiles, and we soon learned its history.

Up on top, the big rock ledges jutted out of the earth in a jumbled sort of way, and under them, hollowed out from centuries of use, were great holes slanting down into crevices of the old snake den. The oldest Indians claimed this to be the largest rattlesnake den they had seen anywhere in the west-river country. In later years, when I owned it, I learned that the snakes desert the den in summer, except for a few old rusty-backs too old or lazy to crawl away. But when fall approached, the rattlers came in from everywhere, crawling miles to the hibernation den. They were weather-wise, for by September fifteenth, cold and frosty nights arrived; flying snow soon after would doom a snake and they seemed to know it.

At the den, they spent every sunny day until well into October lying in the sheltered holes at the den entrance. Twisting and winding about each other, they formed great rolls, not for warmth but to conserve body moisture. Thousands of rattlers were there—big ones, little ones, dull and oddly unmindful of an intruder, in the late fall.

Strangely, at this time, many snakes of an entirely different species denned with the rattlers with no apparent unfriendliness. A foul, musty odor surrounds the den when many snakes are present. Once strange snakes absorb that odor, they are safe from attack.

Rarely can one ride a horse close enough to a den to watch them; he will stampede at the first whiff or rattle. But I owned a wise old horse named Gumbo. I could ride him to the den and he would allow me to shoot off his back into the rolls of snakes. He stood perfectly still and I killed hundreds of them that way.

Once, long after I first saw this den, I piloted a span of mules hitched to a light wagon and, with my brother Frank, drove up the sloping side of the hill, taking a party from

Pierre—Judge Gaffey, Lew Stephens, Glen Martin, two men stenographers, and Bert Moore, the Indian trader from White Horse. We got close enough to the den so they could empty their guns again and again into the huge rolls of rattlers. I believe that few of the rattlers sunning themselves that fall day survived. After such attacks as this, there appeared to be fewer rattlers, although the den will forever be home to countless snakes. I doubt if any of us there that day ever forgot it.

Our first regular work was a big general roundup and tally of the whole range, recording brands and ownership of all livestock on the lease. These were predominantly Indian stock. One condition of the Matador agreement with the Indians and the U.S. Bureau of Indian Affairs was that each Indian be allowed to run one hundred head of stock on Matador range, free of charge, but must pay a fee of a dollar a head per year for all numbers above one hundred. This was considerably less than white owners paid. The Matadors were to handle all Indian cattle as they did their own, and in the same manner as they did cattle pastured with them by white owners. They were to gather what should be shipped to market, or those which needed winter feeding. Not many Indians on Matador lease owned more than one hundred head. The big owners, La Plant, Herbert, Narcelle, Du Pris, Claymore, and others, were on neighboring leases so that their cattle, other than as strayed stock, were of no concern to the Matador.

In our general tally work, only small regions at a time were rounded up as we recorded the stock. Steers of certain brands and age were cut from roundups and held under herd until we got near the shipping pasture, where they were put until fall beef roundup time. After we were through with each little roundup, the stock were turned loose right where they were, on home ground, and we would move on to other parts until we completed the entire tally of everything in Matador range. Horse brands, ownership, and numbers were also recorded.

Before the Matador had secured the Dakota lease, they had pastured many steers with the Three V's, out near Belle Fourche, and a remnant still remained in this range in the spring of 1904. In the first big roundup that year, the Three V cowboys found these Drag V steers, three to five years old. They brought them down the Strip and put them through a gate into the Matador's pasture. Naturally, they hung along the west fence, wanting to go back to familiar haunts, but we found them in our tally work and took them to the shipping pasture.

During the first years of the Dakota lease, it was stocked quite heavily. All through 1904 cattle kept arriving at Evarts and we would bring them out to grass. Besides our own five thousand to twenty thousand cattle, the Matador pastured twenty-seven thousand steers in three brands—nine thousand Three V's, nine thousand Mill Irons, and nine thousand Three C's.

Among the men who had come in the previous year to look at the new range was James Coburn, a Scots banker from Kansas City, manager of the Hansford Land and Cattle company, which owned the Turkey Track ranch on the Pecos river south of Artesia, New Mexico. They branded a turkey track on the left side.

Mr. Coburn, cautious and not too enthusiastic, couldn't come to a decision regarding a lease on this reserve, but Murdo MacKenzie decided for the Matador to lease the entire east half of the reservation, which extended along the Missouri from the Cheyenne River to the Standing Rock line, an almost untouched world of wild, fresh forage about forty-eight miles square.

Suddenly a drouth hit New Mexico, bringing extremely

poor cattle to Mr. Coburn's Turkey Track operations. With no apparent end to the dry spell, he bethought himself of the grassy land far to the north. By then he had hired Captain Burton C. Mossman as foreman for the New Mexico ranch.

Coburn regretted his failure to secure a part of the northern range he had been offered by the Indian Department. Hastily he met with the Matador management, arranged for some of the Cheyenne reservation range, and sent his new foreman north to Evarts to meet with Murdo MacKenzie. Mossman was to look at the new range, agree as to the boundary and decide what was to be done before stocking it.

The range-wise MacKenzie had anticipated other stockmen searching for grass, and while the Matador did not intend using all of this reservation lease (having also leased a huge block of good grassland in Canada), they deemed it wise to pick their neighboring cattlemen in a deal of this size.

Long before young Cap Mossman arrived at Evarts, MacKenzie knew that the Matador would keep the northern half of the range. There his pasture would border the Missouri and shipments of fat cattle would need only to be rounded up and driven the short distance to the shipping corrals on the west bank of the river, opposite the rails.

The whole Matador range could be divided by a fence. The northern half carried a fine growth of wheat grass all over it, a veritable sea of grass. Watering places and winter protection were very good. The big stream, the Moreau, had its many tributaries—North Mouth, Short White Man, Pretty Bear, War Bonnet, Black Chicken, Le Beau, Hoksila [Boy], Black Pine, Beaver, Laundreaux, Ducheneaux, Ducharm, Virgin, Hand Boy, Veo, Swan, Jewett, and White Horse creeks, all of them big, with their own tributaries, too. The Little Moreau, the Cottonwood, and Goose and Powell creeks, with rough grassy regions along the entire course, flowed from west to east through the north half of Matador range, to join the Missouri ten miles below the present site of Mobridge, South Dakota.

This was the way Cap Mossman of the Hansford Company found things when he reached Evarts and looked over the range—as outlined for him by MacKenzie. But it looked good to Cap. After the dry Turkey Track range and dying stock in New Mexico, it must have looked heavenly. He was happy to have the blocks of land the Matador didn't want. Before the two men parted, they had agreed on the dividing line between the two ranges. So the Turkey Track range came into being. Occasional gates in the long fence built between them would provide a way from one range to the other, for it was established from the start that the Turkey Track would have to cross other ranges to get to the Strip and to Evarts to ship.

When the four-wire fences between the Turkey Tracks and Matador ranges and between the Matador and H O's ranges were completed by contractors from Gettysburg, South Dakota, Frank Mitchell, our ranch manager, was notified it was time to "pay off." But Mr. Mitchell decided to investigate how well the fence had been finished, so he came out to the wagon and asked Con to send me to look it over.

I rode the entire length of this new fence and found place after place where the wires across the ravines, the draws, the cutbank places, had not been weighted or lowered in any way. They stretched tight as a fiddle-string ten to fifteen feet above the ground. A whole herd of cattle could be driven back and forth at will, or cattle could wander wherever they wished, for there was nothing to check them. I reported back to Mr. Mitchell, and when he learned the condition of the fence he refused to pay for it until it was properly completed. The contractors were extremely angry and denied that they had left the fence in such shape. But eventually, unable to budge Mitchell, the contractor investigated, found the report to be true and fixed the fence as it should have been. Then Mr. Mitchell paid for the work.

As pasture steers aged and fattened, they went to market, but each spring saw replacements arrive in like number, to be matured to marketable age. There were also three thousand T X and X T steers ranging with Matador stock, which I think Tom and Hugh Chittick were interested in. With all these cattle bringing five dollars apiece for a two-year grazing period, or three dollars for one year, the Matador was able to pay all expenses—the lease of three cents per acre, equipment, fencing, horses purchased, and the cowboy wages and then have a balance left.

One day in late July we got word from Frank Mitchell to come to Evarts to receive a thousand steers that David Bloomfield, Three V's assistant manager, had bought and was shipping from Texas to Matador pasture in Dakota. We broke camp hurriedly, since the message arrived late. Bloomfield had sent the Three V branding irons on ahead with the steers, intending to catch up to the slow freight by boarding a fast passenger train.

At that time scabies, a very contagious itch of the skin caused by a parasite, was rampant on many southern ranges. It was unlawful to ship cattle from these areas without first running them through a dipping vat to kill the pest before shipping the animals. After they reached South Dakota, the Indian Department would not allow them to go to the clean range without another dipping after their arrival in Evarts.

There were big dipping vats at both Evarts and Le Beau. The two at Evarts were 150 feet and 80 feet long, respectively. Weaker cattle went through the short vat, for they hadn't the strength to withstand the long hot swim in the longer vat. The veterinarians used lime and sulphur in hot water, which turned the stock a bluish yellow for a few days. Or they used Black Leaf 40, a nicotine solution made from tobacco, in hot water, held at body heat. Thermometers were used to keep the dip at the proper heat, but it was uncomfortably hot to the hand, and the fumes were sickening. It often splashed into the men's faces, almost overcoming them.

Cattle died in the deep vats; they would get pushed or trampled under and couldn't get up again for cattle on top of them. Sometimes in a busy place like Evarts, where hundreds of cattle went through the vats in a day, carcasses got so numerous in the bottom that we had to stop to clean them out before others could be ducked under far enough to insure complete coverage.

The cattle were forced off a steel slide into the dip; their first leap generally carried them to the bottom, a complete "duck." But men stood beside the vat above the cattle and, using an S-shaped hook, ducked every one of them under several times on the way across. The S hooks were made so that the S lay lengthwise on a steel rod. The curve pointing down hooked a steer's neck to push his head under, for they naturally held their heads as high as possible while swimming across. The up-curve of the S could be used to hook under and lift the animal's head from the dip so he could get his breath.

Indian Department men were always on hand to see that cattle didn't slip into the reservation without dipping, so the usual procedure at Evarts was: branding if necessary, then dipping, after which they were driven down a plank lane to reach the ferry which would take them over to the reservation range.

Bloomfield's contract with the railroad included shipping to Evarts and branding the steers there, where good "squeeze chutes" were available; then dipping and crossing them over to the Matador cowboys on the west side. The squeeze chutes were narrow metal and wood contraptions, wide enough for animals to stand while being branded. Lever controls held them snugly.

When he arrived, several hours late, the branding had already started. The stockyards men at Evarts had gathered a mixed crew of cowboys in town to stamp on the Three V's. On the east side of the Missouri, whisky was plentiful and easily obtained. As the branding progressed, more and more whisky reached the yards until the Three V's, which belonged all in a row on the left side, fell into many patterns. Some were upside down, some slanted one way, or two ways, or any way. Some steers carried four V's; some were branded on the shoulder, some on the hip, and some just any place the iron happened to hit. It was a strange and disgusting sight that Bloomfield found when he got there. He was extremely wrathy. He blistered the men in a most scathing way and immediately stopped the branding.

"We shall br-r-and over on the west side," he said, rolling his *r*'s in his rich Scots accent. "We shall continue br-r-anding over there, I say," he repeated. A more angry Scot would be hard to find. He was well aware that whisky was the cause of the trouble and he also knew it was not permitted on the west side of the river, so he rushed the cattle over to the Matador cowboys. But before that, as the cattle began coming over to us bearing such ridiculous marks, Con had us cut them out and re-do the bungled job as best we could. Finally, we finished the branding of the cattle Bloomfield sent over to us and took them right on out to the back pasture.

When our range was filled, the Matador pastured about sixty thousand cattle. The Indians living mostly along the streams all had some livestock, but in general the whole range was nearly as primitive as it ever had been. The great explorers Lewis and Clark had reached this region a scant hundred years earlier. The nation knew little of this vast expanse of grassland prior to Nicollet and Frémont expeditions sixty-five years before. After the big Sioux reserve was established in 1869, few white men entered the domain. Not many white men lived there in 1904 unless employed by the Indian department or married into the tribe. If a Frenchman, or any other man of white blood, married a woman of Indian blood with her Indian rights on the reservation, she was regarded head of the family. If a white woman married a man having Indian blood, he was head of the family. If both man and wife were of Indian blood, he was head of the family.

Most of the families had hewn big cottonwood logs and built houses and barns. The cracks between the logs were daubed full of gumbo mud; the roofs were covered with dirt, too, with a gray gumbo color that blended well with the surrounding country. These buildings, with their pole corrals, were comfortably cool in summer and warm in winter.

It was a wild, raw country occupied by Sioux Indians just barely reconciled to staying in one place, regretfully releasing their free-roaming habits, learning to hew cottonwood logs for homes along the rivers. Dakotas, Friends, Allies, they had always called themselves, but other tribes in the long-ago knew them as a fierce tribe, warlike and aggressive, taking what they wanted with ruthless force.

The Indian women still clung to the culture of their ancestors—an art which is nearly lost now—making wonderful beadwork and tanning hides as they had in the past. They shouldered heavy burdens as they always had, but were gradually replacing Indian things for clothing and articles like white people used—calico, shawls, thread, food—where formerly they had made everything that they or their families used from the skins or other parts of the animal. They depended on flinty rocks for knives and implements. The buck slid into the new order of things much easier. His hunting days were about over. A shirt, pants, a blanket, and a white man's hat topped off his personal appearance. He was willing enough, in most cases, to allow the white men to handle his affairs.

The half-breeds, taught by the old Frenchmen, were the

ones who questioned much of the administration of their business. But on the whole, the Indians on the Cheyenne River and Standing Rock reservations were friendly, cooperative, progressive, and satisfied with their lot. They were bothered little by hardships, for they knew little else. So we found the Indian life almost as it had been for ages. The few roads were mere Indian trails from one camp to another, for they traveled about mostly in the old way—on horseback or on foot—although by then the Indian Department had issued light rigs called "squaw wagons" to the heads of families and they had harness-broken a few ponies to pull them. But we found that only logs and tree limbs bridged the reservation creeks and the big river crossings were rocky fords that could be used only when streams were running low.

The splendid range was a wild scatterment of little parks, long draws which were stirrup-high in fine forage; wild plums, chokecherry, Juneberry, and buffalo berry thickets bore edible fruit as well as provided shade and shelter. There was water everywhere—deep water holes and running streams, pure and clean, excepting in time of flood.

In this environment, the Matador cowboy worked daily in roundups or on cattle drives, bronc riding, and an occasional fling at hell-raising in the more-or-less "bright spots" to be found in such an isolated region. Now and then, we went to some all-Indian gathering which often proved pleasant, good fun. But in general, we had little time on our hands. Up before dawn, we were busy during every daylight hour in summer, with a few hours' night guard thrown in for good measure—which kept most of us from wondering what to do with our time.

And so we swept through the first summer of the new Dakota range. Spring and summer were extremely busy with so many cattle arriving and then, drifting into the fall roundups, the year slipped away so fast we scarcely realized it.

The pontoon bridge was used in the fall during shipping time, when the river was low. It was built on boats set side by side, with the current, and held together by heavy planks spiked over and between them, all of it anchored to the stream bed by heavy cables. To finish the bridge, a heavy plank railing was built along both edges to keep stock from being crowded over the side of the bridge and into the water.

When a herd was ready to cross over from the corrals on the west shore, a cowboy took the lead, riding his horse out onto the pontoon and the cattle followed. When twenty of the animals got out on the gently swaying walk, someone shouted "Cowboy!" Then another rider would cut into a place just behind the first twenty, and so on, until the pontoon was full clear across the river. Each man carried a stout stick to check the twenty steers following directly behind him, to keep them from crowding too close to the others on the trip across. They looked like a long, colorful ribbon moving on with the gentle swaying of the boats as the river rippled past them.

On the east bank they entered a long, fourteen-foot-wide lane made of snow fences eight feet high, which led to the shipping corrals. Ten loading chutes led up to stock car level from these corrals, so that ten cars could be spotted at one time, and loading continued uninterrupted. Cattle were prodded into the "crowd" pens and through a lane to the chutes. A trainload of four hundred head could be loaded in about an hour. An outfit shipping a herd of twelve hundred head shipped a trainload a day, thus arriving at the market on three successive days, in that way perhaps taking advantage of any price fluctuations. Also, by being allowed but one trainload a day, it gave other shippers the same chance to share in the better prices. It was said that on the three days each week during beef shipping time in fall that a trainload of beef left the Evarts stockyards every hour, establishing this little frontier cow town—only a lost ghost town now—the reputation of being one of the greatest cattle-shipping points in the United States.

3. The Indians

Frank Mitchell established the first Matador range headquarters by leasing an abandoned Indian place adjoining Bull Marshall's place on the west. The old buildings had fallen into disrepair, but they served for a while. The extra cowboys and Con McMurry, the roundup wagons, and the mules wintered there in 1904–5.

Throughout the Matador range, winters camps were established at advantageous sites on the range where two men "batching" together in each camp were to look after the cattle. We were to keep water holes chopped through the ice so stock could drink and we were to watch for wolf depredations among the cattle. It was near the mouth of the Moreau where Ott Cassidy and I were to spend our first winter. Scattered over the reservations were other old, abandoned Indian buildings strictly avoided by the Indians themselves. Some of their band had died in each of these places. You couldn't get them to tell you just why they left or what it was they feared, other than at some time some strange, unexplainable mystery had occurred there, and that was reason enough to stay out!

Ott and I were camping in a supposedly haunted house like this, and Indians watching us settle for the winter warned: "Unhappy spirit not want you! He live there!" I was to remember later how this amused us and we chuckled about their superstitious belief.

The old house we lived in stood upon a bench somewhat above the river bottom, alone and considerably higher than the tree-lined river course twisting into a sharp bend five hundred yards downstream, all of it weed-grown and unused when we got there. Our four winter horses were sharp-shod and grain-fed, and we rode over the region assigned to us most of our time. We would breakfast by lamplight on the short winter days and hardly reach camp again, chores done and horses stabled, before sundown.

As the weeks passed, the weather grew colder, snow fell regularly, but cattle foraged the windswept hills, creeks, and river bottoms, and wintered well enough. There were a few storms, and this being my first winter in Dakota I thought it was really cold. But with warm clothing, and being a youth, I didn't mind it much.

When we would get in from our work in late afternoon, hungry as young wolves, whoever got to camp first cooked food enough for us both. If I was alone, I'd fill up good, then flop on my bunk for a short nap. And that is just what I was do-ing on the chilly winter day when old Crow Eagle slipped into our camp. When I awoke, startled, I already had one foot on the warpath, and I "dug up the hatchet" then and there.

The real cause of the disturbance was something which couldn't happen often in a lifetime, if at all. When we find ourselves sunk in a strange world, halfway between wide-awakeness and deep sleep, the mind, conscious of all that is happening, is yet unable to break away from sleep which pulls so heavily to complete alertness. And that is how it was with me the day old Crow Eagle slipped into our house and nearly scared me to death.

All up and down the streams were camps where Indians lived. They watched us curiously whenever we rode near them and I know I kept an eye on them, too. Even in those days of reservation life, some of the older Indians had not yet lost their yearning for just one more scalping spree—to just once more dangle bloody white man's hair as a warrior trophy. Although they were peaceful and friendly then, probably my subconscious mind was still clinging to the days when it was different.

I had made a long ride out over the river breaks and since the day was almost done when I cleared away my dishes after eating, I removed my six-shooter, which we all wore those days, and laid it on the table beside my bunk while I slept. Ever since we had camped there, Ott and I had given the lower end of beef shanks, usually with a lot of meat on them, to our Indian neighbor, Crow Eagle, who always seemed happy to get them.

This particular day, the old fellow saw me ride in, waited awhile, then ambled over to get his handout. By then I was in that half-awake stage when I heard him come into the kitchen, shuffling here and there. The soft pad of his moccasins was as plain as if I were up on my feet looking at him. I knew he was gatherings things up. I heard him distinctly when he entered the room where I was; knew he picked up my six-shooter from the table, handled it for several minutes and put it down again. The whole experience was as spooky as a wild nightmare from which I couldn't awaken, try as I might!

When Crow Eagle went out the kitchen door, my whole being made a fierce effort to arouse. I awoke suddenly and in time to see the old Indian going along the trail in the timber, homeward bound, his sack of plunder on his back.

I was excited and annoyed by the half-dream. I jumped

out the door, yelled at Crow Eagle, made him come back and dump out his cargo. When I saw that it was only the beef bones, I told him to take them. But his feelings were hurt by my sharp words and he refused, walking away most unhappily. I hadn't meant to offend him, but I did mean for him to let things alone when we cowboys were not present—and I didn't figure I was present if I was asleep.

After Crow Eagle went home, I was bothered because he had looked so offended. Since part of our trouble was because neither of us understood the other, I decided to go over to the Indian camp and see Crow Eagle's boy, Joe, who was my friend and who could talk good English. So I saddled my horse again, took the sack and beef and rode over.

With young Crow Eagle to interpret for us, old Crow Eagle and I got things straightened out. He grinned like a kid when he learned how he had scared me—and that I knew and could tell him everything he did, but couldn't wake up, and that the more I tried and couldn't arouse myself, the more scared I got, like a very bad dream. When I finally broke out of sleep I was fighting mad and spoke meaner than I meant to.

Crow Eagle admitted that I surely knew his every movement. He chuckled and said he didn't want to disturb me; that he knew he could have the meat, so he got it and left. He explained the reason he had so thoroughly examined my gun was because of his deep curiosity about white men's firearms. He promised that thereafter he would stay out unless he saw one of us around in the house.

He was really a good old Indian. After our powwow, we shook hands and buried the hatchet. Then we smoked a cigarette, which served as a peace pipe, and forever after we were friends.

Another old buck, Benjamin Lee, scared me aplenty, too, shortly after that. All cowboys had orders to watch for In-

dians' dogs chasing Matador cattle and to shoot them. Every Indian camp had dogs running around and a lot of them learned to chouse stock. If a man could catch them at it and shoot the leaders, the others generally quit. Most of these dogs had a big strain of wolf in them, so it was natural for them to get after cattle.

One day, I caught four big dogs after about ten head of little steers. They were so busy raising hell that I loped right up on them before they saw me. They high-tailed it back to their owner's tepee with me riding close on their heels, firing at them. I killed two, and kept after the others. They ran like wolves and beat me to the old log house where they belonged and scooted in under a tumbled-down porch.

I came right on, not expecting to find anyone there, but I was mistaken. Just as I loped up to the house an Indian jumped out of the door holding a gun in his hands. For a second I thought he was going to shoot me! But he was after those dogs, too, and he blasted them for me. My nerve returned when I saw him swing the gun away from me, jump down off the porch, and go gunning his own dogs!

After he shot them, he came up to shake hands and said, "How Kola" [Hello, friend]. I was sure relieved that he didn't hold any grudge over his dead dogs. Maybe his squaw made soup out of the whole works and they feasted for a week.

I had yet to learn that Indians are great jokers among themselves and with those they like, so when old Red Water pulled his idea of a joke on me one day as I was riding over hilly country, and would cross over the little wagon road where he was driving, a little ways ahead of him, he just about raised my hair!

I hadn't slacked up my horse any, when out of the corner of my eye, I saw him suddenly jump out of his rig, drop to one knee, and throw down on me with a shotgun! I flung myself over and hung down out of sight on the opposite side of my horse, trying to hide from him. It scared my horse, and he bucked and dumped me off. I hung onto him and swung him around so I could peek out under his neck and see what old Red Water was up to. The way he acted had me more than a little riled and I was tempted to pump a few shots at him. That would have been bad, for when I got a good look, both he and his squaw were laughing fit to split! He padded right over to shake my hand and indicated by motions and a few words I could understand that he knew me and that he wanted to greet me and figured it was a good way to stop me. And it sure was!

I guess I didn't look too pleased to see the old fellow, but we had a smoke from *my* tobacco, with my thoughts dwelling on how I would like to kick him for scaring me so. He might have been the means of my getting badly hurt by such monkeyshines—he and the crazy horse I was riding. But we parted with a handshake, and he went happily on his way. I never forgot him—nor did he ever forget to laugh about his joke whenever he saw me.

Those three old warriors had all taken part in the famous Custer's Last Stand, and Red Water had been known to express his wish to once again peel off a white man's scalp.

I was always luckier than most, perhaps, but a man always remembers an accident like Ed Boynton's—a young fellow who threw a loop which missed its mark and left him a broken man at the prime of life. But his friends were legion.

When I met Ed around camp this first winter, he had been crippled for some time. He was a pleasant-natured fellow who rode a few gentle horses. Everyone at the Matador liked him, gave him clothes and money, for Ed couldn't work. His good humor and uncomplaining ways, in spite of the accident that wrecked his life, endeared him to all.

I think it was just a few years earlier, shortly after the turn of the century that this young Scandinavian came to South

Dakota, ambitious to be a cowboy and to ranch for a living. His first job after he landed at old Evarts was with the French-Indian, Benoist. Soon he married a pretty breed girl and started his own ranching spread on her allotment. With her cattle and horses for a beginning, Ed intended to raise livestock. He took the brand of a connected reverse EB Bar.

One day Ed rode out into the Patched Skin Buttes country and jumped a band of range mares. Running with them was a three-year-old he wanted. Ed was riding a good mount. He tied his rope to his saddle horn and sped after her. There had been a good crop of cockleburs in the gullies that year and the manes, the foretops and tails of these mares running loose all the time, had gathered a big load of these smelly brown burrs.

Ed wasn't very skillful, but he would try to rope anything he was after. Evidently, when he throwed the rope to catch the mare, the loop fell short of her head and settled, instead, around her long, burr-matted tail, swinging out from side to side behind her as she ran. Caught in such a way, the wild mare doubtless redoubled her speed. Any horse can pull considerable weight by the tail. Wild-loose and scared, the mare outran the saddle horse, jerked him down and dragged him over Ed, breaking the rope. That set her free and left Ed on the ground, more dead than alive.

That night when Ed didn't come home, his wife got her horse to hunt for him. She gave the alarm and by morning everyone around had gathered to look for him, too. At dawn, they found his horse grazing close to the corral with about fifteen feet of his rope still tied to the saddle horn.

A few hours later, the searchers found the horse band with the mare dragging twenty-five feet of Ed's rope, still tight around her tail. All day they hunted for Ed and near sundown they found him crumpled up on the prairie, still alive but unconscious.

They took him home. The doctor came out from the

Agency, twenty-five miles distant, in a livery rig, but in spite of his efforts, Ed remained unconscious for ten days, then slowly regained his senses and showed signs that he might live. For a year, he lay helpless and paralyzed in the Agency hospital. Finally, he could walk a little; by grit and determination he could even ride a horse, and after he got on his feet, he found many little chores he could do to be useful around a ranch.

Ed remained partially paralyzed. His nervous system was so badly affected he had trouble mounting a horse. Friends supplied him with the very gentlest horses to ride. After some years of helplessness, Ed's wife left him, and it was then that his many friends proved most comforting.

I think he welcomed all of the new activity on the reservation, which provided new interest for him and someplace to go to mingle with men living the life he loved and had been forced to forsake. Ed often came to the cow camp where we batched. We were always glad to see him, for he was jolly and did everything in his power not to be a burden to anyone. He had no relatives that I ever heard of. He was a fine man and got a lot of fun out of living in the land of his misfortune, where everyone was his friend. He was made of the stuff it took to be a part of a big, wild country such as Dakota was then, but for his accident. In his trunk, packed in mothballs, he kept the rope that caused all of his trouble. His reason for keeping it was his own secret, for he never revealed what it meant to him.

Along about Christmastime, the activities among the natives in our region began picking up. There was a hustle-bustle about us, something similar to Christmas off the reservation. A little white Indian church and a long log building beside it served as the center of all the activities. Contrary to the general idea about Indians and their religion, they were sincerely interested in the church and all it stood for. There was a mixture of Catholics and Protestants among them. For a week previous to Christmas, we saw Indian rigs headed toward the church, and soon tepees appeared there. We could smell smoke on the breeze, and Indian kids seemed to spout out of the tents and ride around on ponies.

This went on daily until, by Christmas, the church was completely surrounded by an Indian encampment. Dozens of kids roamed the place, too, and there were wagons and harnesses scattered over the now cluttered yard. Their hundred or more horses were staked or hobbled on the grassy places nearest the church. It snowed a little, but that didn't dampen their holiday spirit.

Everyone was excited about the Christmas "doings" at the church. And if there was ever a homesick young cowboy on the Cheyenne River reservation at Christmastime, it was me! I was just out of my 'teens, batching with Ott, an older man who didn't care to go anywhere. The excitement of these Indians was contagious and I soon found it was fun to enter into the celebration, too.

The White Eyes Indian family lived near our camp. Mrs. White Eyes was a big-around squaw, always friendly and smiling. Her man was a thin little buck. They had a young daughter who looked like, and was built like, her mother. I used to pass their home often and I'd stop to talk with White Eyes if he was outdoors, so at Christmas they invited me to come to the church affair and feast with them. Our superintendent Mitchell always counseled us cowpunchers to mingle with the Indians on the reservation, go to their gatherings, promote good will all we could. It made it much better, he said, between the Indian owners and the Matador Company who leased their land.

That was all right with me, for I had been up around the Indians camped at the church often enough and close enough to spot some real pretty girls up there. I knew that many of them were breeds—part Indian and part white blood—that they could cook well, too, and had been away to white schools. The more I saw of these maidens, the prettier they became, so an evening of shining around them had a right lively appeal for me. I decided to go—strictly for goodwill purposes, you understand.

In addition to Mitchell's admonishment to keep friendly with the Indians, the Matador Company always presented them with a beef—usually a fat cow—for their feasts. It was a standing rule that the cowpunchers not neglect to drive in a critter for their red brothers, so one morning Ott rode over to tell them that he would bring in a cow and kill her for them. They rejoiced. They assured him they would be ready to receive her. Ott came home and sent me to find a suitable beef for them.

Because neither Ott nor the Indians understood each other very well, the Indians got the idea that when we drove the beef to their camp and roped her, that they were to do the killing. Instead, Ott had planned for me to rope her, he would catch her heels, stretcher her out and shoot her in the head before turning them loose on her.

I got the cow, all right. The Indians had a few old shotguns, and unknown to us, were waiting out of sight while we drove the cow up quite close. I roped her head and Ott moved in to rope her hind legs. But before he got to do that, about a dozen Indians charged down on us and began shooting hell out of the cow. My horse got scared, bucked and stampeded away from them, dragging the cow along. Ott shouted for the "goddam fools to go back," but they didn't know what he was saying, or else didn't care, so they kept coming on and blasting away until the cow went down, and a charge of shot cut my rope in two! Without the cow's weight, my horse sure did take off, but as we went I saw the Indians pile onto their beef, so they finished her up very shortly in their own way. I went back to camp dragging what was left of my rope.

Christmas evening came. All day the preaching had been going on with mostly old Indians taking part and telling about days of the past. Some of it was long talks by some ancient squaw or by an old, long-haired buck who had seen a lot of skirmishes. It took up considerable time to relate all they had lived through, all about the great buffalo hunts or some great sickness in camp. They told anything which seemed great to them—old battles, old powwows with the pale face, enemies captured, floods on the Missouri, and of how the buffalo vanished. It was their idea of taking part in the Christmas celebration. And it was also their way of handing down the legends and information to the young Indians.

After Ott and I had our early supper, I polished up my boots, got out a good shirt and tie, shaved, and dusted on plenty of sweet-smelling powder, while my thoughts jingled around a rather rosy evening just ahead of me. I might even spark one of those pretty breed girls! Might dance a little, too. I saw Ott eyeing me in a sour way, so I asked him if he wasn't "going down to be sociable with our War-bonnet Brothers?"

He snorted loud enough to shake the sod on our roof. "Hell, no, I'm not going down to mingle with them damned, stinkin' Injuns!"

I didn't approve of Ott's further remarks about the doings and the Red Brothers, but then I figured he was getting a little too old to be sociable anyway. Why, he was even getting bald! I brushed my own thick black hair. Ott would be sorry when I came back and told him of all the fun I'd had that Christmas Eve. I didn't pay any more attention to his grouchy glances.

The talks in the church were over for the day and the feasting had begun out in the log house when I got there. I opened the door and stepped into the dusky room, and the first one to spot me was Mrs. White Eyes. Among all the dark faces, her smiling countenance beamed my way. She was dressed in her best calico, shawl, and beads. She came right over to me and we shook hands. She was glad I had come and she took my arm to guide me to a seat at the table, with not a doubt in her mind that I had come solely to feast!

The table was a great long affair with benches on both sides. It was stacked with food. Dishes of fruit, cakes, pies, and bread of all kinds, bowls of meat and others of food I didn't recognize. Around to the back side of the table, Mrs. White Eyes led me! But first she beckoned her chubby daughter and motioned for her to slide along the bench first. Then she pushed me in, and—to hem me in proper—she sat down beside me too. On one side, the little fat daughter smiled up at me. On the other, her mama. Everyone passed me everything on the table. I didn't lack for attention. I wasn't hungry, but I had to eat something to keep from offending my friends. And all the while across from me in a corner, where they had grouped after feasting their fill, were all the pretty maidens I'd had visions of sparking. My eyesight hadn't failed me from afar, either, for there were some cute ones there. They had sparkling stuff in their black hair—bits of isinglass from the hills, which shone like diamonds when they moved their heads. They wore beaded bands, fitted with gay feathers, and beautiful beaded capes covered their shoulders, and their moccasins and white buckskin clothing was heavy with beadwork. A colorful, shining sight. And around the maidens clustered the young bucks, like honeybees around their queen, laughing and showing off! They were right where I wanted to be, but here I was, buttoned in by my good friends—and they never left me. They beamed smiles and Christmas good cheer upon me all evening, and so did all their friends—me, the only Texas cowboy amongst them. I was stuck, so the only thing I could do was to try to look at ease—try to act pleased and polite and appreciative of all the friendliness extended me.

It was late when I made my escape. Gosh, how good to get out in the fresh air! The night was clear and the big moon made the sky so bright you could scarcely see the stars. Far off in the north, the aurora borealis twisted and danced and flung her brilliant banners up into the sky. My breath and my horse's made a frosty cloud around us as we headed for camp.

While I was pulling off my boots, getting ready to roll in, Ott stuck his head out from under the quilts, still giving me the vinegar eye. He flopped his tarp well up over his head and I heard him mumble from deep down under: "Yuh stink like a goddam Sioux!"—and my first Christmas in Dakota was over!

4. First Winter

The Old Muddy hides beneath her turbulent brown bosom many sad tragedies, yet she sweeps imperturbably over them like a furious monster. It wasn't long after Christmas that a man met his doom on the frozen Missouri and wasn't found until spring.

The camp where Ott and I spent that first winter was upstream a mile from the junction of the Moreau and the Missouri, about eight miles from Evarts. All of the rivers were frozen over with thick ice, and in such big ones as the Missouri the water runs deep and that breeds airholes. The water is warmer under the ice than the atmosphere above, and the continual upsurge of the warmer air prevents an airhole from closing.

The airhole is dangerous, always. Many of them are from a few rods to a half-mile long, and nearly as wide. The surrounding ice runs from paper-thin to three or four feet thick back a ways from the hole. No one was ever certain how close you could approach the water without the ice giving way, and many a thirsty creature walked over to these places only to break through and then be unable to get out again. It was into just such as this that Bob Arpan and a horse from Cal Smith's livery barn in Evarts went to their doom.

Bob was a breed Indian living a short ways downstream from Evarts, on the reservation side. He had been in town with others and had been celebrating a bit. It was unlawful to sell whisky to Indians, but there were always men who would buy it for them.

Bob's horse, tied somewhere for the day, grew restless and rubbed the bridle off his head. He went home, leaving Bob in Evarts afoot. Around dark, Bob missed his horse and went to the livery barn to hire another to ride home, promising to bring him back the next morning. According to reports at the time, Bob left town with several other breeds.

The next day, when Arpan didn't return the horse to the stable, Cal Smith rode over to find out why. He discovered that Bob had not come home at all. Late in the night his wife, wondering where he was, had gone outside into the night to listen for hoofbeats that would tell her he was coming home. She had seen his horse come back, and listening, she heard noises she recognized as a group of riders on the ice. Once, as she stood out in the dark, she heard a man yelling down on the river. The voice was Bob's, but she could not make out what he said. When he didn't come in, she decided he had ridden on with the others, all of them drinking and shouting, and she went to bed. But it was doubtless Bob in the airhole, calling for help. Whether anyone was near him, or heard him, no one can say.

Learning that Bob was missing, Cal Smith went back to the road across the river ice and found evidence of where his sharp-shod horse had been raced around over the ice. Instead of staying on the snowy road, Bob had left its safety to spur over the slick, glassy ice, knowing his sharp-shod horse could not fall with him. Whether this exhibition was for his own fun or to show off before others no one knows, but the

sharp-shod tracks plainly told the story that the horse was traveling at a rapid pace in the dark when he went into the airhole.

Weighted by heavy clothing, Bob probably clung to the rim of the ice for a while, calling for help, before he lost his grip and went under. Perhaps, if there really were others with him, they didn't hear his cries for help, or didn't realize what had happened—or else were afraid to try to help for fear they, too, would fall into the airhole. So passed his last moments, while his wife puzzled over the cries she heard.

When the ice went out and the river got low in the channel, the horse was found not far from where he went into the airhole—he was still saddled. But it was considerably later that Bob's skeleton was found by his wife's sister twenty-five miles below the Cheyenne Agency and nearly sixty miles from the deadly airhole. It was long past winter; the Missouri was near normal again, and Mrs. Claymore was washing clothes. She went after a pail of water and saw a spurred boot sticking up out of a pile of driftwood. Looking closer, she recognized Bob's brand cut into the spur leather and knew she had found him. What was left of Bob Arpan was gathered from the water and buried, thus ending one of the many sad stories the Missouri could tell.

In an almost primitive region such as the reservation, the yarns that circulated were often salty and well-colored. Tragedy played its part, but rough humor sometimes flavored the scandalous, enlivening isolated lives. Usually the story gained a little each time it was told.

The story that got out on a lad we'll call Jakie caused him to forever shy away from words he didn't know the meaning of. To understand the Indian better, one must know his life had always been a struggle for food, and he took it wherever he found it. He would ignore meat he didn't kill, unless short on grub. Then he didn't hesitate to use what came his way, no matter how.

The Sioux were always meat eaters. They longed for buffalo meat, for deer and elk and all other wild game that had long since gone from the reservation country. They were grateful for meat. They devoured all of it, without waste. When the cowboys in winter camp, or in summer with the roundup wagons, butchered a beef and took what they wanted, they gave what remained to the Indians, who accepted every bit of it—ribs, flank, shank, hocks, hoofs, neck, and guts. The latter, when cleaned, cut into small pieces, cooked until tender, and thickened with corn meal, made favorite food for them.

One day, the men in one of the camps where Jakie, a kid just lately come up from Texas, was staying, killed a beef. Jakie was riding around looking after cattle and that afternoon as he passed the corral on his way up the creek a ways, the men working out there asked him to go around past the Indian camp and tell the squaws about the kill, and for them to come after the extra meat.

Jakie said he didn't know "Indian talk" and couldn't make them understand. Another man informed him to tell the squaws that there was plenty of *ta-win* down at camp, and to *ki-ga-la* down and get it. Then to clinch it, the helpful one added: "They'll know what you mean and come a-runnin'!"

Jakie rode on and angled toward the Indian camp where he could see five or six squaws out in a sunny spot scraping some hides which they were tanning. He rode up to them and said, "How." He knew that meant "hello." None of them looked up, except one old wrinkled squaw. By Indian custom and as a mark of respect, the oldest squaw always spoke for all. She said, "How."

Jakie told her about the fresh beef down in camp and repeated the words he had been told to use. He pointed in the direction of the camp. "Ta-win," he said, "plenty ta-win down at camp. Ki-ga-la," he urged, "go get it!"

Shawls went up over the young squaws' heads. The old squaw looked down at her work and no one answered Jakie or made any sign at all that they had heard him. Jakie felt that he had failed to make them understand, so he tried again, repeating it all, for them to "kig-a-lap [hurry] to the cowboy camp. Ta-win—plenty of it down there, all ready and waiting for them!"

The old squaw only bent her head lower, muttering, "si-ca, si-ca, si-ca!" (Pronounced *she-cha,* meaning "Bad.") From behind the various shawls came muffled giggles from the younger squaws, and the high-pitched, long-drawn-out sounds of Indian disapproval, "Eeeeeeeeeeeeeeeeee, eeeeeeeee-eee, si-ca, si-ca!"

Jakie eyed them angrily, disgusted with their evident lack of appreciation of the gift of beef and the message he had brought them. He turned his horse and rode away. Meanwhile, down at the camp, as the afternoon waned, the other men wondered why the squaws hadn't come for the meat. Usually they were there at once, chattering happily while they filled buckets and sacks and carted them away.

That evening, after Jakie stabled his horse and was eating a late meal, someone inquired as to whether he had told the squaws about the meat?

"Yes," Jakie snorted, "I told the damn fools that there was fresh *ta-win* down here at camp and to come get it." Still more than a little hostile because he believed the Indian women had poked fun at him in their own way, Jakie added, "But all those crazy squaws did was giggle and hide their heads in their shawls! If they can't understand *ta-win,* why, *the hell with them!*"

The other men listened to Jakie's irate comments, and one of them, his face shining as innocently as a newborn calf's, for here was the essence of a hilarious joke, asked:

"You say they wouldn't *look* at you? Just hid their heads?"

From the back of the room came a gleeful howl which everyone but Jakie joined in. They didn't explain. They just laughed in hearty enjoyment, while Jakie's words scorched them, "If you sonsabitches will tell me the joke, maybe I'll laugh, too."

Eventually, Jakie learned that *ta-lo* [ta-low] means "beef." *Ta-ni-ga* [ta-knee-ga] means "guts." But when he used the word ta-win or *ta-wee*, as it was usually called, Jakie had, in effect, informed the Indian women that if any of them felt the mating urge, that there was accommodation aplenty down at the cow camp, and to *kig-ga-lap*, come in a hurry to get it!

But the squaws didn't come. And Jakie never heard the last of that one!

Not only did the Indians use beef which the cowboys gave them, but they cooked every kind of game—prairie dogs, skunks, beaver, mink, wildcat, as well as dogs and stuff they happened to find. And because the red brothers were prone to such habits, there were once a couple of very worried cowboys.

Dakota winters didn't pass without numerous winter-killed cattle, and the men in the camps usually skinned the carcasses. Roy Vivian had come down from Con's camp at headquarters to spend a few days with us, and he and I skinned a few yearlings that had passed on to warmer regions, and we baited the remains with strychnine. We were after a pack of husky coyotes lurking along the creeks in the willows. Four or five big ones, working together, were not above killing thin and weak cattle. Every evening, whether in bright moonlight or the pitch dark of a starless night, these dozen-voiced yappers yodeled from nearby hills to their own kind on distant ridges, inviting them to help with their blood-thirsty affairs. The range was full of these gray night-prowlers, but when we started out to rid our region of a few of them, we didn't know it was strictly unlawful to poison cattle carcasses on the reservation! We had yet to learn that most of these critters were cut up and used for meat by the old Indians—the main reason for "no poison."

We were considerably disturbed the next day after we had strychnined the steer carcasses to find where the squaws had hacked out the meaty parts and carried them away. We were sure puzzled what to do about it, for we didn't know which Indians had the meat, nor how many had eaten the poison.

We were both just big kids at the time, and we thought the best thing to do was to keep mum about the strychnine, but we certainly kept an ear to the ground listening for reports of dead Sioux. We visioned them dying in droves, from the toothless old bucks who had gobbled up a lot of it, to the little papoose who had sipped the soup!

The weeks passed and we never heard as much as a whisper of an Indian with even a slight bellyache. It was still many weeks before we learned the secret. The Indian wasn't so dumb that he didn't know a dead critter had no tender meat; to eat it at all, it takes hours of boiling to cook the tough, stringy stuff. Hours of boiling destroys the deadly effects of poison and destroys anything else which might be detrimental, too. But we didn't do any more strychnine baiting, regardless. We'd had all the worrying we wanted.

The days ticked off and late January cold deepened. Frost hung in the air; big trees along the river protested with loud pops as they froze and burst open. But the wounds would thaw out and close again with warm spring days, and Mother Nature would go to work growing new bark over the scar to protect it. Snow covered most of the range and time and again on clear nights, we watched the dazzling show of the distant northern lights.

The cold gave way one dawn to warmer air, and by noon

heavy snow fell from low gray clouds. Not a breeze stirred. It piled up steadily until after dark. As night came on, the cold took over again, the sky cleared and the full moon turned the world bright as day. In the trackless, knee-deep, glistening white, the old log house was but a black splotch sitting isolated and alone.

Supper was over and it was nearing time to go to bed. Shins close to the fire, six-shooters on the table between us, we were reading by lamplight in the east room. A door in the northwest corner of that room opened into the adjoining kitchen. The only door to the outside was shut, in the southwest corner of the kitchen, entirely hidden from our sight.

In the evening stillness, the outside door opened, then closed. We glanced up and waited. Again the doorknob turned, the latch clicked and the door squeaked open. It creaked shut with a definite closing sound.

"You heard the kitchen door open and shut, didn't you, Ott?" I asked. He nodded and waited expectantly for the appearance of a visitor.

Once more, the door opened, firmly and wide, then closed solidly, unmistakably, with no attempt at stealth, as when a human hand held the knob! Both of us got to our feet, grinning, for doubtless this was a prankster cowboy from one of the other camps stopping to spend the night, and knowing the "haunted" reputation of the old cabin, was having a little fun with us. We hurried to the kitchen.

Ott yanked open the outside door, but no one was there, not even a footprint, but a few of our own on the doorstep. We stared at each other and thoughts of a friendly visitor vanished. Ott sped past me like a big cat, going after his gun. "That door opened three times, kid! Get your pistol and we'll catch Mr. Spook!"

Going out the door a few seconds later, revolver in hand, Ott said: "We'll go different ways around the cabin—meet in the back. We'll corner whoever is there!" Over his shoulder, he yelled a warning, "Don't shoot ME when I come in sight, meeting you!"

"Hell, no, I can tell you from a spook!" I was excited, too, as I ran around the opposite side of the cabin. In less time than it takes to tell it, we faced each other behind the house— not a thing between us! In the still white moonlight, we two foolish-feeling cowboys stared at each other, breath curling from our faces in frosty circles.

"Ott," I said later, sitting on my bunk pulling off my boots, "do you reckon that was sure-enough one of their Indian spooks?"

Ott grunted. "Injuns would say so. Never saw one myself. We'll look for tracks in the mornin'—might find a cause. Funny doings—" Ott grunted again and blew out the lamp.

Next morning, in the clear light of day, we went over our tracks again. There was nothing there in the deep snow except our own tracks—not even a bush, nor even a jack rabbit track in the hundred yards to the nearest river timber.

Ott shook his head. "Beats me!" he said. "Reckon there are Injun fairies around here?" But he didn't think it amusing. We both knew we heard the door open and close three times, and neither of us fancied things we couldn't savvy.

Suddenly, with a rush of warmer air and chinook winds that cut the snow, it seemed that spring was near. Snow melted fast but cold nights froze the water, so it was still winter. Ott decided to quit cowboy work and went to Evarts to tend bar in the Joe Arens saloon, but I stayed on at camp alone with our horses and poor stuff, for it wasn't near time for spring range work yet. I looked forward to the roundups and the busy summer months, riding broncs and working with the outfit. A few more weeks crept by, slower all the time, it seemed to me.

One day, the wind had been whipping the hills and twisting the timber until it died out with the sundown. While I cooked supper, the horses we had ridden all winter fed at racks in the corral. Came the sudden thud of flying hoofs and wild commotion among them as they raced across the corral, snorting. They whirled to face something, heads held high, then broke away again to gallop to the farthest side of the corral, where they nearly jumped the fence. I ran out there and walked among them. I looked in the barn and down on the river, but I could see nothing at all. After a while, the horses edged back to their feed and I went back to the house.

A few days before that, Con McMurry had stopped at my camp and left his old white bird dog, Jack, until he returned from an inspection trip over the range; and now, here was Jack, crouched by the door, with a woebegone look and his hair ridged along his spine!

"Are you scared, too, Jack?" I patted the old dog—and behind us, the horses stampeded across the corral again. I went back to them, but they wouldn't settle down. I had trouble catching my gentlest saddle horse, for by then I had a mighty urge to go visit the Frenchman living a mile up the river. I saddled up but, easygoing as my horse was, he would hardly let me mount, he was so spooked and wild-eyed.

Old Jack still crouched by the house, and as I rode by he trotted out to follow me. Recalling how the Frenchman's dogs always jumped on him and mauled him severely before they could be clubbed off, I decided to shut Jack in the cabin. As I rode away, I heard the scuffing of his feet as he raced from one room to another, howling pitifully. I pulled up and looked back, uncertain what to do about him, when suddenly, Jack settled the question. He flung himself against the window pane and landed in a heap of splintered glass outside. He bounced to his feet, mane raised, tail between his legs and bounded toward us like seven devils were right behind him—and all three of us took off along the trail to the Frenchman's house!

During the evening, I finally got around to a rather shame-

faced account of what had happened back at camp. But the
Frenchman didn't laugh about it. "You not go back there
tonight," he insisted. "There's something we not see lives
there! He's done things before now! He wants the old cabin.
It's best we let him have it. *I tell you the truth, I would not
stay down there, myself!*"

When I rode back to camp in the next morning's bright
sunshine, all was calm, the horses feeding quietly. Old Jack
and my horse approached the corral with no misgivings. If
there had been anything present the evening before, it didn't
cause any fear now. I always trusted the instincts of a dog or
a horse more than man's.

After Ott left for Evarts, it was a lonesome cow camp in
spite of busy days. I got so I'd stop to talk with the natives,
the French-Indian breeds, whenever I met them, or even an
old full blood, if he could make me understand him. The old
ones were always willing to visit. They were fond of my tobacco, too, I discovered, and liked to smoke and tell of their
past. Sometimes I'd wondered if they were stuffing me, or if
they really believed the tales they told me. I couldn't tell anything by their faces or by their voices. They would spin their
yarns, solemn as an owl, muffled in their blankets or peering
out of a heavy wool wakpomony coat which the Government
had issued them. If I got on the windward side of them, the
smoke smell, the grease, and whiffs of just pure Injun kept
me in touch with the spirit of the narrative.

It was an old warrior who considered himself something
of a preacher who told me about the Indian Ghost Tribe.

In days long past, he said, before the white man came, the
Indians had roamed far beyond the borders of Dakota, Montana, or Wyoming, following the buffalo for meat, going to
the rivers to fish, heading for the lakes to get wild fowl, or to
a favorite wild berry woodland. The whole camp, the chief
and his warriors, squaws, papooses, dogs, ponies, all went

along. Naturally, at times, one of the band died. Most often, a new little Indian, born on a journey, died at birth or shortly after. It might be carried along until the squaw found a tall tree to put it in, but usually the Indian always took time to bury his dead in a manner pleasing to his spirit, surrounded by the earthly treasures needed for his life in the Happy Hunting Grounds.

The burial rites varied, according to who died. A papoose was deerhide-wrapped and buckskin-thonged to a branch of a tree. A squaw usually wound up bound to a thick limb, or shoved up on top of a high rock heap. But a chief or warrior got considerable ceremony. His bier was a scaffold among many tree limbs, or a ledge on a tall butte, and there, with his finest robes and furs, his bow and his arrows heaped around him, they left him for the journey to the Land of Happy Hunting. If a suitable place was not handy, the body was carried along for miles, bound to a travois, to reach timber or high, rocky country.

Contrary to the "stoical" Indian stories, the loss of one of their tribe caused much grief. But their mourning customs differed from the white man's. A buck's harsh "Wah! Wah! Wagh!" snorted above the departed was as piercing as the scream of an eagle. The squaws howled like the wild wolf grieving for her dead pups. Haunting the highest hilltop in the night hours, keening into the blackness, the lonely cries carrying afar on the wind are like nothing ever heard except the she loafer! In fact, the first time I heard an old squaw out on a hill near camp, I thought sure I was listening to the howl of a moon-mad wolf!

The Indian didn't forget, either. When the moon of death came each season, as they traveled the old trails, or in passing, as they must, where one of their own was lost, the squaw nearest the departed sought some distant hill when fires burned low and tepee flaps closed for the night. Her lonely keening floated on the night wind and echoed through the hills. Or, from stormy, gale-lashed ledge, her grief mingled with crashing thunder, whirling, echoing, weaving in the tempest as though the saddened soul would gladly go with the storm and the darkness never to return. So, with all their customs and strange traditions, the Indian lived his life for ages before he knew the white man.

When they accepted the reservation life, the Indians were made to bury their dead as the white man did. Even so, the squaw, howling from the pinnacle in the dead of night, mourned for the dead, free as the wind in life but forced to the darkness of a hole in the ground, from which he must fight his way before he could go on to the Happy Land. To make it easier for them, the Indian buried his dead on the crest of a hill.

At first, the Indians defied the white man's laws and put their dead in the trees as their ancestors always had. These bodies were easy to discover and if the Indian agent heard of it, the Indian police, trained to keep law and order among their own people, were sent to hunt the guilty ones, have them dismantle the scaffolds and bury the dead in a cemetery.

A papoose in a tree was not usually discovered. More often than not, if it was found, it was just left there. The first summer in Dakota, another cowpuncher and I found a little body swaying in the highest limbs of an elm tree and we remembered hearing a squaw howling on a pinnacle near there. The day we discovered it, we were moving a bunch of cattle and stopped to rest our horses in the shade of the elm. The leaves were thick on the tree, but loafing on my back, looking up into the foliage, I saw a bundle swinging on a branch about twenty feet above the ground. Curious about what it was, I climbed up and took it off the limb.

We unwrapped yards of old quilt strips and buckskin, finally reaching a crudely carved piece of a branch. Bound tightly to it was a tiny, shrunken, and completely mummified papoose. Dead probably at birth, it had dried to dark, skin-covered bones. Very carefully, we rewrapped it, put it on the branch, and securely tied it in place. We made no report of it to the Indian agent. If the squaw howling on the hills in the midnight hours was happier with her little buck high in a tree near her, instead of mouldering in the grave as the white man insisted, then she could have him there. He belonged to the ages now, anyway, no matter where he was. But we remembered whenever we rode by the old elm or when we heard the squaw keening in the darkness.

One of the strangest stories told on the reservation concerned an Indian woman's attempt to keep her dead brother. He had no family. When he died, she could not give him up to be buried deep underground. She knew she couldn't put him on a high ledge, either, nor on a tree scaffold. So she had his bowels removed and his body packed with salt to preserve him, and so she could keep him with her. She was so unhappy at his death that she caused him to be laid out in a separate building for the salt treatment. But somehow word leaked out. Reportedly, a white man who had been working for the dead man rode to the Agency and told what was taking place out on the reserve. Several Indian police made the trip out there to investigate, found the already pickled body which had been in salt for several weeks, and made the sister bury it. They stayed there to see that their orders were carried out. But had it not been discovered, it is very possible that the body could have remained in good condition for years, filled with salt.

5. Spring on the Missouri, 1905

It was when the chinook winds of March released the snow-bound winter range to the warmth of spring that the wolves ran in pairs, the bitch heavy with her coming pups. From lofty pinnacle or brush-choked dip on a ridge, they scented for likely denning places. Before April, the female sought a lonely spot to have her young. She hovered over them during their blindness while her mate hunted and brought food to the den. Soon the pups were eating partially digested food she disgorged for them, playfully tumbling about, already snapping and vicious in their fun.

The great menace to livestock, other than the continual battle with cold, snow, wind, heat, flies, mosquitoes, and drouth, was the gray wolf. We were constantly watching for wolves, and they were thick on the reservation range. These wild hunters possessed almost-human intelligence. They had always lived where red meat could be had and as the cattle crowded the northern grasslands, the big loafers came in from everywhere. They knew where hunting was good. In fact, I've often wondered if they didn't send out scouts to look up

new hunting grounds. It was an everyday occurrence to jump
five or six of the big fellows on a day's ride, and sometimes,
we would bring one down with a six-shooter.

Where the buffalo roamed the prairie in endless brown
waves, there the loafer had always made his home. When the
great, shaggy beasts disappeared and the longhorn steers
came to follow the ancient trails they cut, there also the
big wolves loped at their heels—wary, slant-eyed, with thick,
erect fur protecting their powerful necks and shoulders.

The wolf's color ranged from white in the frozen north
and near black in the timberlands to the gray-brown of the
winter storm clouds on the wild ranges of the Dakotas and
Montana—the gray wolf, buffalo runner, timber wolf—name
or color mattered little, for the animal was the same, and his
long, deep-noted hunting howl in the night struck terror
to those he preyed upon.

Every cattleman knew the wolf for the cruel wastrel he
was. The cattle companies paid a bounty of fifty dollars for
the scalp and ears of a mature wolf and five dollars each on
the pups. The Matador cow camps were furnished with the
best available books on wolf habits and ways to exterminate
them, and we cowboys got every loafer we could.

But the gray wolf is much too sharp for ordinary man to
cope with. Hunting over a wide area, killing whenever
hungry, eating only the choicest parts, they rarely if ever
returned for a second meal off the same carcass. During the
time they trained their pups, the destruction and losses in
killed or maimed-and-left-to-die livestock attributed to one
pair of loafers was appalling. The young wolves were but a
few months old when they began following the old ones on
the hunt, and from then on we would come upon mangled
stock daily that bore the loafer sign.

Newborn colts were favorite meat. The wolf displayed uncanny wisdom as to spring foaling time and was smart
enough to watch the horse bands. Through field glasses,

cowboys observed loafers going about their deadly work, but the intervening rough terrain prevented rescue before the kill was made.

When cutting down a colt, wolves cunningly isolated their quarry. Hidden on a rocky hill, several loafers—usually an old pair and their pups—working together, waited until a mare and colt grazed somewhat apart from the others. While one wolf charged down to stampede the horse band, the others cut the mare and colt off. The mare, with her colt hugging close to her flank, instinctively tried to get back to the others, but the wolves closed in with their vicious attack. Her colt was too young to get away swiftly, and the mare stayed to protect it, but unless her frantic nickers brought the band circling back to her, she had little chance of saving it or even herself. And if they came upon a mare gone alone to a quiet place to foal, their deadly work was much easier.

Hamstringing was a favorite trick of the gray. He did this by ripping the flesh just above the hocks where the cords of the leg are close to the hide. It took but a few fang slashes to cut an animal down. Crippled in one leg, it was easy to cut the other from under it. With the critter almost helpless, a wolf moved in for the throat. If he wanted the colt, it took but a snap or two of the jaws to snuff out the little foal, while the other wolves kept the mare fighting for her life. In the open-range days, horse bands lost a high percentage of colts to the wolves.

Fed all his life on raw meat, the old gray wolf grew large and powerful. Fully matured, he stood up to thirty inches at the shoulder and weighed 150 pounds or more. Cold weather meant little to him, with his long, heavy hair matted around his throat. He possessed the keenest instincts. Rarely could he be lured by scent or by poison bait. It was said that if a loafer reached two years of age, he was pretty apt to live out the fifteen-year average span of wolf life.

But with all their predatory ways, they were loyal to their

own kind. If a litter of pups were left orphans, other wolves learned of it either through direct contacts that only they knew of or by the long, lonely howl of the surviving mate, in the event only one of the parents was killed. Perhaps that was the way they called for help. Anyway, it was not unusual that orphaned pups would be moved to a den where other pups were and the old wolves together hunted for and trained them. Dens have been found to contain pups of three different ages—proof, time and again, that the gray will look after his own kind.

But to stockmen they were vicious, yellow-eyed killers. They hated them and exterminated them to the last one.

It was no unusual thing for a man to ride across a brownish stain on the grass or the snow, which, if followed to the end, revealed the twisted carcass of some luckless critter. Perhaps every bone would be chewed and polished, indicating that a whole litter of hungry loafer pups had filled their bellies. Again, little of the animal would be gone, and a man recognized the sign that the wolves, not really hungry, had cut down a likely victim, partly for sport, yet never ignoring a fill of blood and tender meat. Coyotes, lurking shadows along the trail, careful to keep their distance while the big fellows feasted, took what was left and grew fat on what their big cousins wasted.

One cold day, I watched a gray wolf cut down a four-year-old steer. The snow was a foot deep on the level where the killing took place. A few days of mild weather had thawed the snow on top, then freezing nights had crusted it. Scouting for cattle over in that end of the range, I topped a hill two miles from a commotion near a fence. Through field glasses, I saw a wolf at the heels of five big steers plunging in a dead run through the snow, while the wolf, working alone, skimmed along on top of the crust. Near the corner, he cut a steer off and stampeded him up the fence. Fear-crazed, the steer jumped the four wires in the corner, but the wolf circled him back and he unhesitantly jumped the four wires again. While the steer floundered in the deeper snow in the fence corner, the wolf slashed the cords in his legs, and when the big critter went down, moved in and ripped his throat wide open.

Fighting through snow as fast as my horse could go, I almost got into pistol range before the loafer left his kill. He had filled up on blood spurting from torn neck arteries and some of the rump meat when the crunching sound made by my horse breaking through snow crust sent him loping easily over the packed snow, comfortably full. I know the gray didn't eat on the carcass again, but coyotes took over and cleaned up on it.

My adventures for that winter weren't over with. If I'd felt my scalp tingle a few times during the past months, it was nothing compared to my last ride across the Missouri ice that year. I "cut my eye teeth" on the big stream that spring, in a way that I never forgot. Sometimes one can crowd Old Lady Luck almost too far!

When I rode C Heart out onto the ice road across the Missouri, it came near being my last ride. But for the big gelding's stout muscles and fighting courage, we would never have finished as we did.

During the cold months, the Missouri ice froze four-foot thick and everyone crossed on the ice. Before it froze to a safe depth in the fall, and in the spring when it was breaking up, there was no way to cross the river. The ferryboat "wintered" in open water downstream. Government engineers had made many soundings of the river bottom at Evarts, but failed to find suitable bedrock there for the pilings needed to sustain a big bridge. Eventually, they did find a solid granite site twelve miles north of Evarts, at the present-day Mobridge, named for the river and the bridge. But there was no bridge anywhere for miles, in 1905, except the pontoon bridge at shipping time.

As people drove back and forth in sleds, wind-blown snow and dirt piled up over the tracks and horse sign until, by spring, an additional solid, frozen three or four feet, had built up above the ice. It stayed that way all winter, excepting for the airholes here and there, where one could see the water racing along down under. Men shod their winter horses with never-slip shoes, renewing old caulks with sharp ones as they dulled. But spring winds kept biting away at the remaining snow, melting it, and water crept from snowbanks. It stood in pools everywhere, covering even the river ice, though as yet there was no hint of the ice breaking up.

I was still in winter camp, still restless for spring to come, when Frank Mitchell, driving a snappy bay team to a sidespring buggy, drove out and spent the night with me. He had been scouting over the range and counseling with Con on this last inspection of the winter, before he left for Texas. After winter was well over, he put Con in charge of things in Dakota while he went home to Texas.

Mitchell always kept a private saddle horse, C Heart, in the livery stable at Evarts, as well as his buggy team. But since he would be gone for a few weeks, he wanted to turn C Heart out. So early next morning, we loaded my saddle in his buggy and headed upriver and across the ice to Evarts, for I was to bring the big blood-bay gelding back to my camp. I hadn't been in town for weeks, and the day was pleasant as summer. I found Evarts full of lively people I knew, and I spent considerable time with the Darling girls, too, so it was well into the afternoon before I felt the urge to go home.

C Heart was named for the brand on his left shoulder. He was grain-fed, good looking, and a treat to ride. I saddled him, and we pranced away to the river. When we got there, it looked plumb scary. The whole of it was not only covered with water, but I could see that the ice was honeycombed all over. C Heart was afraid of it, too, but I had to get back to camp and this was the only way over.

I'd been a mite "bravery-fortified" at the various bars in town, but C Heart hadn't sampled any of the peppy stuff I had, and he sure wasn't wanting any part of that river road. We had a little argument, which I won. I made him get out on it, completely against his will and better instincts.

As we went along, C Heart was just plain scared—and my own bravery was seeping out of me mighty fast! The ice looked too brittle on either side of the road to hold even a man's weight, but everything was all right until we neared the far shore. I was fairly holding my breath when there came a thundering crash right behind us! I looked back to see fifteen feet of the road we had just passed over falling through to the water below. Even the ice under C Heart's feet was going down! Once he was in a hole clear to his hips, but he kept on clawing and lunging, the never-slips on his forefeet holding until his hind feet caught, before it began to give. While it was sinking C Heart jumped ahead, and he kept that up for an unearthly long time, it seemed to me. I let him have his head completely, which is probably all that saved us.

C Heart battled the falling road until we hit ice that held up, and not long afterwards we climbed the shore to solid earth. When we stood safe above the river, C Heart looked back out over the wide expanse of ice. With head held high, he snorted and whistled the loudest, keenest blast of horse-talk I ever heard in my life. And I felt like doing the same. Both of us were thankful to get off that river.

By sundown, the ice burst apart, booming like a cannon as it split in a thousand directions. Before dawn, the whole river was moving, great ice chunks bumping along, gouging and grinding against others; some were flat in the water; some were upended or double-decked, and the noise they made was deafening. One could hear the river moving for a mile.

C Heart and I were the last ones to cross the river ice there at Evarts that spring and I knew for sure that I'd never get myself or my horse into a spot like that again, for in a brush with the big river man is rarely victor. The great streams of our West have ever been dangers, like living things, menacing man if he crowded too closely. Frontiersmen considered them a necessary hazard, and crossing over their frozen forms hardly rated any thought. But those streams brooked no carelessness! To forget or to overlook their power could well spell doom for the offender, and the Big Muddy had reached out and grasped many things.

It had reached out for me and barely missed.

Grass came early that spring. Flowers made gay patches everywhere. Many kinds of birds winged in for nesting, and larks sang with the wind. Stock got plenty of green feed by April and shed their heavy winter coats. One day I got a message to bring my horses to headquarters. The roundup wagon was about to start work. I was to ride the rough string again and go along with the wagon for a while. I wasn't sorry to leave my winter quarters, either. It was a sorry place. Because of its poor location, it wasn't used again for winter camp, although the big hay meadows proved useful, and at times were used for a temporary horse pasture and camp. I rode some rough horses there for a few weeks, but the usefulness of this place to the Matador lay mostly in its grass.

So, with its secrets and mysteries still unsolved, I turned my back on the old cabin. It still crouches on the river bank, rotting, its roof caved in, weeds and brush crowding around and over it. No Indian ever goes near it, any more than they did years ago. Perhaps the unhappy spirit has ceased its lonely vigil ere now, while the old logs sink further into decay until, one day, all will be completely hidden, and what happened there forgotten.

6. Horses

Western people seldom tire of hearing about horses—any kind of a horse—and certainly cowboys didn't tire of telling about them! "Bad" horses generally got the limelight, standing out in a spectacular, vicious way. But the kind, reliable horse is a pleasant memory always. A man would become as attached to a horse belonging to the outfit he worked for as to one he owned himself. It was what the horse did for his rider, the energy he put out, the easy way he carried himself, his reaction in emergencies that won a cowboy's regard. And if a man wanted trouble, let him try to take a rider's top horse! For that reason, when a cowboy was given a horse to ride, the horse was not taken from him unless he was unable to cope with him and turned him in. This happened lots of times and was one reason why the outfits kept a rough-string rider who rode horses other cowboys couldn't or wouldn't ride.

Riders seldom showed emotion toward a horse, often treated him rough. The life itself was rough. A cowboy rode hard and demanded his mount's best. He sat on him so long he liked to slip his rigging off his back, pull the bridle over his ears, slap his rump to dismiss him—and turn to other things. And the horse was always glad to be turned loose, no matter how willing he was. Seldom did a cowpuncher speak other than pridefully of the horses he rode.

"He's a hellova good one!" he would say, or he would admit, "He's a rough-gaited old sonovabuck, but he'll take you away over yonder and bring you back again!" Sometimes he cautioned other men: "Have to watch him or he'll hurt you, but he's got wind and power to burn."

Every cow outfit had its good roping horses, trained to carry a rider close enough to other animals so they could be roped, and these horses knew what to do then. The cutting horses, equally important, were used to cut cattle out of a roundup. Man prized the river horse that liked to swim and work with cattle in water. The night horses, with eyes like a cat's in the dark, were ridden while night-guarding a herd. The long-legged, strong, seemingly tireless circle horse was ridden when a big region was to be encircled for a roundup.

Then there was the outlaw horse that could be "rode" and was useful, and the one that required so much constant watching he was useless.

The all-around, competent horse, excelling in nothing yet capable in everything, rated high with everyone. Horses, all kinds, were as much a part of a cowboy's life as his hat, his boots, and his spurs!

A horse that a cowboy called tops possessed near-human understanding and his rider gave him credit for it. Perhaps a man prized his cutting horse most—a mount having so much natural know-how that if given his head he needed little to guide him once he knew what was wanted. In working cattle for a roundup, if he was shown a critter, he never lost him. No matter how a steer maneuvered out of sight among other cattle, the horse kept his eyes on him and cut him to the roundup edge, where a few swift steps beside him pointed the steer toward the "cut." The stock that were cut out were held in a separate herd. These horses worked quietly and didn't excite a roundup. Most of them rode easy —they possessed a gait which didn't jar or discomfort a rider —but they were so quick and active while working that a man had to be careful he wasn't unseated.

I was privileged to know many outstanding, knowing horses. There was TV, a speckled gray horse named for his brand. I have watched Homer Willingham, son of Cape Willingham, riding him to cut yearlings from a big roundup. Sometimes TV found himself working a little too close to the yearling, and on his own initiative he would back away a few feet until he again caught sight of his quarry hiding behind other steers. He was never mistaken, either. Once he saw, or had a steer indicated to him, he knew him, even if momentarily lost among milling stock. Sometimes, while watching intently for the hiding steer, he would hold up one foot in his eagerness to spot him. When he got him to the edge of the herd, he paid little attention to the bit. He was fast and had such a very rough gait he would almost unseat a rider, but nothing got away from him. He put the bovine character into the cut!

What made horses "rough" or "easy" to ride, while working stock at a fast pace, was, I think, their ability to move or run easily. A close-built, short-backed horse was usually as active as a cat and handled himself better than a long-geared horse, although that is a flexible statement. I've ridden long-barreled horses that were excellent mounts, and easy riding, too. Certainly, there is a vast difference in horses.

Bird Rose, one of South Dakota's early-day pioneers, became manager of the L7's on the Standing Rock reservation. He rode Frazier, a sorrel, blaze-faced, stocking-legged horse that was squirrel-light on his feet. Bird could sure cut cattle from a roundup on him. He looked very much like Pat, also a sorrel, ridden by Con McMurry from 1901 to 1909.

Pat was six years old when Con got him. He watched cattle with an eagle eye, padding along as easy as a coyote, and with as little noise. He knew how to get a steer out of a roundup and what to do with him. If Pat jumped at the steer to head him in the direction he wanted him to go, he didn't need to turn loose a lot of grunts and snorts to start the steer out to the cut mighty fast.

Warrior was Con's horse, too, branded a Campstool. He was black, stocking-legged, wild-eyed, and very active. He never let a steer run in a roundup or stirred up the cattle.

Bill Smedley, Sword & Dagger wagon boss, rode Silver, a palomino horse raised by the Indian, Lone Eagle. Silver was sharp as a fox in a roundup. He knew what steer he was after and never let him out of sight, and he never aroused a roundup, either.

It is hard to describe these horses in action—so alert, so wise-eyed, so gifted with natural cow-horse sense. If you have ever seen a sharp-eyed saddle horse, ears alert, his face and whole body keenly alive, and as interested in what he was doing as ever a human being could be, then you will know what these horses meant to a cowboy. I've ridden my share of them.

Dick, my night horse, was a blaze-faced black with white stockings. He showed the whites of his eyes a lot—a pretty fair sign that he could see good in the dark. Gentle and smart, he watched the herd as carefully as I did. He was raised by an Indian, Takes Him Standing, who lived on the Moreau. He branded Dick TS.

A cowboy trusted no horse as much as he did his night horse. On a dark, stormy night, Dick would drop his head low to the ground, to see better. He would stop dead still, not even breathing, so that no squeak of saddle leather broke the stillness, while he listened for the herd or watched for stock edging away from the bed ground. He worked his ears a lot, listening. On good nights, when the darkness was friendly and meant for sleep, he knew when a steer had wandered off from the others, and would, of his own accord, turn out to him and put him back where he belonged. It was never so dark that he lost track of the wagon—just give him his head and he would go to it.

I rode Dick on many a stormy, troublesome night when the herd would run. In going along with them, there were times when Dick stopped right where he was and waited for lightning to flash to see what was before him. More often than not, he would be on the rim of a washout that another jump would have landed him into, probably breaking both of our necks. I have known him to stop and feel with his foot when he couldn't tell what was ahead. In these wild runs, I let him have his head so he could figure out what was safest for both of us.

It was Dick under me one night when lightning hit the herd at Coffee Buttes, knocking us, as well as a block of steers at the edge of the roundup, down, leaving a few there permanently. After that, Dick was so afraid of storms that I had to quit riding him on night guard.

I liked Club, a coal-black horse named for a wire-cut foot which didn't heal unblemished. He had exceptionally good eyes, was sure-footed and watched and listened a lot of the time. He was easy riding, easy handled, and made little noise himself.

On extra-black nights, he too had a habit of stopping to listen, and of holding his breath to avoid saddle squeak. He'd watch intently out into the dark, and I knew he could see how the herd was acting—if the steers were restless and moving. If he turned away from where I knew the herd was, I let him have his head, and pretty soon I'd know we were bringing cattle back. He always knew where the other night guard was. When he circled the herd to the side where the saddle-horse *remuda* was being held, he turned his head that way to look but didn't nicker, which was one thing a good night horse must not do. A nicker more than once has caused a stampede. The cattle knew we were there and remained quiet, lying down, as Club moved by them. They paid no attention to my humming a song, either, but a sudden noise could start trouble.

The hardest to hold and the easiest to spook were those herds that were newly rounded up, but after a few nights of quiet night-guarding on the bed ground they wouldn't spook even from the flare of a match. A night horse could move around them as they lay close to the edge of the herd and not disturb them at all. But if they ran the first night they were guarded, they were ringy and hard to hold the whole drive.

Stormy nights, with electricity hanging above us and crackling along the edges of the clouds, were a different matter. Then most of the cattle would be on their feet, anxious for the weather to hit and have it over with. A cowboy could well look for a stampede then, and if the herd ran, he hoped to be riding his best night horse.

Croppy, a red-roan Matador horse, raised in Colorado and branded a Drag Y, was another horse a night guard cowboy could depend on. He got his name from his ears, frozen off short when he was young. Croppy had good night eyes, seemed to see and avoid holes, washouts and cut banks, even when traveling fast. He watched the oncoming weather, nickering his nervousness, like he was talking to himself in soft little undertones, cussing such unnecessary troubles in the night. He was a good cow horse, too, and Con often borrowed him from me when he had stock work to do.

Great roping horses had to be intelligent, fleet, and interested in the work, and have a natural sense of accuracy. Each one had some little personal trait that helped him. A rider recognized this and often went along with it, for above all, man and horse must be in tune with each other.

Perhaps two of the greatest roping horses of my time were Red and Rowdy, both sorrels. They belonged to Ellison Carroll, steer-roping champion of the past. Carroll's method was different from most ropers. He used a short, twenty-two-foot rope, tied hard and fast to his saddle horn. He rode straight for the steer and roped his horns, but made no attempt to flip the rope over the steer's hips for the trip. Both horses were very fast. They raced on past the steer, jerking him off his feet—even dragging him along, if necessary to keep the rope tight so he couldn't get up, while Carroll made the tie.

I was a fifteen-year-old kid when I saw Ellison Carroll and another great steer roper of those days, Clay McGonigle, rope five big steers apiece in a match roping for the fastest time at Carlsbad, New Mexico. It was an unforgettable day in my life, and here I saw a fine act of real sportsmanship.

Clay McGonigle's rope broke when his steer hit the end of it too hard. Carroll loped right out to McGonigle, and gave him his own rope to make another try.

I've known many wonderful roping horses, and have trained my share of them, and I knew when one had outstanding individual ability. Some horses like roping. They are as eager for the catch and to work with the roper as others are to shirk it. A horse that likes roping will do his utmost to carry his rider to where his loop will catch, and he doesn't mind the jerk that follows. But a horse that doesn't like roping can cause a loop to miss, even if he has been spurred to the right place and can do a good job of working the rope once the catch is made. A split-second of slowing up by his mount can mar a roper's timing and these wise old shirkers know it.

The rope horses with the big cattle outfits had to be trained for every kind of roping work. If a man needed to catch cattle on the open prairie, his horse needed to know not only how to throw the animal, but how to hold him down. And in calf branding, these horses knew when a loop caught and the next stop was the branding fire. Most of them liked these light stock and fast work.

A man can only describe a good roping horse by telling what he did in action. One would have to see the sharp look in a horse's eyes, the set of his head, and the way he pointed his ears; his attention to the man on his back, while never taking his eyes from his work. Any old cowboy roper will know what I mean. There have been hundreds of good roping horses that no one ever heard of but the men who rode them and the men that worked with them.

I recall several horses that were so wise that in such work as calf branding, if the rope somehow got on the wrong side of them so it would pull across their breast while dragging the calf to the fire, they would swing their head down and under the rope, thus getting it free and straight. They kept their feet and the rider from becoming entangled, and no calf or steer was ever fast enough to twist it about them. If need be, they would spin like a top to keep their feet clear of the rope.

Outfits had different methods of roping calves and of branding. Some penned the stock in a corral and "heeled" the calves, dragging them to the fire by both hind feet.

The Matador branded from a roundup in the open, usually, with the branding fire out a ways from the edge of the herd. The ropers caught by the head and took the calf to the fire where "flankers" took over. These men threw a calf to the ground by reaching over his back, catching his opposite flank and rolling him over their knee. A quick step backward, and the calf hit the dirt. With the first act of throwing a calf, the rope was flipped from the calf's neck, freeing the rider to go back for another. Generally, two men roped calves, averaging a calf a minute. Each roper had two flankers who held the calf for the men with the branding irons and the knife.

A man's arm would swell from so much roping, and a couple of hours of fast work was about the limit of a horse's efficient endurance, then he slowed down.

Polo, a blue-roan Matador horse, was one of the best of roping horses. His hair was blue, but his mane, tail, head, and legs were black. I broke and trained him and knew when I roped anything, no matter what, I had it.

But Shorty Brown stands out by himself. He was a Matador horse, too. He had run as a stud too long, but I liked to ride him. He was powerful on a rope and was tops to pull cattle out of boggy places. He liked to do that.

In calf roping he'd hit a slow lope from the herd to the fire, dragging his calf, where he hesitated but a moment until he saw the rope come off the calf, then he was gone again in his slow, steady lope to get another. Rarely did he fail to distinguish the unbranded. At first sight, this statement might be questioned, but remember the branded calf carried visible signs—the smell of fresh blood of his ear marks and the odor of burnt hair. So, in his own way, Shorty Brown took you to a calf with little help, for he was a dead-jawed horse and his effort was his own idea of getting the job done.

When my rope sailed out, it had better catch right, for Shorty Brown went to the fire, whether you caught a calf that had already been branded, or a cow, or had missed. He went to the fire. That was his job, to get to the herd, then back to the fire, loping powerfully along. If he found the rope on the wrong side, he'd swing his head down under it with scarce a slack in his gait.

It took long hours of this sort of work to make a cowboy's roping horses good. In those days, there was plenty of such work, so horses didn't get rusty.

One of the first things to be done when rounding up is to start men driving all stock from a certain region toward the center. Bunched together, they became the roundup. To accomplish this, shortly after dawn the wagon boss or some man he selected, together with eight or ten men, set out. At intervals along the route of the vast region from which cattle must come, he turns off men to drive that part of the circle. As he goes, he keeps dropping men off at the head of the creeks or near a wide group of hills until finally only himself and another man remain, and they ride on to a place which will tie in with the place where the first men turned off, and so, roughly, enclose the "circle." Their yells soon start cattle trotting to the center.

Riding the circle was for horses with stout muscles and long wind—horses that could run for miles without breaking down. Usually, the craziest horses were good for this. They liked to run, and while they were good in their job, they didn't rate as high with a cowboy as did his other horses. By their very nature, most of them didn't appeal to a man because they were often untrustworthy—horses that had to be watched all the time. I remember any number of circle horses, but none had any outstanding traits except that they liked to run for miles with little rider interruption. They knew we wanted them to run, so if we guided them in the direction we wanted them to go, they would do the rest.

The Dunn Stud, a horse that came from Colorado, made a good circle horse. He was a pretty palomino with white mane and tail, but he'd buck hard and often. I had him in my rough string. He was silly about snorting and cavorting after the mare mules. When the *remuda* was penned, the mules were trained to duck around the rope corral and go to the chuck wagon to be fed and harnessed. The Dunn Stud would cut the corral, too, and go with them. He was a a troublesome cuss that way.

One morning, Con got tired of his monkeyshines. He tightened his saddle down on old Love Letter, got a firm tooth grip on his pipe and rode out to rope "Dunnie." Con's loop was too big and Dunnie loped right through it, but Con yanked up the slack just in time to catch both hind feet. He drug Dunnie down by his heels, the men pounced on him and tied him down, and in no time at all the Dunn Stud was just plain Dunnie. After he healed, he gave no more trouble nosing after the mare mules.

The Dunn Stud had always bucked, even when only slightly provoked. The last time he gave me trouble was early one morning while he was still intact, as nature made him. Several of us, including Con, were riding out towards Dog Buttes, intent on making a circle. Jogging along, looking up at the high pinnacles, Con idly remarked, "I'd like to be on top of them. A man could see a lot of country from up there."

And while all eyes were focussed on the Buttes, George Carlton, riding close beside me, reached out a boot and raked his spur across Dunnie's flank. Scared, snorting, busting wind, the Dunn nearly ran over Con and Love Letter. He kicked, bucked and raised hell, giving me a rough time. But, then, I welcomed bucking practice. I spurred the Dunn considerable and he put on a good show.

When things got quiet again, me and the Dunn Stud jogging along with the others, but out of reach of any more spurred boots, Con chuckled and indicated how high the Dunn bucked when he asked me, "What could you see over the other side of the Butte, Ike?"

Con liked to watch a lively skirmish now and then, if there wasn't a herd to get stirred up.

Wild, rough country, rocky ridges, brush-tangled coulees, crisscrossed by trails known only to wild animals that seldom saw any but wilder, warrier neighbors, in a region so big a good fast crow couldn't wing over it in a week—that sort of home ground is bound to encourage outlaw tendencies. It breeds the will to resist, to break away and keep freedom—or die trying. Every man who ever rode horses has known at least one real outlaw horse. Stories of the range wouldn't be complete without them.

Possibly there is a bit of outlaw in all horses, even gentle ones. Certainly they are highly sensitive to the sound of men's voices, and their natural tendency to revert to the wild can easily be increased in proportion to their irritation or reaction. To be ever watchful is bred right into them.

Every stockman has seen gentle, rested saddle horses spook at the sight of a rider on a ridge. Up go their heads and tails; they'll circle and high-step, nostrils flared, and likely it will take a lot of fast riding to pen them in the corrals they have been in a hundred times.

It is a strange fact that a band of wild, untamed horses will follow a rider on another horse, loping in the lead of them. This is an exciting job, staying in front of running horses. It is a beautiful, thrilling sight to see them swing or swerve with the slightest turn of the rider ahead, colorful, easy as a dancer whirling to rippling music. Yet they are ever mindful of the riders behind them. The wilder the horses are, the easier they follow, indicating that horses, like people, look to leaders to point the way.

Sometimes a new man just starting to work for an outfit could well suspect the nature of the horse he was given by the name it had, for most of the cowboys' mounts were named for something associated with them. If a mean horse, the name usually indicated it—Danger, Rollers, Skittish Bill, Jessie James, and Widow Maker were names that revealed something about the horse so named; but Happy Jack, a black horse branded with a Drag Y on his left rump and IL on his left shoulder, came all the way to Dakota from Cimmaron, New Mexico, to acquire his name from a man he kicked. It was the only time I ever knew him to kick, for he was gentle. I had ridden him to Evarts and left him tied to a hitch rail in front of the Phil Du Fran Saloon. The saloon swamper, known to everyone as Happy Jack, generally drunk, invariably approached every horse he saw tied to the rail and tried to stroke his nose. Most horses resent being touched on the nose, and the drunk man's strangeness didn't help, either. Before his hand reached them, they would sag back, break the bridle reins and run off. But Happy Jack, the swamper, could not understand, and never tired of trying to touch the next one's nose.

Annoyed by the man continually monkeying with their horses, some cowpuncher told him, "Don't touch a horse on the nose. Pat his hips!"

Good or bad as this advice was intended to be, when Happy Jack saw the black bronc tied in front of Du Fran's, he started over, remembered to by-pass his nose and stumbled up to his hips. Slapping his rump soundly, he yelled, "How's the hoss!" The black "hoss" looked around and kicked Happy Jack for a roll of fifteen feet; and that is how the black "hoss" got his name. Somehow, the swamper wasn't hurt. I went out and got on my black horse and left town, decided to give him the name of the old swamper who got such a rough deal for his friendliness.

Then there was Rainbow. He changed colors from chestnut-sorrel in summer to nearly jet black in winter.

Love Letter was a red-roan whose many brands had healed and haired over in a darker red, giving him his name. Ring-Eye showed the white of his eyes completely around the iris.

A cowboy generally expressed what he saw in a horse—and very likely that had a lot to do with naming him.

7. Storm and Stampede

All spring the weather had been mild. Plentiful rain and sunshine brought grass up by leaps and bounds, so the Matador began working through their pastures early. Since I was to ride the broncs again, I took them and others of the rough string out to the wagon, for I was to help with this work.

We started clearing the Strip of stock that had wandered in there during winter. April drifted into May and animals had shed their winter hair. All of the other big outfits were moving herds or working their ranges, too. The H O had started from their ranch out near the Black Hills, to their reservation lease with a herd of over twelve hundred cattle. The H O men rode big horses, carrying a lot of Belgian blood, the only outfit to have these big horses. They were pretty tough to ride. With this drive, they were also bringing several hundred mares. One band was headed by a big eastern stud, the others by range studs. The Sword & Dagger, an outfit just to the south, straightening out their livestock also, were out with their wagon. There was nothing to indicate that anything other than summer was near at hand.

Certainly, the cloudy, warm morning of May 5, 1905, was pleasant enough. But rain began falling before noon, the summery breeze became icy, and the rain changed rapidly to snow, blanketing everything—the makings of a blizzard growing by the hour!

Our Matador wagon was on the Trail near Tony Akers Corners. Con, sniffing the north wind like a longhorn steer, felt from this storm's approach that we could expect a bad time. So he ordered the wagons to move and camp down on the Moreau, in the timber between Pete Le Beau's and Landreaux' place, where there was plenty of wood for the cookstove. The tents kept us dry while the snow pelted us continually for two days and nights. It fell in huge flakes that at times so filled the air that objects ten feet away were not visible.

We turned the horses loose in the timber, except a few that we kept close to the tents, and they fared all right. While it got pretty cold, there was little wind in the timber and the horses stood bunched together a good deal of the time. Snow piled up on their backs like a blanket, but we didn't lose any horses at all. The ones we kept up were blanketed and saddled, which helped to keep them warm.

But other outfits, caught on higher ground where wind could hit them, lost many horses, especially those that had been stabled all winter in log barns and were slick as seals. The H O's held their big herd in the whipping gale for a while, but had to let them go. They drifted into the rough country along the Cheyenne. The band of mares with the big stud from an eastern farm all died, but some of the others, with native studs that kept them moving about, got through all right.

Art Bivins, a Sword & Dagger man, told me later how he had wrapped his pet cow horse, Papoose, in his best quilt to save him. Long years afterward, when Papoose was in his twenties, he became my children's cherished companion.

After this terrible storm, the sun came out again, the weather warmed up and the snow melted, revealing the frightful livestock tragedy. Range cattle and horses had died like flies in a heavy frost—some of them still standing up against a fence or a tree. Dead animals lay everywhere. One Indian owner, Herbert, who branded his horses with the figures 24 connected, lost twenty-four of them in one pile. It was the same all over—livestock died due to chilling from the sudden, extreme change in weather so late in spring. The May 1905 snowstorm remains historically the worst killer of range animals, and doubtless was the worst spring storm ever known on the reservation.

For a while, the weather held nice, and we went back to work. Then, with June, came the heaviest rains I can remember. Lightning and thunder were frightful. Once, during a week's downpour, the soppy ground was totally unable to absorb any more water and we had to dip deep holes to drain water away from the cook's tent. We were camped on Bear Neckless Creek, northeast of where La Plant is now. Virgin Creek, to the west, was flooded out of banks. We couldn't work, nor even move camp to higher ground, because of the deep, sticky gumbo mud. The wagons simply couldn't be pulled through the heavy underfoot for the gumbo would roll up on the wheels until they became so wide and packed they couldn't turn. Had we undertaken a move, we would have mired down completely, and so would the teams. Fifteen years later, where the saddle horses bogged nearly to their knees when penned and circling the rope corral was plainly marked by a different, darker green type of grass which came up where the gumbo top soil was stomped and churned under by their hoofs. This, to me, was a strange thing, suggesting that perhaps several feet down under the present soil of that region might be a far different sort of plant life which was somehow covered over in the long ago.

While we were forced to stay there, I saw my first Indian killed by lightning. Gray Bear lived on Virgin Creek, west of the crossing. One morning, while waiting for drier weather, we were sunning beds, pulling mud balls from horses' tails, braiding them, and tying them up out of reach of more mud. We saw a team of Indian ponies hitched to a squaw wagon inching through the gumbo, coming our way. It was the Gray Bear squaw with four or five youngsters, and in the back of the rig lay a large, tarp-covered form. She drove up to the roundup tent and stopped. Con stepped out to her rig and Mrs. Gray Bear told him that lightning had killed her husband when he went to the pasture to catch a horse. She and the kids had loaded him into the light wagon and waited for Virgin Creek to go down so she could cross over. Now she was taking him to the Agency, twenty-five miles distant, through all that mud, to bury him.

It was noon, and Con invited her to eat with us, which she did. We all helped the kids get plates and heap them with grub. The woman had been married to Charley Ducharm before Gray Bear and her hitched up. Charley was with our wagon then. Some of the kids were his and went right over to him. He helped them fill their plates but didn't speak to the squaw, and she took no notice of him.

Some of us took a quick look at Gray Bear under the tarp. He had been dead several days and was a rough-looking sight.

After the team had rested, Mrs. Gray Bear started out again. Con offered to send an escort with her and the corpse, but she refused. She said she would get there all right by herself, and she did.

Lightning was an ever-present danger to a cowboy. Working livestock in natural lightning country, we had many close calls. Among ourselves, we had a theory that hot, sweaty cattle or horses "drawed" electricity; that they were a likely target when the fire-devils in the clouds got to splitting the sky apart. Most any old cowboy can tell of the way a horse's mane and tail almost sparks just before a storm. The hairs stand out separately as if a little hurricane is blowing in from underneath. On nights when a black storm hovers overhead, soft phosphorus lights glow on the tips of a horse's ears, like little candles, moving as he twitches and turns them while watching everything out in the dark. On many bad nights, I've seen these same little balls of light on the tips of the cattle's horns, and the glow is considerable when many cattle are bunched. Such are a cowboy's memories of the stormy nights, night-guarding a herd, and to claim that a man is without fear of lightning just isn't true.

Those were the nights that a herd was hard to hold, for they were fearful, too, and would run with the storm. Weather has stampeded many a herd, and not always from lightning and hail, either. Snow and a fierce gale with it has turned many a herd and sent them drifting in a lope with the wind. But lightning has the strongest grip on creatures of the outdoors, man or beast. A stampede has led many a cowboy to a near miss with death while riding to stop a running herd. But not all to the bad was lightning those times. By its dazzling flashes, a man could see mortal danger ahead, affording a split-second's time for his mount to leap aside or over it; or to stop in his tracks, to save his and his rider's life.

Lightning is full of strange tricks. It runs a crazy pattern that is as unpredictable as the streak it cuts across a dark cloud. I've seen it strike one horse, yet not harm the one beside him. I saw it kill a man and burn everything off of him except his shirt collar, tie, and boots—even his socks were burned.

Contrary to the old legend that lightning never strikes twice in the same place, I know that it will not only strike in the same spot more than once, but I've watched a bolt

hit Coffee Buttes, saw it keep on bouncing, striking with
fire flying as it went from ridge to ridge a half-dozen times
before it grounded. And more than once on the same night.

Coffee Buttes is a series of high ridges that were in the
Matador pasture near the Missouri. They were noted for
fiendish lightning, and we rarely had a herd to hold there
but what a hellish mean storm got set to give us the works.
The worst lighting I ever saw in my life was near these
buttes the night the herd was hit.

We had been working the beef pasture nearest the Missouri, gathering all of the two- and three-year-old winter-
drifted stock out of that end to take them to the back
pasture where everything not going to market that fall belonged.

We had worked the range to Coffee Buttes and had a
herd of a thousand. That afternoon, away off to the northwest, we could see a storm brewing. Oscar Buford and I
rode out to relieve the others on day herd. The storm by
then looked cyclone-black, edged in ruffled hailstone-and-
wind green. It was right over us by then, as I circled around
the cattle and watched it. We couldn't bed the steers in the
face of such weather coming up. They simply wouldn't lie
down, but we had to try to hold them if at all possible.

The wagon was camped just over a little knoll not far
from us.

I had gone around the herd and met the other guard a
couple of times, and I was singing a little, if you could call
such sounds singing. I had just pushed a few edgy steers
closer to the others and rode on around the outside of others,
when a bolt of chain lightning split the sky wide open! One
blinding prong shot straight down and hit the herd where
I had just passed only a few moments before. One hundred
steers went to the ground, and the tail end of the strike
flattened me and my night horse, Dick. Twenty steers lay
in a heap that never moved again. The others stumbled to

their feet, stunned and wobbly. I cannot recall having any feeling at all. I just didn't know what had happened. I was dazed and scrambling around on the ground the first I remember. Dick was doing the same, trying to stay near me, nickering pitifully.

Oscar saw everything that happened from the other side of the herd. He didn't wait for anything or even look back. Scared as ever a man could be, he swung his horse around and rode like hell to tell Con and the men that "Ike and half of the herd are dead!" Everyone in camp rode out to us and saw me trying to get on my horse, both of us still staggering from the shock, while the lightning doubled its violence. The herd was moving, too, gathering speed for a stampede. When the bolt had hit, the steers had bunched and milled for a time before the leaders led off. But the men from the wagon got there just in time to hold them, and Con had the whole herd moved a half-mile away from the dead steers, out onto a flat place for the night. He sent me to the wagon and to bed. Extra men stayed to help guard and the black tempest swept on over us with very little rain. After a night's sleep, I was all right again, but ever after, my best night horse, Dick, was spoiled. He went completely frantic in an electric storm, and could never again be used for night-guarding.

There couldn't help being many wild stampedes where thousands of half-tame cattle were handled on a semi-frontier where virgin soil had never known the plow; where the rocks, the streams, the butte landmarks with their tall Indian water signs on the highest point seemed to have existed always; where the wild life and the forage, down through the centuries, were changed only by the hand of Mother Nature. Her forces—sun, wind, rain, snow, blizzard, hail, drouth—all these had changed the land but little. Not yet had the destructive hand of white man torn asunder the ages-old region, in his quest to make it over into something he believed was better. And only time would tell the havoc he wrought.

Although there were stampedes of frightened cattle, they were not always the bloody, hair-raising affairs some "tellers" would have you believe, but wild enough to stir up plenty of excitement, and they were always dangerous.

Once, at Short White Man Dam, six miles out on the Strip from Evarts, we had a mixup that was a dandy. A half-dozen outfits, the L7's, H O, Turkey Track, the Sword & Dagger, Matador, the H A T's, and possibly other outfits, were all in to the rails receiving the spring shipment of thin stuff from the south. All of these cattle had to be taken to their ranges and turned loose, no matter where they were. The wagons were camped about a half-mile apart. Some of the shipments were short—that is, not all of the stock arrived at the same time, so it caused some outfits to delay until everything arrived. All of the outfits were anxious to leave just as soon as they could. These were the times when Evarts swarmed with cowboys, and many a hilarious night that wild little cow town knew. Every outfit had from eight to twelve men, and with time to spare they made things lively. Some of it was cheerful hell-raising; some of it wasn't, but actually the happier side predominated.

One day, the L7's received all their cattle and were ready to leave at daybreak. But for some reason that night, their herd broke away and overran half of the surrounding herds, some of them ready to start out, too, the next morning. The Sword & Dagger let their two thousand head go, under pressure. Some outfits held part of their stock out of the stampede, but more than six thousand were well scrambled in the night's run.

Next morning, the L7's sent out word that their men would round up everything, which they did, but of course, the other outfits sent men to help, too. When the cattle were thrown into a big roundup, ten or twelve men went to cutting cattle according to the brands they were representing. The big roundup was separated into quarters, and each one moved back far enough so that the men had room to work and to hold the cut from each quarter. I helped with the separating. We cut cattle to the center, cut them to the sides —just wherever the different brands belonged, while reps took them away as fast as they could. Twenty-five cowboys held the big roundup together as the brand men rode among the stock, separating them. Other cowboys held the different cuts from mixing again with the main roundup, no matter who they might belong to, and as night came on the guards were doubled. Eventually, all brands and herds were back again where they belonged.

This job was just over when an amusing incident touched off another stampede that was as wild as any, but didn't involve so many herds. It happened in daylight, which helped some, but it showed how little it takes to set off a stampede.

A man on a pinto horse came riding down a trail near one of these ringy, or edgy, and well-spooked herds still being detained, waiting for late trains. A big black dog trotted close to the horse's heels, minding his own business, excepting for an occasional side trip to sniff for a rabbit, and maybe to yelp a little. A young fellow, not much more than a kid, who was helping hold the herd saw them coming, feared that the pair might cause trouble when the cattle spotted them, since they were still cranky enough to run at a sudden puff of wind. So he rode around to the wagon to tell the boss what he saw in the distance. "Man coming over yonder," he said. "Got a dog a-follerin' his horse," he added helpfully.

The wagon boss was grouchy enough at best, and without considering what the kid said, he growled, "Mind your own business, kid!" The kid turned away and rode back to his place at the herd. Shortly thereafter, the steers saw the approaching pair. A bunch of them jumped, rattling their hocks; others caught the cue and inside of minutes the whole herd, heads up, tails curled over their backs, and horns cracking against others, stampeded completely out of control. They ran for two hours before they could be turned into a "mill"—or run in a circle and stopped.

But the granddad of all stampedes I ever took part in was on Bear Neckless Creek, with a Matador herd. There is usually some reason for cattle stampeding, but a lot of the time, no one knows but the cattle themselves why they take off. "Some instinct" men will tell you, but I don't know. Sometimes a man on guard causes it by doing a careless thing— lighting a cigarette, or getting down off his horse. At times, a hard cough will do the trick. It could be something in the wind, or a night horse nickering for a reason known only to himself. There are times when a herd will "break" in broad daylight, but it happens mostly at night. Cattle are slow animals, but they are fast enough when scared. A herd of a thousand can get to their feet as quickly as one can, hoofs rattling, running before they are half up—a mystery how they get the "flash" to go at the same instant. Herds have been known to "jump" but not run—that is, to get on their feet from the ground where they had been resting an instant before. There would be a heavy roll of sound and every steer would be standing, alerted and on his feet, ready to run, and if they did take off, every head would swing in the same direction at the same moment.

Most of us old cowmen have seen some lively stampedes in our time and we like to recall them, remembering that the cattle we handled back in those unforgettable days weren't slow to put up a fight if molested a little—yet we handled thousands of them with little trouble. A man had to know the nature of these wild critters.

The stampede on Bear Neckless, when the Matador herd split wide open, happened while we were taking cattle to the back pasture. Besides the Matador men, there were at

least a dozen reps from other outfits, as well as Indian owners looking for their strays, so our horse *remuda* numbered
at least 175 head. Each rep had from eight to ten head, and,
of course, the Matador men had theirs.

In spite of muddy, rain weather, we were getting along
pretty well with the roundup of that part of the range, and
had a herd of about two thousand head when we reached
Bear Neckless. The wagon camped for the night on a little
knoll above the creek. As night came on, away off in the
north, a whole skyful of bumpy clouds began to show up
and move toward us. Each man with the wagon always kept
a night horse. If he was gentle, he was staked out with a
rope, but if he was bad about getting loose, he was tied to
the bedwagon wheel. Most of them were saddled and ready
for their owners to go on night guard when their turn came,
or so they would have horses if anything happened in the
night.

Among the reps was a young Indian named His Horse Is
Fast. He lived on the Moreau, and that night he kept up a
sort of a cream-colored horse. He had saddled him, and with
the oncoming storm in mind, he had covered his saddle with
his big yellow slicker, tying it down so it wouldn't come off.
Somehow, during the night the horse got loose and wandered along the creek, probably grazing and looking for
other horses. We were holding the steer herd just north of
the wagon, and north of them the night hawk guarded the
saddle horses. The loose horse had worked around north of
the *remuda,* when just about midnight a helluva rainstorm
hit us and the lightning flashed almost continuously. The
stock in both herds were restless, all on their feet, heads
pointing south and backs humped to the storm coming in
on them.

When lightning began tearing the sky apart in dead earnest right above us, with deafening thunder crashing right on
its heels, the gelding belonging to His Horse Is Fast made

a run for the other horses. In the zig-zag lightning, the night hawk saw him coming, and just as he reached the *remuda,* a terrific bolt of chain lightning and crashing thunder streaked over the entire Up-Above, plainly revealing the big white thing charging down on them, white "wings" (the sleeves of the slicker) flailing and flapping all about him as he tore in among them. The rising wind struck, too, just then, and he chose that instant to nicker just as loud as he could! Who knows what he told the others? Perhaps he screamed that the devil himself was riding his tail. Anyway, in a short split-second, the *remuda* whirled away in a wild run. They swept through the steers, who were ready for action, too, and they broke away also, and the whole works ran over and around camp, breaking loose nearly every night horse—and they ran, too.

A night guard is broken up into four shifts of two hours each, between eight P.M. and four A.M., and that night I was to go on the two o'clock guard. I wasn't asleep, but had rolled out my bed on the south side of the wagon. Not far from me was old Dick. He would stand staked with just a little pin shoved into the ground. We used little iron pins shaped like a corkscrew, with a handle on top. They were easily twisted into the ground. A swivel around the top allowed the rope to turn about it without tangling up.

By the lightning, I could see he was still there, and after the uproar had mostly passed by, I got on him and followed the stampede. We ran steers and horses the rest of the night, and daylight found us—Dick and me—about ten miles away, on Stove Creek. I had lost track of the steers, but had kept up with about seventy-five head of saddle horses. A dozen of them were saddled or dragging a rope around their necks. One was Con's old white night horse, Walker, and he had Con's saddle on his back.

Dick was nearly played out by the night's run. I turned him loose to travel with the bunch after I caught Walker, and started the others back toward camp. Men who had a saddle and horse were out looking for me, but most everyone was afoot until I got there with the horses. That was one stampede we never got together again. Some of the scared horses headed south and ran over the Turkey Track fence that night. Most of the reps were completely afoot, for their horses had headed for home as soon as it got daylight and they got their bearings. His Horse Is Fast had neither horses nor saddle. He lost all of them in the night's run. No one was hurt, but we sure had a stampede to remember. And we had to begin all over getting the same region rounded up again.

About ten days later, we had a good-sized herd at Coffee Butte, and once more hit the same old bad night. I often wondered why Con continued to camp there when we so seldom escaped trouble. It certainly was a mean place to be when an electric storm moved in, but this time a rather comical incident occurred there.

As night came on, we had no sooner bedded the herd than a threatening storm began building up just as the first guard was going on. All of us were jumpy and wishing we were anywhere but there—especially me. But the worst scared one of all of us was a long-legged, big-mouthed fellow named Rufe. He came from Georgia, and "Suh, he was a much a-feared of the damnable lightning, Suh!"

Con was a quiet man, but he didn't like to be told his business. All of us hoped he would turn the herd loose in the face of what was about to hit us, but we kept our mouths shut and let him decide the matter. We knew that to start bellyaching was a good way to get to stand night guard on those cattle. But Rufe wouldn't shut up. He kept advising Con against "holding the herd," until we wanted to plant a fist in his mouth, for some of us who knew Con well could see faint signs that he might turn loose.

As Con rode by, we heard Rufe yell: "Con, you suttinly

don't intind tryin' to hold this here herd an' that helluva storm 'bout to pounce on us?" Con didn't answer, and all the more we wanted to choke the mouthy Rufe.

After Con rode around a while longer and everything got blacker by the minute, he said, "Just drift the herd up to the head of Stove Creek breaks," which wasn't far. "Turn them loose and everybody go to bed tonight. If the storm stampedes them they will hit the Turkey Track fence and we'll round up in the morning." That sure sounded good to all of us. The storm beat over us, but we were snug in our bedrolls and didn't give a damn. We could soon gather the herd again, come daylight.

Right after that, Frank Mitchell came out to the wagon and talked to Con. He had word that Matador steers were in Turkey Track range, so a rep had to go and work with them. Next morning, Con told me to take my horses and go to the "Tracks," the short-cut name we gave to the Turkey Tracks. Since I had several broncs extra, I was to give them to the cowboys I thought could ride them, leaving me with a regular ten-horse string. So I cut my horses from the *remuda*, packed my bed on Dick, saddled up, and started the rest of my mounts toward the Turkey Track range to the south.

8. Rep at Turkey Tracks

The first glimpse I ever had of Cap Mossman, manager of Turkey Tracks, was in Joe Green's hotel in Evarts, the previous spring 1904. He was a young man, not too tall, and wore a black moustache. His gray hat was set at a jaunty angle on his head, and from under its broad brim his blue eyes had a way of looking sharply at each and every man he met. He was a colorful character, and as I jogged along, my thoughts dwelt on Captain Burton C. Mossman and what I knew of him, his outfit and men.

I was scarcely out of my impressionable teens, so I never forgot what Cap was doing the first day I learned who he was. He was standing at the hotel bar with a drink before him, lighting his cigar with a hundred-dollar bill! He folded the greenback lengthwise several times, then, reaching over to the cigar lighter which always stood on the bar for customers' use, Cap dipped the end of the bill into the flame. When it blazed up good, he put it to his cigar. Spectacular? Of course! The Captain had everyone's attention, too. He pinched out the fire, pocketed the bill, puffed his cigar, and

took up his drink as if lighting cigars with a big greenback was an everyday occurrence with him. What a showman he was! To my delight, I saw him do this trick several times afterwards, and watched men's eyes bug out.

On this particular morning, I was going to the Turkey Track outfit as Matador rep and I wondered what Mossman's outfit was like. We knew the Tracks had shipped in a lot of cattle the year before because they crossed Matador range to reach their own, and the opinion was that they had about ten thousand head on their lease then.

In 1904, when the cattle concerns on the Cheyenne River Reservation began stocking their ranges, Cap Mossman sent in the Turkey Track vanguard to unload at Evarts. From there, they crossed to west-river grass by boat. The man Cap Mossman selected as his Dakota superintendent was Homer Willingham, son of the noted Cape Willingham, first sheriff of the renowned old Tascosa, Texas. He started him north in charge of the saddle horses, cattle, teams, harnesses, branding irons, stove, tent, and other things necessary for efficient cow work under outdoor conditions. They entrained from Mossman's New Mexico sources, but Cap intended hiring most of his men in South Dakota.

Homer was unquestionably an able cattleman and first-rate cowboy. I worked with him many a day and knew that his good qualities far outweighed the bad, but demon drink dogged his heels all of his days.

The Turkey Track trains left New Mexico and headed rapidly northward. The first stop for unloading and feeding was at the Sioux City stockyards. The city was a lively place on the shores of the Missouri and there temptation hit Homer again. Hard. He got gloriously drunk and stayed that way, somewhere in the city, while his horses, cattle, and all the rest of it, being billed right on through, were loaded again by stockyard men and the train pulled out on schedule for South Dakota, without Homer.

Upon arrival, there was no one there to attend to unloading the cars, so Hugh Chittick, the Milwaukee railroad man responsible for all shipping in or out of Evarts, enlisted the help of Ernest Eidson, Sword & Dagger manager. He was busy with cattle coming in, too, but his men gave Chittick a hand and they got the Turkey Track stuff off the cars and out onto the Strip across the river. They arranged for men to guard them on the Trail until a Turkey Track man with authority to take them to their range came along.

The horses were left in the stockyards at Evarts, for Mossman's ranch boss was expected hourly, so Eidson went on about his work until he heard of, or discovered, that the horses were still corralled several days later. There was water in the corral, but they had grown so starved they had chewed the manes and tails off each other. Since no Turkey Track boss had yet appeared, Eidson took the hungry horses from the corrals, crossed them over the Missouri, and put them with the Sword & Dagger *remuda*.

Following the first trains with more loaded cars, Cap Mossman caught up with and passed the slower freight on a fast train. He also passed Homer, not knowing he was stranded in Sioux City. He was anything but in a good humor when he left the train at Evarts and heard about his previous shipment. Someone gave him a telegram from Homer. It informed Mossman that the train "ran off and left me!"—that on account of his new boots he couldn't walk to Evarts, and to wire him fifty dollars. If this jolly message was intended to cheer Mossman, it missed its aim, but he did wire Homer the cash to come to Dakota.

Homer didn't come. When he got the money, he immediately retraced his steps to the dance halls and the friendly gals, where he stayed until the fifty was gone. Once more he wired Mossman for money, but Mossman sent a train ticket instead, with not one red copper to buy anything to eat en route. So Homer landed in Dakota about as starved as the

Turkey Track horses were when Eidson took them from the stockyards.

By then, some of the Track cowboys had followed Mossman north—Tom Cage, "Peavine," Ed Truit, and others. While still waiting for Homer to come, Mossman hired more men and rigged up his wagons for the work that was piling up on him. Amadee Rouseau, a young Frenchman native to the reservation region and married into the Sioux, helped Cap buy more horses and went to work for him, too, as temporary manager. But Amadee rode his own horses, which were good ones. He would have nothing to do with the skinny little New Mexico horses, manes and tails chewed off and ragged, although they were good enough cow horses and couldn't help their shabby looks.

Cap had not weakened any on Homer; he still intended that he run the Dakota outfit. But he certainly reprimanded the repentant cowboy when they met. He hustled Homer on across the Missouri without tarrying at all in Evarts, determined for him to keep sober and to manage the Tracks, for he knew Homer could do it.

Homer was sober enough by the time he caught up with his outfit, which Rouseau and the men had taken out to the head of Virgin Creek, in Mossman's range, and there Rouseau turned things over to him.

Engrossed in getting cattle to Dakota, Mossman had hurried back to New Mexico to try to interest men in sending stock to his northern lease. He found many who needed grass, but they were also skeptical about the severe winters. Meanwhile, in Dakota, Homer settled the stock on the new range where grass and water were abundant, and returned to Evarts to await other trains, along with his outfit. There they found time on their hands, but Homer always knew how to fill idle hours. He liked the bright lights and gaiety, and he knew where they could be found.

His roundup outfit had a good cook, and besides the men's

beds, the bedwagon carried a tent for sleeping out. Instead of pitching camp out on the Strip away from Evarts to await the cattle, what did young Homer do but cross over to the east side and pilot the wagons down to a spot near the Missouri. Here he set up camp on the flat, within short sprinting distance to the hotel-like structure where the painted and obliging Gals plied their trade. Not a livelier place could be found even in Evarts, wildest of all wild cow towns. And there the Turkey Tracks stayed, convivial as could be, until Cap Mossman, rushing back and forth between Dakota and New Mexico, appeared without warning, just hours in advance of his cattle. He routed Homer from his camping place, reprimanded him again, in typical Mossman vernacular, which never left a man in doubt about what Cap thought—and put all the men to work dipping cattle.

Being in our range or on the Strip a lot, we often met the Turkey Track men and knew much about their affairs. We knew that Mossman had rousted Homer and his outfit across the river again and left him to take the steers out to the Track range. But after these few short weeks, Mossman already knew he couldn't trust Homer as his Dakota manager. He couldn't be watching him continually, so he arranged with Amadee Rouseau to oversee things in his absence. Amadee worked for Mossman for a time as manager, but he was a snappy, independent little man who would take but little of the explosiveness which Mossman so often indulged in.

After Amadee quit, someone mentioned Jess Knight, who had once run a wagon for Scotty Philip, and Mossman, in a limited way, turned the Turkey Tracks over to Knight until the extremely hard winter of 1906–7. Knight was wagon boss when I went to work with them that first time.

Mossman never completely lost faith in Homer Willingham. Even as he installed Jess Knight onto the Turkey Track range, he had sent Homer with a string of saddle horses to the noted early-day Three V's. Their range was west of the reservation line. The grassland beyond the reservation was a vast, free-grazing region, where many outfits ran cattle, but all of it was under a "Gents Agreement" not to trespass any more than could be avoided on range claimed by another man and his outfit, and out there the Three V's operated.

Homer was to receive three thousand steers which the Three V's had been pasturing for another man and were to be released to Mossman. Cap wrote Homer a letter to take to the Three V's, but he met them on the Trail, taking the cattle to Mossman's range, and right at the outset he had a lively brush with the cowboys doing the driving. They had their ropes down and were hurrying the steers along like saddle horses. It didn't take Homer long to notice the lolled-out tongues, the puffing and slobbering, and other evidence of too much haste. He rode to the lead and held them up. Since these steers were to go to market that fall, Homer had no intention of allowing such treatment. His action in stopping the herd met with loud protests from the Three V's men.

"We'll slow down!" Homer said emphatically.

"We're not working for you," he was told. But nothing daunted Homer. He went to the wagon boss, showed his letter from Mossman, and asserted his own authority. Consequently, ropes were coiled and tied back on their saddles and they drove the stock as Homer directed, turning them eventually through one of the numerous gates in the Trail fence. The steers were watered at a crossing on the Little Moreau River in Matador range, then driven on south to Turkey Track grass.

The reservation country was free of mankind then, except for the Sioux Indians and French-Indians, descendants of early trappers and explorers who had married Lakota women. White men who had joined the Indians lived out there, too, but otherwise, white people did not go into Indian country without a U. S. Indian Agency permit. So it was just cattle and grass, mostly.

Early summer had come and every little draw held thickets of wild plums or chokecherry bushes. They still flooded the air with sweetest blossom perfume and were starting to "set" green fruit. Many southern cowpunchers had not known the wild plum, a really toothsome fruit when ripe. Most plums were deep red, but sometimes a patch of huge yellow ones could be found. They were a prize. Meadowlarks, blackbirds, and little brown field birds by the score nested and warbled melodiously. Native prairie chickens and the chunky, feather-legged grouse, whirring up suddenly out of grassy hiding places almost right under the cattle's hoofs, spooked both horses and steers, and more than one nest of these game birds were probably destroyed, yet they abounded everywhere. Coyotes and gray wolves left padded trails to tell of their presence on the range. Now and then a wildcat left his sign, too.

Already, the Three V steers that Willingham was receiving for Mossman were putting on tallow and meat. They were counted into Track range, after which Homer returned to the Turkey Track wagon.

Here, shortly after he reached Dakota, Willingham met with something of a surprise when he found Jess Knight in charge of the Turkey Tracks. Jess was not slow to let Homer know about his authority, either. But, even so, Mossman had left another letter for Homer, instructing him to take his string of horses and go to the Matador to rep for the Tracks. Mossman was well aware that Turkey Track steers had been lost in our range as the herds trailed through. Although not too happy over circumstances as they were, Homer took Mossman's letter and came to the Matador wagon. A top hand such as Homer was always welcome, and we were glad to see him. Most of us called him Jack Bean—a name his father had given him when he was a boy. Homer always needed quite a few horses to keep him mounted. He rode them hard, and worked hard himself, so his dad claimed that Homer "got their bean," meaning the last ounce of energy. Homer and my best friend, Roy Vivian, son of the first Clerk of Courts of old Tascosa, Texas, were cousins.

The Matador was engaged in its first big work—the roundup and tally of the reservation livestock—when Willingham joined us. Roy and I were both with the Matador wagon, too—all three of us young, full of devilment and life. It was a joyful time of year. Sunshine warmed the Dakota winds. Our cook was a good one, which added to our feeling of well-being. And our horses were getting fat on the fine pastures.

The Matador men worked well together. Only occasionally would there be a sharp little argument among them, but Con could be as deaf to these things as a stone, and never interfered unless the talk became loud.

When Homer came, he fitted right in with us, and he worked well until we had to go to Evarts for cattle. Then old pal whisky would get him by the arm and delay him there. He'd leave his horses with the Matador *remuda* while he lingered around Evarts. When he decided to come out to our outfit, he would somehow smuggle plenty of forbidden whisky across the Missouri, and while it lasted he would stay drunk on the range, allowing the Matador men to do his work, cut the Turkey Track cattle from the roundups and keep them in herd without his having to stand guard either night or day. But in spite of his hellion ways, Homer had a pleasing personality and was well liked by the cowboys.

His trouble came from Frank Mitchell, who violently disliked seeing him loitering around the Matador outfit, half drunk. Invariably, he had enough whisky hidden in his bedroll to keep some of his Matador buddies pie-eyed, too, if they were so inclined.

One day Mossman, always on the move, popped into Evarts unannounced and found Homer drunk as ever he could be. Cap got him into his buckboard and started the thirty-five miles or more to the Turkey Tracks. On the way, he sighted the Matador outfit rounding up, so he looked around for their wagon, saw it in the distance, and headed for it. Homer was asleep in the rig by then, and he was still slumbering when Mossman drove up, intending to leave his passenger.

Mitchell happened to be there that day. He, too, was a short-tempered man at best, given to quick bursts of anger which equaled Mossman's. The sight of Homer peacefully sleeping beside Mossman in the rig aroused his wrath and when Cap drove up to leave his rep with the Matador wagon, Mitchell yelled: "Take him on with you, Cap. He's a damn nuisance here. We do his work, anyway."

Mossman remonstrated with Mitchell and when the two men fell into a sharp argument, Homer roused up momentarily and cast a neutral eye over them before returning to his slumbers, for he didn't care how they settled it. Although he took Homer onto his own wagon with him, the fiery Cap aimed a parting shot at Mitchell as he drove away. Referring to Homer, he said, "Yes, he may be a drunken little sonofabitch, but he knows more about cattle, dead drunk, than any of you Matador men—and that includes you!"

So Cap carted his sleeping ex-manager along with him to the Track wagon, where he left him. As soon as Homer sobered up, he got a horse and came back to our outfit, to rep. He was a good cowboy, and we could use him.

There appeared to exist some sort of bond between Homer Willingham and Mossman, for no matter what his faults were, Cap never let Homer down. He kept him at work when he would have scathingly berated any other man for far less an offense and fired him. It could have been that the friendship between Cap and Homer's dad had a deep hold on Mossman. At one time, Cap had replaced Willingham as boss of the New

Mexico Turkey Tracks, and everyone had expected trouble between these two men, for both were hard-bitten veterans of many range feuds, but no such thing developed, and Cap's loyalty to Cape Willingham's son often made men wonder.

Homer continually defied and ignored Jess Knight's authority. He did as he pleased as long as he worked for Cap. If he was with the Turkey Track wagon and Knight attempted to give him orders, he used his own pleasure as to whether he would take them or not. He seemed to bear an amused contempt for Knight's management of the Tracks, although he was never quarrelsome about it. He was never quarrelsome at any time.

I didn't know then that some years later Homer Willingham was to die by his own hand. Or that he would leave his silver and gold mounted spurs to me. The note he left behind read in part that he wanted "the best cowboy and bronc rider I know to have my spurs."

I joined the Tracks in their northeast corner near the Agency, instead of on Stove Creek where they were supposed to be. They had made one roundup already and were camped on Bull Creek. I worked across their range with them, which took about three weeks. We caught one hundred or more cattle belonging in Matador range, and I took them back home.

It was on this trip to the Tracks that I saw the reservation's most cantankerous character, Elmer Perviance, get into trouble. Cowboys all called him "old Peavine." He had come to Dakota with Mossman, but he didn't work for Cap many months at a time. It was standard procedure for Peavine to work a few months for the Tracks, get mad at them and quit; then he would go to the Matadors. Con always gave him a job, for he was a top hand, no matter what he did for the outfit. When something irked him again, he'd quit and go back to the Tracks, and there, too, he always had a job waiting.

It was he who once quarreled with Mossman in a most heated way, for Cap was as explosive as Peavine. To end it, Cap told Peavine he was fired, and to turn his horse loose. To which Peavine retorted, "You go to hell! I came up here to Dakota to work for you and I won't be fired." He got on his horse and rode away, leaving Cap to shrug his shoulders and ask, "What can you do with a fellow like that?"

The morning I left the Tracks to go home with my cattle, Peavine, cranky as usual, had a most amusing disturbance with a little bay horse that was as irritable as he was. Grasshopper, the fiery little bronc, appeared to carry considerable Steel Dust blood. He had a long, silky mane, and that morning when Peavine saddled him, a strand of the mane was left under the saddle blanket. He neglected to pull it out, and it worked up in a little loop in front of the saddle where it attracted Peavine's attention. He'd hook his finger in the loop to pull it out so it wouldn't make a sore there, and every time he tried it, the salty little horse would bow his neck and threaten to buck. Finally, Peavine lost his ever-short temper and yanked the mane out, regardless of Grasshopper's threats—which was all the bay wanted him to do. He dropped his head and bucked like a scalded pup! He throwed Peavine off and he sailed away out to one side like a big bird, landing flat on his belly in the grass. It took us an hour to catch Grasshopper, for he bucked, cavorted and snorted and had a lot of fun, same as we did, laughing about it.

9. Cowboy's Romance

When I got back to the Matador wagon, they were leaving for Evarts to bring out more cattle. I was glad to get back in time to go along, for here was another opportunity to see the Miss Darlings. By then, Roy Vivian and I imagined we were really tops with these young ladies. Frank Mitchell had a room at the hotel owned by their mother and step-dad, Joe Green, and whenever the Matador wagon came in, Mr. Mitchell would round up a few guests for an evening in the hotel parlor. Both Violet and Rose played the piano and sang nicely, and they were very fond of Mr. Mitchell. He enjoyed their attentions, too—a kiss and a hug now and then, and doubtless he supplied the money for various items that girls are fond of, for he was a liberal man.

When we reached Evarts, we camped out on the Strip and then rode horseback down to the ferry to cross over the Missouri. The first person I met after I stabled my horse at the livery barn and entered the hotel was Mrs. Frank Mitchell, who had come back to Dakota with Frank when he returned from Texas. I had known her in Texas, had been to her home, and thought her one of the loveliest ladies I knew. She was a slim, very pretty woman who had always been nice to me, so it was most pleasant to meet her again. But before the evening ended, I learned from Miss Violet that Mrs. Mitchell hadn't been at all pleased when she and Frank got off the train in Evarts a few days previous.

It seemed that Mr. Mitchell hadn't mentioned that his wife might come back to Dakota when he did. Perhaps he didn't know it himself. Certainly the little Darlings didn't know it. In fact, they didn't even notice the lady with Frank. They saw him get off the train and without waiting for him to reach the hotel, they fairly flew down the street to meet him. They flung their arms about him, and both of them kissed him affectionately. They called him some pet names and appeared so joyful to have him back in Dakota, and for all this attention, Frank looked and acted most pleased, while Mrs. Mitchell, ignored momentarily, took it all in!

When Frank got around to introducing her to his young friends, she was somewhat chagrined. The girls were more than a little squelched by the dignified Mrs. Mitchell, whom they hardly knew existed, and they retreated to the hotel about as fast as they had left it.

By the very manner and familiarity of the greeting extended her husband by the girls, Mrs. Mitchell suspicioned that he might have other lady friends just as affectionate. She didn't leave Frank in doubt about her thoughts, so it wasn't long after we got to town until he called Roy and me up to his office. He told us about the meeting at the train and enlisted our aid in helping him soothe his wife's ruffled feelings. He told us not to be bashful in our attentions to the young ladies that evening, so that Mrs. Mitchell would see they were *our* friends and that he had only an "unclelike" interest in them. Since Roy and I were about like his own boys, and Mrs. Mitchell was fond of us, too, he figured that would remove him from the hooks.

We did our best. We sang with the girls in the parlor and buzzed around them all evening. The girls knew what was up, too, and between us, we figured we had fixed things up just dandy for "Uncle Frank" and that the bee wouldn't be on him any more. Mrs. Mitchell was just as sweet as ever, and little did I suspect that she was wise to us, until she came out to the wagon one day a month or so later.

We crossed the new cattle over the river and the next day went on back to the range. Mitchell came out to the wagon right away and stayed with us for a while, going along with us, getting first-hand information on the grass situation, the water, the amount of "gain" the steers were making, and something of the number of cattle that would be ready for market early. He was an excellent range man. He had worked for Murdo MacKenzie for years, and his experience as a cowman was vast and varied. And that was how he came to be present and saw Skittish Bill.

The men of the wide open spaces went in for all kinds of rough fun, unless it involved abusing a horse. For a cowboy to buck one out for pure fun, if man and horse had equal chance and no herd to disturb, was never frowned on. In fact, it spiced up their plain, everyday diet of hard work and little amusement. But what happened to Skittish Bill was another matter.

He was a white horse, a little spooky but active and well able to do a day's work. The man who had him in his string was a rough-tough Texan who was inclined to fight at any little excuse. He had ridden Skittish Bill to Evarts when we were in and had lingered on in town after we left. He stayed drunk for a day or two and when he started out of town, he used his spurs on the horse for some reason. Probably it was the liquor in the man that found fault where none existed. But for pay, Skittish Bill dumped him unceremoniously off his back and sprawled him on the ground before the people of the town who had gathered on the street to watch the performance.

Wrathfully, the man went to the blacksmith shop and sharpened his spurs. He tied Skittish Bill's head back to the saddle so he couldn't get it down to buck, and spurred him until his white hair was red with blood. When he rode into camp that night, still half drunk, the horse was in a shameful shape. Next morning, he asked me to help clean the blood off. It was an outrageous sight, but I helped him wash the wounds for the old horse's sake, and just as we turned him loose and this man was saying, "That's good enough. Turn the old sonofabitch out," I saw Frank Mitchell standing just outside of the roundup tent. He stepped out farther to watch the horse as he limped away to the other horses, then Frank went back inside the tent.

Con, range boss, and boss also of every other wagon working in Matador range, was in the tent. Had he seen Skittish Bill before Frank did, he would have fired the rider on the spot. As it was, Mitchell was the man who had seen the hellish mistreatment the horse had been through. Short-tempered and with his anger greatly aroused, he ordered Con to fire the man. Con refused, purely on policy—the manager must not interfere with the wagon boss' men. Doubtless, had Mitchell waited, Con would have let the big Texan go later that day. But Frank wanted action then, and Con's refusal didn't delay things any longer than it took for Mitchell to open his grip which contained his business papers, get out his checkbook, and write out the man's wages in full. As the Texan was walking away from Skittish Bill, Frank called him into the tent. Realizing he was fired for his offense against the horse, the big man turned on his meanest. "No Matador man or Matador horse can run it over me and make me like it." His loud tirade didn't intimidate Mitchell one bit. He roasted the man to a proper dark brown, gave him his check, and pushed him out of the tent. And that was the complete end of one cowboy's job with the Matador's Dakota spread. Skittish Bill got well eventually, but never before or since have I seen a horse more spur cut than he was.

With long days of work our daily fare, and having only occasional entertainment, we could become just as interested in some cowboy's romance as if it was our own. One, especially, held our attention that summer. Rufe, our big-mouthed cowboy, was fixing to marry into the Indians. He was answering an Indian love call. We explained our methods of lovemaking and how the maidens, both white and copper hued, all thought we were just dandy lovers.

But Rufe, being rather a bold young man, figured he could handle his own romance better than any of his advisors. He kept reporting the fine progress he was making with his maiden fair until he had all of us over half envious.

Early-day white men came to the Dakota Indian country for many reasons—trade with the Indians, or freighting with ox teams, but mostly with trapping, fur-trading, or ranching inclinations. Our bright, young Rufe came to Dakota primed for adventure, and he regarded the Indian country as the land of opportunity, if a man were but aggressive and far-sighted. And Rufe certainly was ambitious—rather on the rough gun-toting side, but not at all hard to look at. He spoke a little loudly and entirely with a Georgia accent. Being a man of quick decisions, it hadn't taken him long to think pleasantly of marrying an Indian maiden and setting up a ranching spread of his own, right on the reservation. Other men had done it and had prospered. Everything would be free to him—free grass, free housing, free cattle—from his Indian wife's tribal rights. And free land—a half-section of grassland for every young one he fathered. Yes, Suh! Given a deal like that, a man was bound to prosper. Yes, Suh!

The family Rufe selected as quite elegant enough for him was headed by a snappy old Frenchman. He and Rufe hit it off like brothers, right from the start. And Rufe's romance was most properly conducted all the way through. Yes, Suh!

When Rufe went sparking the buxom maiden, he sat throughout the evening, mostly talking to the old Frenchman, who constantly assured him that his daughter, besides being the eldest, was the very prize of the whole family. In fact, she had any other maiden around there completely outclassed. Her father listed her assets to Rufe. She could cook extremely well. She could attend to any chore whatsoever that needed doing, from cutting up a deer to make a jerky from fresh venison, cut in strips and dried in the sun, to making doeskin moccasins that a man could take comfort in. In fact, the maiden had little to do with the romance other than to act agreeable.

Rufe's courting was well chaperoned, too. His "love" sat primly on the far side of the room from him, her full skirt billowing to the floor, her shoulders draped with a bright shawl, her brown hands busy with beadwork. The young couple smiled at each other and love-talked with their eyes—bold, bright blue man eyes, and dark, shy maiden eyes—while between them sat both the Indian mother and the old Frenchman.

Eventually, the wedding came off, with all of us cowboys and all of her friends and relatives present. Great preparations had been made for the feast and dance afterwards, for this was to be a "white-man style" marriage with all the frills. And that's just what it was, too. The priest was present, and before him, Rufe promised to love and cherish the maiden. She agreed to love old Rufe, give heed to his wants and to obey him. They were made man and wife. After that, the whole throng of us whooped it up. We sang, danced, feasted, until after midnight. With the guests all departed,

Rufe and his bride could finally retire to their bridal chamber.

When alone at last, and for the first time with his maiden, and during his natural lovemaking and caressing his new bride, Rufe made a suspicious discovery. The young squaw was distinctly heavy in a certain place! Her naturally plump waist didn't fold in softly with the ardor of Rufe's bear-hug embraces. That solid bump was there to stay, at least for a time, and it was none of Rufe's doing either!

He backed away and eyed his woman angrily while he accused her. He got no answer to his questions and he didn't wait around for any, either. Swooping up the boots he had pulled off his dance-weary feet, he yanked them back on and stomped across the room, putting on his hat and coat. As the door slammed behind him, he was swearing vengeance on a certain Frenchman—who had disappeared also.

Rufe went out to the corral, saddled his horse, and lit out. He didn't come to our wagon. He rode over twenty-five miles to the line camp of a cowboy he knew. He stabled his horse and stomped into the kitchen, swearing to himself: "No, Suh! By gad, Suh! They can't hand me no Injun Buck's youngun'! She can go get a daddy for him some other way."

Rufe punched the sleeping cowboy. "Get ovah, you stinkin' sonofagun! Ah'm a spendin' m' weddin' night in your bunk! Get ovah, Suh!"

Rousted from sleep, the astonished cowboy challenged his dressed-up and perfumed guest. "What 'n hell's ailin' you? Thought you was gettin' hitched to a squaw and bedding with her tonight?"

"Like hell ah'm beddin' down with that'n!" Rufe snorted. "No, Suh! Not by a damsite! By gad, Suh, *that filly's done just about to foal!*"

And that was that! No more did Rufe visit the old Frenchman's end of the reservation—not for many months. And he plumb got over the notion of a ranching spread with an Indian wife!

The long heads of the wheat grass and blue-joint ripened up early and beef steers began to round out in fine shape. Already, cool nights topped off the hot August days. Rains had slowed down and the cured feed was getting to its best. Mitchell got a wire from Mr. MacKenzie that fat cattle were bringing good money. He advised that Con work through the range and top out a herd of these. Mitchell drove out to the wagon to tell Con about it, and Mrs. Mitchell came along with him. They had a little private tent and stayed out there with us for several days.

During this time Mrs. Mitchell, who was an excellent rider, requested a gentle horse so she could ride around some. Of course, a dozen horses were hastily offered, and several of the boys shouldered each other to see who would escort the lady over the range and to the roundups. But Mrs. Mitchell gracefully settled that question herself. Much to my delight, she said, "I'm sure Ike has a gentle horse in his string, and he will ride with me, thank you."

I set my hat at an ace-deuce angle and caught my best horse, put her saddle on him and brought him to the tent for her, and before long, we rode away together. She wore a trim-fitting riding skirt and blouse. Her boots and Stetson hat were the best and she was pretty as a picture riding old Dick. I was freed from work by Con, since Mrs. Mitchell had chosen me to accompany her.

We rode around several hours each day. I showed her where the sweetest wild plums grew. I pointed out the distant buttes and named them all for her, as well as the various streams we could see from some high pinnacle. We jumped several grays and dozens of coyotes. Half-grown prairie chickens and grouse could fly as well as their parents, and we saw hundreds of them. The wind blew moderately—just enough to make riding pleasant during the hot days. She enjoyed watching the cowboys work the roundups and hold the herds.

She relished Krump's good cooking and complimented him for the variety of good food he could prepare under such limited conditions. All of the cowboys about split themselves to outshine the others in her presence. But before she went back to Evarts I knew from what she told me that she did not like Dakota. I couldn't blame her. She had a lovely home in Amarillo, and Frank could have most any job with the Matadors that he wanted, right there in Texas, so why stay up here in this crazy stampede of wild cattle and wilder humans? From the day she had first set foot in Evarts, she had seen and heard things that, in those days, were very much frowned on by a woman of her character—drunkenness, wild men and women, promiscuous romances, the House down by the Missouri, the whole little frontier cow town—they didn't appeal to her.

Without being told, I knew that a predicament involving a well-known cattle operator whom the Mitchells as well as the rest of us knew very well, was not amusing to her, while most of us chuckled over it as a prime joke, which doubtless gained volume as it was repeated.

As is nearly always the case, most everyone was well aware of the quiet little romance between this cattleman and a married woman, but what happened came as a spicy surprise.

Late one night, this gent was found shouting for help from beneath a pile of boards in a lumber yard. A whole stack of planks had fallen on his leg, fracturing it and pinning him down. The story making the rounds told of the loving twosome stealthily seeking a quiet spot to be alone. In scrambling around in the dark trying to find a comfortable place, they somehow disturbed a tier of lumber which had toppled suddenly and caught Romeo's leg before he could get out of the way. By examining the high-heeled tracks there, it appeared that the woman had been caught, too, but not enough to pin her down, although she had been unable to extricate Romeo. There was little that Juliet could do except to summon help, and "someone shouting and groaning from the direction of the lumber yard" had been her story.

As we rode around, Mrs. Mitchell asked about various things, rumors and people in that country, and I told her the little I knew. I was more interested in showing off the dandy mosquito bar which one of the little Darlings had made for me. It fitted around my hat so that the stinging little insects couldn't reach my ears. I was mighty proud of it and had been careful not to smudge or tear it, and Mrs. Mitchell was wearing it then, while she was out at the wagon.

I berated my buddy, Roy, for spitting tobacco juice right out through the meshes of the one these girls had made for him, without raising a hand to lift it out of the way. I told Mrs. Mitchell that the ungrateful wretch had thrown it away after it became so foul that even *he* couldn't stand it. She smiled and listened to my stories of the girls we knew, the dances and other things we did for fun. But somehow, I had a persistent feeling that she was gently "picking" me for information that for some reason of her own she wanted to know.

Later on that summer, different incidents shocked and irked her, and when she went home to Texas it was for good. Nor would she let Frank stay on as Dakota Matador manager, and she jolted the motley collection of Evarts citizens with a parting shot: "Evarts is a disreputable bawdy house which lacks a big tent to have it all under one cover—an annex to the House by the Missouri shore." Right or wrong, that was her opinion, and she cared little who knew it.

But I had no forewarning of this when I loaded her saddle into their rig. She smiled and waved goodbye to all of us as we rode away that morning, and she was going back to town with Frank. My vacation was over and I got back into the roundup work.

10. With the Sword & Dagger

As the summer passed, the bright green of spring disappeared in the golden brown of maturing forage on the reservation range. Summer-heated breezes stirred the dry grasses, rippling them gently, inviting fire havoc. There were no warnings which would bring fire-fighters and fire-control equipment. There were no "smoke jumpers" to parachute into the worst areas.

Old cowboys will recall that when flames hit grassland, it meant clumsy fire drags, galloping horses hitched to squaw wagons bouncing over rough country to the nearest streams to fill water barrels and rush back again to men fighting and beating at the burning grass with saddle blankets, coats, or anything else handy, while often the head fire roared skyward in a leaning arc funnel one hundred feet ahead of the ground fire racing along with the wind, in an inferno that couldn't be stopped. Such was the big fire that swept the South Dakota prairie in 1905, where cattle grazed by the thousands in west-of-the-Missouri-River country.

It was scarce mid-afternoon when somebody yelled, "Fire

is sweepin' the whole country back west!" Almost at once a high wind whirled in from that direction, bringing the smell of burning grass. Yellow-gray smoke billowed up, and wheat grass rippled in the breeze like a farmer's grain field.

With the strong wind behind it, the fire spread rapidly, thrashing forward almost as fast as a horse could run. It came on so swiftly that all stock work stopped and the cowboys turned to fighting fire. Con McMurry ordered the roundup turned loose and sent the chuck wagon, with its water barrels hanging on each side, to be filled at the river. He sent cowboys to take the beef herd out of the path of the approaching flames in an effort to hold what had already been gathered. But this herd had to be turned loose, too, for so fast was the fire traveling that every man was needed to try to head it off. Before dusk, the Turkey Track outfit, also gathering a beef herd in their range twenty-five miles south of the Matador roundup, turned their stock loose and came to the fire. The Sword & Dagger, the H O, the 73 and many other outfits saw it and came to fight it, too. In fact, it hit the H O and 73 ranges before it got to us, so we set out to help them first.

The main fire-fighting contraptions, the big fire drags, were brought from the cow camps along the rivers, where they had been stored handy to the few accessible roads. They were made of chains and twelve-foot-square asbestos sheets. Interwoven over and across the bottom sheet like a bed spring were heavy steel links, and on top of that was another asbestos sheet, the whole works welded together by steel chains run through and through. Steel rings in the heavy bar across one end provided a place for a cowboy to tie his rope; with the other end snug to the saddle horn, the men pulled the big drags with horses. It took the combined efforts of six saddle horses to move them. So great was the strain, and so foamy-hot would our horses get that we had to change these heaving-flank mounts for fresh ones every two hours. The horse wranglers kept the saddle horse *remuda* as close to the fire-fighters as possible, and the chuck wagon followed the outskirts to feed the men.

In a conflagration the size of this one, already spread to a wide front, little could be done about the head fires that were swallowing up grass before such a wind except to get far out in front and attempt a backfire, or to drag it out along the edges. To backfire at such times was a tough job. Often after a broad backfire had been accomplished, the lead fires burned so fiercely that sparks leaped the blackened ground and blazed up on the far side.

In a matter of hours after this fire started, it had gained a front more than twenty miles wide, and every man who saw it came to battle it with everything he had. Breaking away nearly a hundred miles to the west, this blazing menace swept on to burn to the Missouri River in two days and nights. Not far from its source, one prong swept a little to the southeast, jumped the Moreau River and burned down the Big and Little Cottonwood creeks to the Cheyenne River. Changing winds in the two days turned the course of the fire several times. With one prong driving east and the other southeast, the wind helped to check it in those directions, only to have it turn to the southwest, gobbling up all it had by-passed in the first sweep. Before it was finally put out, it had blackened more than a million acres.

Most of the control efforts were directed to narrowing the fire to a point by use of the big drags, followed by men on foot beating out what it had missed. After hours of contact with hot, dry earth, the asbestos in the fire drags wore out completely, leaving but a tangled mass of steel and asbestos pulp. To remedy this, a big four-year-old steer was driven up close by and shot We cut him open, his hide, carcass, and entrails replacing moisture and weight. Ten or twelve steers were killed for this purpose by the Matador, and doubtless each of the other outfits used as many.

With sweating horses straining to pull, ropes tied to saddle horns creaking fit to pop, Indians and white men beating flames, it took two full days and nights of fire-fighting, even with the help of natural barriers and changing winds, to control this fire.

Cowboys had rushed most of the livestock to safer regions, so cattle losses weren't high. Natural instincts sent the remainder, as well as deer, antelope, coyotes, wolves, and even buffalo, hurrying across streams or scurrying over burned ground to patches the fire had somehow gone around.

There were two stories reported as to how this fire got started. One had it that lightning from a passing thunderstorm struck the dry grass and it blazed up. The other story was that a homesteader—one of the very earliest beginning to trickle out into what was later Perkins County—had found his first rattlesnake. In his zeal to destroy it, he started a fire to burn it. The fire got away, swept on for miles, into all of the reservation outfits' leases, and burned parts of five present-day counties. In has gone down in history as just about the biggest and most uncontrollable fire ever seen by white men in the west-of-the-Missouri country.

For a time, the fire slowed down our beef roundup, but eventually we turned toward Evarts with this herd of Indian cattle. It always took about three days to ship a herd of twelve hundred, for only one train a day from each outfit went out—about four hundred head each. This was to allow other shippers the same chance to get to market for the better prices. Usually, the cattle shipped from the range on Monday, Tuesday, and Wednesday (reaching the market on the weekend), were ready for sale the following Monday, Tuesday, and Wednesday—thus with the rise and fall of prices, a marketing hazard shared by all, there was no feeling that the Milwaukee was showing partiality to one shipper over another. In the busiest seasons, it was said that a train-

load of beef left Evarts almost every hour of the day for the first three days of each week.

After our last train was loaded, Con took us back to the range. He and Mitchell decided that I was to take my horses and go to the Sword & Dagger outfit to work with them through the shipping season. There had been reports of Matador steers and other brands from our range among the Dagger stock. The Sword & Daggers, shortened to "Daggers" by cowboys, operated the big range southwest of the Matador, handling thousands of cattle, many of them the wild longhorn type. Those that were sent to market each fall were replaced by other stock from the south somewhere.

It was a hundred and ten miles or more from Evarts to the Sword & Dagger headquarters on Cherry Creek, a tributary of the Cheyenne River. The Cherry Creek Indian substation was at the mouth of Cherry Creek, but the Dagger headquarters was five or six miles on up the stream. I left Evarts and went by way of the White Horse Trading Post, crossing the Moreau up further, near the Matador west line. The gates in the Matador–Turkey Track fence were spaced four or five miles apart, with big, high gateposts which could be seen for a long ways. I went into Mossman's range and spotted the Track wagon, where I stayed the first night. Next morning, I passed through the Dagger gate, southwest of Eagle Butte, near the present town of Eagle Butte, and stayed with Quill Ewing the next night. He had married a breed girl and had a family out there. The next day, I reached my destination.

The Sword & Dagger were known and named by other outfits for their brand—a sword on the left side just back of the shoulder, and a dagger on the left thigh of both cattle and horses. At one time, their horses were branded with the sword on the left shoulder, too, but that was discontinued. Officially, they were the White River Cattle Company, owned by Webster and Brown, whose offices were in the Minnesota twin cities, Minneapolis and St. Paul. They were a rough and ready outfit, and because of this they were also nicknamed "Shoot 'em and Stick 'em" cowboys, but a better crew of all-round cowboys would have been hard to find anywhere. This was my first trip to the Daggers as Matador rep, but I felt at home with them, for I had known their manager, Ernest Eidson—affectionately called "Booger" or "Boog" by his friends—most of my life in Texas. He was tall, exceptionally well-built—a rugged young man—keenly intelligent and well-fitted for the job he held. He was one manager who was different. He stayed right with his outfit. He was one of the boys, for all anyone could tell when they came to the Sword & Dagger outfit. Bill Smedley, a cowman tough as a boot, was his wagon boss.

They ran two wagons in the busy season, with Art Bivins the second wagon boss, and always worked from twelve to twenty men, depending on the season of the year. They were easily the largest operators on the reservation. They joined the Turkey Tracks on the west, excepting for a neck of land that wedged up between them from the Cheyenne north, but not very far. It belonged to the Mississippi Cattle outfit, run by Jeff Carr, and they branded DEL, LDT, and TLD. They had a larger lease south of the Cheyenne, but came to Evarts to ship, using the same Trail, usually, that the Sword & Dagger did, all of them crossing Matador range to get to the rails.

Ernest had no thought nor desire to run the Sword & Dagger outfit before he actually became manager. He was hauling corn with a four-horse team from south of Cheyenne River to the Dagger headquarters. Henry Hudson was manager then. Suddenly, and unknown to Ernest, there came a change of management. Mr. Webster, the owner who was most active in the Sword & Dagger affairs, had seen Eidson at work with the other cowboys. He could tell he was a good cowhand and a good worker. His whole general appearance and personality impressed Webster, and he knew Ernest was familiar with every phase of range work.

So Mr. Webster, a gentle, soft-spoken man, asked that Eidson be sent in to his office. There he told him that he was putting him in as Sword & Dagger manager. But Eidson refused to take the job.

"Why not?" Webster asked. Ernest explained that he lacked experience enough to run an outfit of that size—that he couldn't keep books.

Webster brushed Eidson's objections aside, "We have bookkeepers who can do that job. What I need is a competent man to run the Sword & Dagger, and you are it."

After a night of deliberation, Ernest agreed to take the job under certain conditions. "What I say goes," he said. "No changing orders, and no taking charge of the outfit once I become manager. I'll keep my records on the stubs of the company checkbook."

"That's the way I want it, too," Mr. Webster replied.

So, while Ernest ran the Sword & Dagger—closing them out in 1907—there was no book work involved on his part, except that he gave checks and filled in the stubs with the information.

In over seven hundred thousand acres of Sword & Dagger range, there were many Indian homes along the creeks and the Cheyenne River. These log houses—and barns, too—were built of native timber, hewn logs set one upon the other to make the side walls. The cracks between them were daubed and chinked with wet gumbo soil that held like plaster when dry. A heavy ridge log supported the roof logs and the two-foot-deep covering of the same sort of grayish dirt. These buildings were warm, windproof, and dry. The deep dirt pack on the gently sloping roof was kept from sliding off by logs laid along the edge, notched to fit, and spiked to the wall logs. Once "settled," the gumbo soil resisted rain or snow penetration—in fact, moisture tightened its texture. With the exception of a few big two-story log houses, this type of building was a general pattern of the Indian house. Sometimes they had two or three rooms, but more often just one. In summer the Indian took to his tepee outside, and a brush arbor for shade and a place set up for cooking in the open replaced the log dwelling through the warm months. The squaws did their work seated on the ground in the shade of the arbor. There were few wells in this whole region at that time. Water for cooking was brought from the river or water holes, but if the job at hand required considerable water, it was taken to the river. When washing clothes, cleaning berries and other foods, the Indian women carried their tasks to the edge of a stream. The old-time theory was that water which flowed over rocks or swept along in a swift current was "purified" every three hundred feet.

Most of the cowboys working with outfits on the range drank coffee—morning, noon, and night—for one main reason: boiled water.

Often in late summer, the places where we would have to camp had a low water supply, usually well-inhabited by water bugs and the like. Once during hot weather, we reached camp grounds late. Thirsty, we stumbled through the dark to the creek and filled up. Next morning, we discovered that not far from us in this stream, which had stopped flowing temporarily, were a couple of steers, dead and decayed. We were pretty suspicious of what we drank thereafter unless we had a daylight view of the water, and more than ever we stuck to *boiled* coffee.

The Sword & Daggers were a fast-working and agreeable bunch of men. I liked to rep with them. We were well into our day's work before the sun tipped the horizon.

Altogether, I found about three hundred head of stock from Matador range. As fast as I cut forty or fifty head,

Ernest would send a man along and we would take them back to the pasture where they belonged.

Busy days were not monotonous, but if ever we lacked entertainment, we could always rely on the "Dagger Twins" to come up with something. What a pair of little hellions they were! Their nefarious schemes turned peace into bedlam more than once and the whole outfit was wary of them, for no one ever knew who they would be plotting against next. That fall, I saw those two pranksters at work for the first time.

The two little cowpunchers, Art Bivins and Johnny Dorsey, Sword & Dagger top cowboys, were the eternal nemesis of the cow camps. Most of the time they escaped punishment for their monkeyshines, though occasionally they ran into trouble they could not evade.

The Daggers had a new roundup cook then, a big man, and during the past weeks he hadn't put himself out any to feed the cowboys. His meals were scanty and he hadn't kept his cooking or his person very clean, either. He was cranky and none of them dared ask about a meal, or to wish for pie to eat. All of this aroused the ire of the Twins, so they set up a plot.

Fall days were still nice. It was a good, warm noontime when I first learned that things had reached the explosion stage. It all began with a commotion in the tent. I was stretched out in the shade of the wagon when, through the open flap, I saw the cook pounce on Johnny. Then I saw Art grab the big man by his heels, and after that, there was the dangdest swearing, thumping, thudding, and rattling of pans in the cook tent!

Ernest Eidson was resting under the wagon, too. I saw him raise up and take a look at what was happening. Everyone got around where they could see. Anyone could tell the Twins had the affair well in hand, so no one interfered while they piled all over the big cook and mauled him plenty.

Done with their job, they quit the cook tent, and the cook, roaring like a mad bull, charged out after them.

"I can whip any man in the goddam outfit, one at a time," the cook shouted. He cussed cowboys in bunches, and the region by sections, and fairly frothed through his teeth in his rage.

Ernest scrambled out from under the wagon so fast he bumped his head, knocking his hat off and his sandy hair stood up like a fighting wolf's. He tore into the wild-eyed cook who was waiting for him, and they had one helluva battle, with Eidson the winner. After the fight, the defeated cook said, "Well, now that you have licked me, and those two little bastards have licked me, I guess you'll fire me."

Eidson said, "No, that's not my intention. I'll raise your wages instead, but I want you to clean yourself up and cook. Feed these men like you should. Stop your bellyaching around and you won't have any trouble." The cook took the advice and everything went along fine after that.

It wasn't long afterwards that these two little devils pulled a trick on the wagon boss, Bill Smedley. Bill was past middle age, and his teeth had gone bad. Most of them were missing, leaving one here and one there in his mouth. Without a doubt, Bill needed teeth.

On the morning's ride, Art and Johnny found a skeleton of a real young colt bleaching in the sun, apparently dead about a year. This gave them an idea. They put about a dozen of its smallest teeth in their pockets, while they cast about for a way to put their trickery into operation. They knew very well that they couldn't carry out their scheme without help, for old Bill was too big and powerful, and besides, he was a little on the mean side. He would not hesitate to perk up their attention with a few close six-shooter shots in their vicinity if he was riled up enough, and they feared him a little. As they rode toward camp, they met Eidson and put their proposition before him, claiming that Bill surely needed teeth, but that he might be resentful if they approached him all by themselves, and wouldn't accept the gift they had brought him. But with Eidson's help . . .

Eidson was a big, husky man, well able to hold his own anywhere. I never knew him to get the worst of anything he got into. He considered their plot awhile and decided it was a friendly gesture that few men would take the trouble to make for a cantankerous old wagon boss! Certainly old Bill could use some teeth. After all, the wagon boss should be grateful and cooperative, even if he had to be forced somewhat. So he agreed to help Art and Johnny.

Old Bill had a habit of seeking his bedroll when things got quiet, flop down, and lean back on it to catch a short nap. His mouth would invariably drop wide open, completely exposing his almost toothless gums, and it was with him in this position that the three nabbed him.

Ernest pinned Bill down. The two little dentists hopped upon his person and began setting the teeth in his mouth. Bill fought them off in a seething fury. He clamped his jaws, making it a difficult job to pry them open, but it got him nowhere. As the three "do-gooders" struggled with Bill, the would-be dental experts encouraged him by telling him how much better he could eat with the new teeth. They dwelt at length on the pity they had felt for him, watching him bobble his food around trying to hit first one tooth then another, and they could no longer bear it, so they had brought some teeth for him.

Bill spit, sputtered, and pushed the teeth out with his tongue until they wadded his mouth so full he couldn't, but as long as he could move his tongue at all, he seared the very air with his cuss words. He threatened to kill everyone implicated in this outrage. He was mad enough and mean enough to do it, too, but the dentists kept on with their work. They finally got the teeth crammed against his gums in a fashion to suit themselves, and tied his scarf around his mouth to hold them in, then wound a towel up over his head and under his jaws, and turned him loose for the teeth to "set."

Bill's wrath was horrible to see, but the dentists kept out of his reach, in view of Bill's threats. It was well to be alert if you did Bill for a joke, for the one he would return was certain to be plenty miserable, and there would be nothing to do but grin and bear it. Eidson had taken Bill's gun away from him at the start, so the "payoff" was delayed for a time.

Before autumn chill settled over the range, one of the Twins was punished, probably for himself and his partner, too.

On payday, little Art had scooted under the bedwagon, out of the way, and flopped down on his belly to take a nap. His head was on his folded arms, and his crossed feet left the sharp little heel of one boot sticking high enough up above the other to make a good target. Bill, sprawled as usual against his bedroll, saw the little imp resting peacefully under the wagon. Bill was a famous marksman. He eased his gun out of the scabbard on his hip, cut down to a fine line on Art's boot heel and pulled the trigger.

Bang! Off went the heel! The stinging jar to his foot brought Art up fast and hard, howling with pain. He hit his head on the wagon reach and howled some more. He cursed with an affluence that even Old Bill couldn't match. He looked at his wrecked boot and shot a murderous glare at Bill, who neither smiled nor commented. He spun the gun cylinder, pushed his spine more comfortably down against his bedroll, and eased himself for his usual nap. But Art was wide awake by then, and his heel kept him that way. He had a hotfoot the rest of the day, and a cobbled-on boot heel.

Not only did these two little cowboys trick their companions, they also bedeviled each other. One morning about dawn there was a noisy rumpus coming up from the bedroll they shared.

Johnny, who had been raised in the north, never wore an expensive boot. Footwear, other than for usefulness, meant little to him, while Arthur's boots were of the best leather and keenest make that he could buy in his native Texas. Both men wore exactly the same size boot. After Art had gone to sleep the night before, Johnny had exchanged boots with him. He painstakingly strapped his own spurs onto Art's boots, and put Art's spurs on the old boots Johnny had nearly worn out. Next morning, Johnny rolled out of the blankets first and pulled the neat boots onto his feet. About that time, Art discovered that somehow, in the dim dawn light, he had put on Johnny's old boots. But his searching fingers identified his own spurs. Amazed for the moment, and puzzled over the "how come," the truth suddenly flashed upon him. He was a victim of skullduggery, and he woke up pronto! Without delay, the battle was on.

Johnny swore an accusing protest: "You know damned well that you swapped boots with me, fair and square, last night! And you're going to stay with your bargain! A deal's a deal."

Art pronounced Johnny a liar, a night prowler. He told him he never owned a decent pair of boots in his life, to which John replied, "Well, that's why I was willing to take these sorry, scuffed-up boots off of your hands. It was your own deal, and you know it. You said I'd have a better pair of boots than I can get here in Dakota, and that you would order new boots for yourself from your own bootmaker. You know these were always too tight for your big feet."

"Like hell!" Art exploded, but he only wasted his breath. Johnny kept the boots. Art vainly tried to swipe his boots at night, but Johnny slept with them under his head. Day after day, Johnny wore them and refused to give them back, saying that he would "teach the little rogue from Texas to make deals and then try to back out again."

No one interfered in the Twins' business, and Johnny pranced about in the boots that Art claimed. For two weeks, Art shuffled around in Johnny's old boots until we got back to Evarts where he bought another pair that would do until he got his made-to-order boots from Texas.

About the only time the Twins met their match was when their scalawag minds tinkered with the idea of doing Ernest Eidson a trick. He generally caught wind of it in time to turn the tables on them, and it wasn't long until the three of them had a round.

Suddenly the nice fall weather turned cold and clouds began banking up every afternoon. We gathered and shipped one Sword & Dagger herd and were after another. It was still September, but one chilly dawn about time to get up, Eidson dressed and stepped outside where he found the water hole beside which we had camped was not only fringed with ice, but was lightly frozen over. He scooped up a small sheet of ice, went to Art and Johnny's bed, whipped the tarp back off of the still peacefully sleeping pair, and crumpled icy pellets on their bare feet, at the same time telling them it was "chuck" time.

The cook had put a washpan and towels out by the water hole and Ernest was out there preparing to wash up. Art and Johnny hopped out of bed, pulled on boots and pants, and loped out to the water hole just as Ernest was humped over, splashing his face with water. Although not apparently watching them, he knew that the two were approaching. Art and Johnny had been in the trickery business so long that it took but a nod or a lifted eyebrow from one to the other to get the idea of what might be crackling around in the other's head. And here was a fine place to pay off the manager for dropping ice in their bed. A quick push would up-end him into the water hole and break the ice.

The hole was three or four feet deep under the half-inch layer of ice, and it would take but a few motions for the two little pests to heave the big man overboard. So they advanced confidently. But the wily Eidson sensed their intentions a split second before they got to him, in time to reach behind him as they set upon him and grasp one of the offenders in each powerful hand. He had a good grip on them as they gave him a shove, and he took them along, too, when he overended into the water hole.

They crashed through the ice, hit bottom and came up gasping. Crawling out, each in his own fashion, they headed for the tent and dry clothes. The Twins promised dire consequences to Eidson, and he returned the threat. But it was all in fun, and no hard feelings, for a joke was a joke. If a man could take a joke as well as perpetrate one, he was a "good Joe," but if he was the other kind, no one bothered him. And he could not, himself, pull a joke on others, or ever be a really close friend.

I stayed with the Sword & Daggers while they gathered and shipped two herds, and in these two drives through their range I caught just about every critter that belonged in the Matador pasture.

While we were taking the first herd to Evarts to ship, a most memorable incident happened on the Trail. The Matador, the Flying V's, the H A T's, and the L7's were all driving in herds, too, and we came up behind them at Dog Buttes crossing. It was one of the meanest places on the Strip to get through. The crossing was springy and boggy at any time of year, especially after a wet spell, until frozen solid in winter. There we found the three roundup wagons sunk to the hubs. When the Matador wagon rolled up, with Walker Krump driving, he pulled right through the crossing and set up camp on the other side, some distance away.

The four mules that pulled the Matador wagon were the

wheelers, Pete and Jack, big black mules weighing about fourteen hundred pounds each, and the leaders, slick little twelve-hundred mare mules. Kit was black, Molly mouse-color. No one ever saw the tugs slack when these mules were in the collar. They pulled together with no shirking. If a load could be started at all by mules their size, they'd move it.

Charley Hamer was the L7 cook, and his wagon was mired the deepest. He asked Con to loan him Kit and Molly to hook on the lead and help him pull the L7 chuck wagon through the crossing. He insisted that he only needed the leaders, but Con told him no.

"We'll just take all four mules," Con said. "They're used to pulling together. You take your teams off," which Hamer did. The Matador mules were hitched to the L7 wagon, and Con took the lines. They tightened the tugs and tested what they had behind them. They dug in and loosened it, then snaked it clear out to dry land. They were the best roundup wagon teams I ever saw.

11. Second Winter, 1905-1906

After I reached Evarts with the Sword & Dagger herd, my work with them was done for the fall. Frank Mitchell told me where Con was, so I cut my horses from the Dagger *remuda* and went to the Matador headquarters on the Moreau.

The Matador had shipped the one herd besides the Indian herd and were gathering another one. Then Con got word from Mitchell to "turn loose" and take the roundup wagons in for the winter, which meant that no more steers would be shipped that fall.

Murdo MacKenzie believed that prices did not justify selling and had decided to hold everything over. Every cowboy who heard it thought that MacKenzie had pulled a boner, but he hadn't. By the next fall, the extra growth on the carcasses and better prices—two dollars more per hundred pounds—well rewarded the Scot pocketbooks. This was one more example of MacKenzie's wisdom.

Murdo MacKenzie, Matador general manager, was always in the background of our operations; though we didn't see

him often, we all knew him as a great cowman. He built
the nationally known Matador Land and Cattle Company
into eight hundred thousand acres of Texas plains range
for a Scots syndicate in Dundee. He came to the United
States from his native highlands of Scotland in 1885. He was
thirty-five years old then, and knew little of large-scale cattle
operations, but he lived to become one of the most colorful
and great cattlemen of his era.

He held the highest regard of President Theodore Roosevelt, of the fabulous men of the meat industry, of the West's
foremost stockmen—as well as hundreds of small operators
and working men whose friendship he commanded, men
who looked to him for honest leadership.

In the beginning, he became manager of the Prairie Cattle Company, also a Scots syndicate, with ranches in Texas
and on the Sweetwater and Chugwater, in Wyoming. He
managed the Texas LIT's for twenty-five years before closing them out and was advisor to other outfits, including the
Cross L's in Colorado and New Mexico. But his greatest
activity was as over-all manager of the vast and ever-spread-
ing Matador, with their Drag V cattle brand and the straight
50 on the hip of the horses.

Murdo MacKenzie's ability and stature were in tune with
the wide, unlimited ranges of his day and the big herds he
dealt with. He lived to see his beloved Matador expand to
one of the greatest cattle empires in the world.

During his life, he continually fought for better conditions
for the stockgrower. As a member of the executive commit-
tee of the Cattle Raisers' Association of Texas, he helped
break up the Big Packer's Trust, a combine which was
rapidly throttling the western stockgrowers.

He had a big part in ridding Texas of the tick which
spread deadly Texas Fever wherever it went.

He battled the unfair practices of the Stock Commission

Houses and was mainly responsible for the winning of the long fight before the Interstate Commerce Commission regarding regulation and control of the railroad freight rates to cattle shippers. He saw this legislation go through considerable litigation and be eventually ruled constitutional by the United States Supreme Court.

Murdo MacKenzie, great man among great men! President Roosevelt wrote of him, "During my term as President, he [MacKenzie] was on the whole the most influential of the Western cattlemen. He was a leader of the farsighted and enlightened element; a powerful Government supporter in the fight to conserve National Resources, forests, pastures and for the honest treatment and reshaping of governmental policies in the interest of the small settler, the home-maker. . . ."

Mr. MacKenzie served as president of the Texas and Southwestern Cattle Association, 1901–03. When he retired in late life, his son, John, took over active management of the Matador, with his father acting as advisor until his death.

Murdo MacKenzie didn't live to see the nearly unbelievable happen in 1950. At a time when this sprawling beef outfit was bringing in a million dollars yearly, it was suddenly sold to nonranching New York speculators for nineteen million dollars. They resold it in smaller tracts.

There came a September snowstorm which was as sudden and in many respects as damaging as the one in May of that year. It took everyone by surprise. From warm, pleasant fall days, the thermometer plummeted down, down, down, and real midwinter was upon us. It didn't last long, and stock—having summer fat to fall back on—survived. There was no such loss as in the May storm, but it was hard on the animals, regardless.

When the weather cleared, Con sent me to the mouth of Swift Bird Creek as there were changes in winter camps that year. There were much better corrals, houses, and barns than at the camp of the winter before.

Since the Swift Bird Creek camp was near the line between the Matador and Turkey Track, Jim Seals, who worked for the Tracks, batched with me. During the winter, several other men stayed at our camp, but as it turned out I didn't spend all my time at Swift Bird. Toward spring, I went back to our first winter camp for a while, to ride broncs.

As we went into the winter, we followed the old, familiar routine. We kicked our blankets off long before daylight, fed the horses, had breakfast, and were ready to start out on our rides as dawn broke. Swift Bird bottoms were wide and brushy. Thickets of chokecherry, plum, buckbrush, and willows, with grassy places between, made good protection for stock, and they gravitated toward it. Cattle instinctively seem to know where to go—like a mustang horse will skirt around danger; or he will unerringly pick the side of a hill where the most grass lies beneath the snow, once it is pawed away. With canny awareness, the semi-wild bovine fought for existence in a harsh world where storms and savage animals sought his life, and man ceaselessly guarded him solely because he, too, wanted his life in the end. The sale of hide and carcass would load his pockets with money. So the steer played a losing game all the way round. But while life remained, he battled to keep it.

The first heavy snow in the early fall stayed on, for the most part. Stock got plenty of snow with the grass they ate, to quench thirst, but they preferred water, pure, running water, if they could get it.

Swift Bird, "La Chapelle," a short tributary of the Missouri, was established as far back as 1829. Here the notable mixed-blood Swift Bird, son of David La Chapelle and a Two Kettle Sioux woman, was born. In his youth, Swift Bird was one of the heroic "Fool Soldier Band" who rescued the Lake Shetax white captives from hostile Indians. He died in August 1900.

But the historic Swift Bird Camp was to us just another old Indian place along the Missouri, about three miles north of the fence dividing Turkey Track and Matador range, but inside the Matador pasture. From here, we riders could fan out, up and down the Missouri and the creeks. Jim went south into Turkey Track range. I went to the Track fence and then up Swift Bird. Oscar Buford, who stayed with us some, rode north to the mouth of Four Bear Creek, where it joined the Missouri. We kept water holes open in the river for cattle to drink. Using a heavy axe, we cut long troughs in the ice about eighteen inches wide and fifteen inches deep. At each end, we chopped a hole clear down through the ice to the water running underneath. The hole at the lower end was opened wide, but the secret of a fine flow of water through the trough was the care with which a man opened the hole to water at the upper end. It had to be broken out only partially. To break it completely through would allow too much water to burst up into the opening, and overflow the trough and flood the surrounding ice. But if wisely done, a little stream would gurgle up to the level of the trough, filling it and escaping back under the ice to the lower hole.

All day long, and often for days in mild weather, there would be a constant flow of fresh water from under the ice. Cattle could not fall into a place like this. Besides, we put dirt, barn litter, and even snow around the hole. Cattle made litter themselves, so it wasn't slippery and dangerous around the trough.

In cold weather these holes had to be watched, for they would "grow up," that is, the deep holes at either end, even the trough itself, would gradually freeze over solid if the weather was severely cold. So we had to keep watch on them every day. Stock fared much better if they had plenty of

fresh water, and also, these watering places were a good spot
to look for thin cattle or wolf depredations.

Perhaps the worst pack of wolves in Matador range, and
the wariest, were led by the old dog wolf who made his home
on Blue Blanket Island, but the winter I was at Swift Bird
he was finally trapped.

The little town of Evarts set back from the Missouri about
a half-mile. Blue Blanket Creek was just north of town, flowing into the Missouri from the east. From its mouth, Blue
Blanket Island, varying from three hundred feet to a half-
mile wide, extended for a mile downstream. It had built up
so high it was never flooded—a veritable jungle of uprooted
trees, debris, and gravel brought down through the centuries
when the Missouri was in flood stage. Brush, cottonwoods,
and water-willow thickets were rampant, harboring a multi-
tude of birds, rabbits, and rodents. The Missouri split its
channel on the northern tip. Towards the lower end, the
island tapered and became a gravelly, low-brush beach which
lay almost directly between the Evarts stockyards on the
east shore and those built on the west side.

Actually, for a considerable distance the island formed part
of the pontoon bridge constructed over the two channels of
the Missouri. Snow fence panels were set up to make a lane
the same width as the pontoon, thus making it stronger and
shorter, anchored to the island.

In this natural, almost impenetrable island wilderness, a
pair of loafers lived for years and raised six or eight pups
each season. Small game being plentiful, they had no trouble
feeding their young until freezing weather arrived. By then,
the pups were half-grown and ready for the hunt. The whole
family would cross over the ice, and from then on, they
wreaked havoc among the livestock drifting into the big
bottoms for feed and winter shelter along the river. With so
many hunting them, eventually someone shot the loafer's

mate. Their grown pups scattered, and the old dog was left alone. Following a custom found more often among wild creatures than one would suppose, he never took another mate. He hunted alone and never deserted his island home except for the hunt. His savage way of making a fresh kill every time he was hungry set a big price on his head, but he eluded every "trap set" for months and months. He simply ignored poison bait, or he scratched clods and defecation onto it with his hind feet. Trappers tried luring him with a she wolf. They coaxed his interest with scents and with choice meats, but he'd have none of them.

The scheme which finally proved so completely absorbing that the wolf let his caution desert him was cruel and excusable only because of the scores of animals that had suffered torture and death by him.

Baldy Sours, the man who caught the old depredator, worked with the Missouri River boatman, Captain Sours, during the summers, hauling freight up and down the river, crossing Indians rigs over the big stream, and ferrying the thousands of incoming cattle across the river. But when winter ice ended river work, Baldy turned to trapping and swore he'd get the Blue Blanket Island wolf. He used every snare he could devise to get him, without success, until he hit on the dastardly one that worked.

In setting his deadly contrivance, the man concealed many traps under an overhanging willow, to which he fastened a stout cord. To this, he hung a live rabbit by its heels, in such a way that it kicked and dangled, squealing pitifully, directly above the traps. After so long a time, the rabbit died, but the man hung another in its place. Finally, the cries of one caught the ear of the wolf and he came to it. Circling the set, eyes intent on the struggling rabbit, he stepped into one trap. His efforts to get free got him into a couple more, and there the trapper found him, completely helpless. The old warrior didn't fight or show any sign of ferocity as the man approached. It seemed he welcomed the bullet which ended his life and cut short the torture of broken bones. Thus ended the reign of death by the wolves of Blue Blanket Island.

Snow fell regularly as winter came on. Our work kept us too busy to think about going places. Still, if a "doings," where music and dancing and a chance to swing a pretty girl in a good fast square dance, was whispered from camp to camp by chuckline riders—those unemployed newsmen who rode from place to place, dropping a good story for a meal—every one of us perked up his ears.

We'd haul out our best wool shirts, shake the wrinkles out of our Sunday pants, and wait for the word to come. When the date and place were set, everyone was invited.

We wore high-topped boots and folded our pant legs neatly about our shins and pulled our boots on with them tucked down inside. Winter weather made overshoes a necessity, and they were made to fit our boot heels—not flat as for shoes.

That winter, Con McMurray, Roy Vivian, and I each bought a coonskin coat from Whitlock & Dean at the Agency. They were full length, with high collars, and they cost us fifty dollars apiece. I bought a muskrat cap, too. Its long earflaps extended well over my jaws and when I tied the strings under my chin, my head and neck were well protected.

About this time, we all knew that a young fellow, Leon Poitras, who clerked in the store at the Agency, was coming up the Missouri every chance he got to spark Miss Josie Brown, who lived with her mother not far from our camp. Both were breeds. A chuck-line-rider rumor had us keyed up for a wedding dance and a feast before long.

When we got the word to come to it, we scrubbed our necks and ears, uprooted our whiskers, polished our boots, parted our hair just so, and dashed plenty of scented talcum powder inside our shirts, for the cowboy who smelled the sweetest usually got the most attention. With bright scarves about our throats, we donned our coats and mounted our gentlest horses. We were going out to an all-night good time, which I recall as one of the highlights of those early reservation days.

The marriage had been performed before we Matador cowboys arrived at the fine old Narcisse Benoist place down the river from the confluence of the Moreau and the Missouri, where the bride lived. Her mother had married Benoist after her first man, Brown, died and left her with three children. Two more daughters were born before Benoist died, too. Then the widow married Charley Ducharm and he moved right in with his bride.

Guests overflowed even such a big two-story log house as the Benoist home to celebrate with the bridal pair, a handsome couple.

The musicians were breeds who could play a violin or chord on an organ, and they cut down heavy on both instruments. Our dancing partners were breed girls, too, very pretty in their long, full skirts, and hair curled and pinned on top of their heads like white girls wore theirs. Most of them had been away to school and talked good English, and all were good dancers.

Cowboys and breeds in wool shirts swung gay Indian maidens wearing silks and satins through rollicking square dances, lively two-steps, and the sweet, slow and tuneful waltzes that were our delight.

The feast was spread out on a long table in the kitchen where many of the older women sat visiting. There were cakes, pies, bread, biscuits, fruit, meat, jelly and ham. Coffee simmered in a big coffeepot on the stove. Whenever anyone felt hungry, they were welcome to come in and select anything that appealed to them. One of the women would pour a cup of coffee to go with it. This was the first time I ever tasted "Indian coffee." It was boiled with plenty of sugar already added. It had an odd taste when made that way, but it was economical. Sugar was a treat to most Indians and they were apt to overdo the thing if allowed to sugar their own drink. If it was already sweetened, everyone got the same amount.

One incident came near to marring the fun that night and we cowboys squashed that as soon as possible. A man we will call Joe, because it wasn't his name, had come out from Evarts and brought his wife. She was a snippish, sarcastic, and rather ignorant female who seemed to take pleasure in scoffing at others. People didn't like her, although few disliked Joe.

During the evening, our Matador Ott Cassidy heard this woman ridicule the cook from Matador headquarters, who had torn his coat, but had mended it and wore it to the dance. Ott had a few drinks too many from the various bottles smuggled down from Evarts and here, he considered, was a prime excuse to take a poke at Joe for something his woman had said. It was strange logic, but he straightway began a search for Joe while he—innocent of any wrongdoing —was enjoying the party.

When warned that Ott was hunting him for a fight, Joe got his mouthy woman and went home, while we kept our overheated cowboy under guard. Joe had smuggled in some of the liquor, and by rights he rated a punch in the nose, but we wanted no fights which might bar us from further bids to reservation good times.

So we danced and feasted until dawn and the Home Sweet Home Waltz. Reluctantly we got our horses from the barn and set out for camp.

We rode right up the frozen river, for our horses wore "never-slip" shoes, and ice didn't bother them. At first, a horse would be pretty spooky about going out on the ice, but they soon gained confidence on the glossy river when wearing never-slips. Horses that were inclined to kick and were shod with this kind of shoes were dangerous and they often crippled a rider.

Not only did the chuckline riders bring us news of dances, but they told us of all kinds of reservation news which we had no way of knowing otherwise. Once, someone brought in a tale of an accident which was both serious and amusing. It concerned a bachelor cooking beans. He was short of wood and had taken the stove lid off to set the kettle right down on the flames. He failed to notice that the beans were nearly done and somewhat mushy. They had used up all the water, too, and were getting pretty hot. The victim was sitting very near the stove, absorbing the heat, when he bethought himself to put in more wood. He was hatless, and as he leaned over to pick up wood and was poking it in among the coals, head right alongside the kettle, he was heard to remark, "Bile, bile, you sonova-bird-dog, bile!"

At that instant, the steam built up under the beans and exploded. It blew the whole works out of the kettle and most of it landed smack on his head, plastering his hair down. He jumped to his feet, yelling like a Comanche, and ran outdoors pawing the stuff off. But the boiling mass had so scalded his scalp that he completely lost his hair, and after the painful wound healed, he was bald from then on.

That winter gave us a rough January. In daytime, sun dogs rode through the cold sky guarding the sun, and northern lights flickered in the dark hours, but as the sun swung back north, the cold began easing up. It was nearing February when Frank Mitchell stopped at our camp while making a trip over the range, and he told me he was going back to Texas for good. Dode MacKenzie, Murdo's son, was preparing to come to Dakota, and Mitchell would take over at

Alamocitas in his place. To make it short, Dode and Frank were changing places, and Con was in charge of the Dakota spread unti Dode arrived. This was rather a blow to me, for Mitchell was almost like my kinfolk. I didn't see him but once more, and that was when he again turned C Heart over to me when he left for Texas.

Before long, we heard Dode was in Evarts, and Charley Brown, who rated pretty high with Dode and had been his straw boss and pal at Alamocitas, was on his way, too, with Dode's string of saddle horses, and some broncs he wanted to bring to Dakota—horses he favored, and he had authority to bring along. Charley was to run the second beef wagon. The Matador had so many cattle to go out to market in fall that two roundup wagons were necessary. Con, range boss and boss of the beef roundup, always put up the herds himself out on the range. Twelve hundred head of steers of a certain age made a herd, and when Con got done with them and they were ready to be trailed to the railroad by the boss of the second roundup wagon and his men, they were mighty even in weight, color, and size.

Some of us cowboys were uneasy about Brown coming, though, and I think Con knew there might be a change. Dode and Con had often disagreed in Texas, while Con was wagon boss at Alamocitas. He had some trouble with Brown, too, so naturally, apprehension floated through the cow camps. None of us wanted Con replaced by Brown as over-all range foreman.

The fall before, the Matador had bought five hundred three- and four-year-old Colorado broncs and shipped them to their lower ranch in Texas. Here, Claude Jefferies was bronc buster supreme and it didn't take him long to spot more than one outlaw horse in the bunch—horses which showed a mean streak and signs of having been monkeyed with and spoiled by someone not able to handle them.

Accordingly, when Mr. MacKenzie gave orders that a

carload of these horses be shipped to Dakota, Mr. Jefferies selected them. And a good job he did, too! They turned out to be the rankest buckers I ever saw, among them being horses deserving of such names as identified them later— Danger, Widow Maker, Rollers, Fighting Red, and Panther Piss and others that were cheerfully and consistently ready to paw a man apart at the least excuse. They were mean to bite, kick, and buck whenever a chance presented itself, and rare was the day they earned the grass they ate.

When Charley Brown arrived in Evarts with Dode's horses, they were taken to the Willy Jones place, where I had spent the winter before. The pasture and corrals were suitable for bronc riding and when the carload of horses from the Lower Ranch in Motley County, Texas, came, they too were driven out to that place. Charley Brown took over there, just down the river from Con's headquarters. Before long, another cowboy took my place and I was sent to stay with Brown and ride the broncs—and right here began a year that for me was simply loaded with hard luck. It seemed that wherever I went, the devil kept on my trail.

12. The Rough Broncs

Dode MacKenzie was no stranger to me. I had known him well in Texas. He looked like his father, Murdo, rather heavy-set and under six feet tall—a blue-eyed, sandy-haired Scot, as likable and fine a young man as ever lived, while sober. Liquor was his deadly enemy, but even when drunk I never knew him to do a mean thing or cowardly act. We were always good friends and even when I saw the rascally broncs he'd brought from Alamoçitas for me to ride, I knew it was because of his confidence in my ability to make usable horses out of them. Dode was an experienced enough cowboy to recognize intelligent horses.

As to the horses from the Lower Ranch, that was a different matter. Obviously Jefferies didn't want to ride those broncs with the hell-bent streak, so when the opportunity came, he shifted them on to Dakota, to me, after they had been bucked out a few times.

Long, tall, and dark, Charley Brown was a Texan, and like most older men, wore his brown moustache long at the corners of his mouth. He had a never-ending taste for the bottled firewater.

When I rode up to the pasture to look at the horses I was to ride, it didn't take me long to spot the meanest horses among the new ones, so I decided to let them alone for a while, until I started riding those Dode had brought up. Most of them gentled right down. Charley Brown picked several to round out his string of mounts, and we kept them under saddle a lot of the time. When I was ready to start on the Colorado horses, I selected the first bunch and put them in the corrals. But I had yet to top off Spokane, the horse Dode had especially brought to Dakota for me.

Spokane had a reputation as a hard-bucking horse. He was a slim blood-bay, weighing 1050 pounds. He had good shoulders, high hips, and was probably a good deal thoroughbred. He had been handled some and didn't fight saddling; in fact, if a man could ride him until he had his buck over with, he worked willingly. But there was the pinch! Spokane saved himself for furious, hell-to-set pitching after a rider mounted. It was sport for him, and he had thrown more cowboys than had ever ridden him farther than three jumps. Spokane's reputation followed him when Dode shipped him to South Dakota and came north himself as manager. Dode liked the horse.

"I want to see what our South Dakota bronc rider can make of him," he said, preparing to leave Texas, and from the time that Spokane snorted down the chute, filled his belly and ran free a few weeks on rich grass, he was primed to jar the gutfat off the best of riders. He was one of the really snaky ones to come to the Dakota outfit.

Brown knew that Dode had brought Spokane along for me to ride, and he was present the day Dode pointed to the horse and said, "If a man can stay on him, that bronc has the makings of a top cow horse."

Since I could ride my horses wherever I wanted to while

training them, Brown saddled up, too, and went around with
me considerable, looking at the new range and getting acquainted with it. He got quite friendly, and jogging along,
he continually preached "hell-roaring Spokane" to me. He
declared the horse was one of the worst buckers ever when
he cut loose with all he had, and hinted that even Dode was
skeptical about my being able to ride him. The more Brown
talked about Spokane, the more I wanted to get a rope on
the salty cuss and see for myself how tough he really was. I
had found few horses that were hard for me to handle—still,
I also knew that "for every man, there's a horse he cannot
ride."

Brown conceded that I might possibly ride Spokane, but
he confided a little fear that he wouldn't pitch his toughest
without help, so he came up with an idea.

"We've got to convince Dode," Brown said, gently smooth-
ing his moustache, "that Spokane was pitching his damndest,
in case you do ride him. So I'll get my bullwhip and wrap it
around him a few times. That will put him to tearing up
the sod. That way," he confided, "Dode can't dispute he was
doing his best, 'cause a bullwhip puts plenty of outlaw into
a hoss. If he pitches wicked, you will have good excuse to
spur the fire out of him and rake him up good and plenty."

Looking back on it, I believe Brown had three deals
rattling around in his skull. He wanted Dode to see Spokane
spurred to a finish. He hoped to see me get the rip-roaring
ride of my life, and he wanted to give Spokane a damned
good blacksnaking. His idea that a bullwhip would "double-
spark" a horse was new to me, but it sounded good. I figured
if I was a bronc such as the unridable Steamboat, the famous
bucking horse of those days, a whipping would irritate me
plenty, just as it did him. If anyone dared flick him with
a whip or quirt, he became a real devil. Since I, too, wanted
Spokane to do his worst, I was all for Brown's pep-talk, but
that was before the fracas started.

One morning I flipped a loop on Spokane as he stood in the little corral and started saddling him. He would kick a man, but aside from watching for such things, he was easy saddled. He had a frosty gleam in his eye, like he was counting on a lot of fun just as soon as I dropped a leg over him. Brown came along and saw what I was doing. While I was busy, he disappeared inside a shed where he had a little jag of hay stored for our horses and pretty soon out he comes with his bullwhip and gets on his bullwhip horse, Buck, who had been standing there saddled.

I twisted Spokane's ear to make him stand still while I stepped up on him. I didn't intend to start any trouble with him, so I let him set the pace. If he would be peaceable, so would I. He trotted out away from the corral ten paces, nice as anything, looking all around real pleasant. Then, without any urging from my girl-leg spurs, he snorted loud and keen, dropped his head, clamped his tail, and bounced into stiff-legged, hell-to-set bucking, zig-zagging as he went. And that was a signal for the bullwhip artist to sting his back end with a few well-placed snaps of the braided leather, and it wasn't long until I heard the first crack somewhere behind me. From almost the first jump, I knew I could ride Spokane, but my big trouble was coming from the bullwhip. The artist hit me more times than he hit Spokane. He nicked my ears, stung my back, wrapped a good one right around my belly and I could hardly stay on the horse for the beating I was getting.

Once when Spokane dropped half to his knees, I raised in the saddle a little. The whip lash caught me across the seat of my pants, and I thought it jerked my whole endgate off! Brown swung the leather for another try, and the next pop caught Spokane smack under the tail just as he was hoisting himself for a headstand. Roaring like a lion, he doubled up sideways with backbreaking force. I settled back down into the saddle, cussed Brown to hell and gone, and

spurred the living daylights out of Spokane, until he threw up his head and outran Brown's horse, which was the only thing that could save either of us from that bullwhip.

When that son-of-a-bird-dog Brown finally caught up to us away out on the flats, he was happy as a lark, praising me for a great ride, patting his own back for putting the "pitch" in Spokane, completely ignoring the times when he had snapped me—and me pretty cockeyed certain that not all of his poor aim with the bullwhip was purely accidental! But it didn't sting so much any more, and I knew I'd made a good ride, so when Brown suggested we go to Evarts to report to Dode and show him Spokane, I was more than ready. I pulled my mount right around and we trotted up the Missouri road at a lively clip.

Dode and Brown met at the hotel steps, greeting each other like long-lost brothers and with a hearty handshake. They vowed me the best rider on the reservation. They rejoiced that Spokane would become a useful cow horse now that a man had been found who could ride him.

I was pleased because they were, but if I entertained any notions of tarrying around in town awhile to celebrate my victory, I soon found it was no go! The two of them rushed me right back to work and by the way they talked, one would imagine I was the most important cog in the outfit! But Brown stayed with Dode, for by then they discovered much essential business to discuss—besides, the utter defeat of Spokane as a bucker had to be drowned in a series of good stiff ones across the bar!

Me? Well, I went back to camp, rubbed linament on my welts, speculating that the most probable business those two had to discuss pertained to which brand of Scotch whisky packed the smoothest wallop. That evening when I forked hay out of the shed to my night horse, a tine hit something that wasn't hay. It turned out to be a Sunnybrook bottle, empty. It likely accounted for at least part of old Brown's wild swings with the bullwhip!

As long as I rode Spokane, he bucked whenever the notion hit him, usually bucking far harder than when Brown was after him with the bullwhip. And Dode's prediction was true: Spokane was a good cow horse—if a man could ride him.

But the jolly Brown wasn't done with me yet! One evening I reached camp in considerable pain. A few hours before, the half-broke bronc I was riding that day spooked at an old prairie chicken whirring up to wing away from beside a buffalo berry bush, almost under his nose. The bronc ducked back and broke into high, hard-hitting pitching. I always rode heavy in my stirrups and somehow I got a hitch in my groin, just where the cords of my leg joined the rest of me. It grew worse all afternoon, and by the time I got to camp, I could hardly stand on that leg. I unsaddled and limped to the house, and as soon as Brown learned what had happened, he goes and digs out his bottle of red arnica linament.

This was a concoction I'd never seen before. He praised it to the clouds for ligament strain, and that is what he insisted was my trouble. Just a little, temporary strain! He advised me to put plenty of the red stuff on it and rub it in vigorously. Then he drove away in his buggy to go to Evarts to meet Dode again.

After he was gone, I decided to try the arnica treatment, so I pulled off my pants, dumped out a palm full of the cure, slapped it into my groin and thumbed it thoroughly into my hide.

The stuff was strong enough to scorch a buffalo bull's hide, and in a matter of seconds the whole sore spot was red hot, burning and spreading like wildfire. The more I tried to stop it, the hotter it got. I looked out the door and saw the horses drinking from the trough plumb full of clear water. Water! That would put out the fire! I'd wash the dang stuff off, and the trough was the nearest thing to a bathtub that we had. I left my pants on the floor, grabbed my hat and hopped for the tank.

What a mistake! The water, and my efforts to scrub it off, spread the arnica into every nook and cranny where it didn't need to be! The bath was a howling success, and me the chief howler.

There wasn't a thing I could do but let it burn itself out. I limped back to the house, eased myself down on my bunk, stuck my feet in the air and fanned my blistered quarters with my hat—and began thinking up the most diabolical, painful, and prolonged way to maim or murder one son-of-a-bird-dog Brown, if I could but get the chance.

That fellow Brown was a *character,* and the ideas that blossomed forth from his cranium were never dull ones— for the other fellow, anyway. But I got to see him get his dues one day, and I should have let his pals have their fun. There is an old saying that water seeks its own level. Apparently those individuals who hanker after whisky do. Anyway, the three fellows whom another rider and I found in camp the day we got home late after a long ride out among the cattle, beat anything I ever saw. And Brown was one of them. Why they came out to camp to celebrate, I don't know, unless it was to get drunker than usual. The whisky they brought was smuggled over the Missouri, for it was forbidden on reservation land. But there they were, and things had livened up plenty for them as the day wore on.

At the time, the first greatly advertised rubber camp mattress, with its neat little pump to inflate it, was just out, and someone had bought one for his bed. When these three celebrating buddies reached our camp from town, they were rum-soaked to the gills and two more swigs so stupefied Brown he couldn't wiggle.

The other two, examining the empty jugs, grew resentful

toward their buddy. They said he was intoxicated! They claimed they were ashamed of him, and to teach him better manners than to hog down so much liquor, they got out the little mattress pump. They pulled the britches off their helpless, muttering, swearing comrade, flopped him belly down and pushed the pump nozzle up into him. They pumped him so full of air he looked like a bloated steer, then they jerked out the nozzle. The resulting raucous racket made by escaping air tickled them mightily. They even discovered that by punching Brown's belly in a certain way, they could turn a thin eerie whistle into a loud blast! The two had become so hilarious we could hear their shouts and laughter away out to the corral where we were unsaddling our horses.

When they heard us ride in, and so that we might laugh and join in their fun, they got busy and pumped in a double charge of air, so much so that the victim struggled with all his might to escape. When we stepped through the door, what a sight greeted us. There, flat on his face, was the funlover who had treated me with red arnica and the bullwhip! One of his chums was sitting straddle of his shoulders while the other sat on his legs and kept the pump busy. He couldn't get away to save himself, and no matter how he pleaded, they paid no attention.

"Hold still, you unmannerly son-of-a-bitch!" cried his chief jailer, who was directing the pumping. Turning a merry glance on us, the chief shouted, "Jerk the cork!" which the pumper did. "Allegheny Pack Jack," the chief shouted, doubling over with laughter. Pack Jack, indeed! Never did I hear such curious bangs, boops, and blow-offs in my life. A wonder they hadn't ruptured the man's guts! And did the two pals roll and howl in boisterous glee!

We took the pump away from the two fools, of course, and stopped their sport. Next day, Brown was humping around camp with a sure-enough sore posterior, while his buddies went back to Evarts, after they sobered up.

I didn't even try to ignore the warm glow inside me while I watched Brown trying to soothe his hurts. "Why not use a little red arnica?" I inquired. "It's mighty useful for most any sort of strain!" But he just gave me a sour-vinegar look and didn't answer.

There were some horses in the carload sent to Dakota by Jefferies that I hated to tackle, so I delayed breaking them as long as possible. One was a big dappled gray horse branded Down F on his left jaw; the long bar of the F lay lengthwise along the jaw with the two short bars pointing away from the eyes. In order that a rider might be fore-warned about him, I named him Danger. He was deliber-ately mean about kicking or pawing a man, and he bucked like a scalded hound every chance he got.

He had a mate in the bunch—a smoky-gray, who was branded Down F, too. He was every bit as mean, but he would give warning of his temper by blowing violently through his nostrils, making a whirring, rolling noise inside. His roller-racket snort always meant trouble and earned him the name of Rollers.

Then there was Fighting Red. I had to keep him in my string for months and always had to "ear him down" to mount. But twisting his ear generally kept his attention un-til I could mount. He was a big red horse, blaze-faced, with white legs—a powerful horse—also branded Down F. He came from Colorado, and was a murderous-natured horse if anything annoyed him. If anything happened which he re-sented, he would immediately lay it on his rider and jump on him, fighting, biting, and pawing him down. I think he would have killed a man under certain circumstances. But if all went well, he did lots of work, especially as a circle horse. I also used him a lot for cow work in a roundup. But a man couldn't trust him. He was the shortest-tempered horse I ever saw.

I had too many horses to ride, so I finally turned Red into Con's *remuda,* and he gave him to a man that he thought could handle him. If I happened to be with the outfit, I always helped a new man get started with this horse, for he was really dangerous. Once a slim little Arizona cowboy, Tommy Smith, joined us and Fighting Red was assigned to him.

I started to show Tom which was the easiest way to mount Red, and I nearly got killed.

Tommy didn't have his own saddle, but had borrowed a big, heavy one that belonged to Murdo MacKenzie, and which he used whenever he came to the outfit. I think it was the feel of the saddle that irked Red. When I walked over to him after he was saddled, he suddenly jumped all over me. His teeth snapped off my shirt; he pawed, kicked, and tried to get me down under him. I hung onto him with my arms around his neck and my body close so he couldn't get hold of me or paw me very much either.

With Tom's help, I finally got free from the maniac. Then he stood all bowed up, watching me with hate in his eyes, but I was done using patience on him. I got on my horse, Happy Jack, and roped him. He struck at the rope as it sailed at him and I got him by his head and forefoot. I yanked him down and Tommy mounted him there on the ground. Tommy always had a bad time with him. He wasn't big enough to handle such as Fighting Red, although he was an excellent rider. Once when we were in to ship, somehow Bill displeased Red when he started to tie him up for a few minutes. As usual, he took out his temper on the rider. He bit Bill, ran over him and knocked him down, and chased him under a coal car standing on the track. Red kept Bill under there. Bill throwed chunks of coal at him, and that fired Red's temper all the more. He circled the coal car, even getting down on his knees trying to reach under far enough to get his teeth into Bill's hide.

After an hour or so, some of the Matador men came along, roped Red and rescued Bill. He was about over his mad spell, so Bill mounted him and rode along with the others.

Fighting Red was one of the most savage horses, to have been ridden so many years, that I ever knew. Such horses as these were too mean for most men, even after I'd spent weeks breaking them. As a rule, most cowboys were good riders—they had to be—but they couldn't be blamed for shying away from an outlaw. As a saddle horse, I considered these horses worse than useless, and I thought they should be discarded, for they didn't earn the grass they ate and were a continual menace to those who rode them. But I was being paid to ride them. I didn't have much competition for the job, either. And only rarely did some cowboy complain because I drew more wages than other men. If Con or Mitchell ever heard a man complain, they shut him off with: "If you want to ride the kind of horses our rough-string rider does, then we'll pay you that kind of money." But I never had anyone ask for my string of horses.

Dode was always ready for what looked like a "good deal," and he hadn't been in Dakota long until he met with a drinking pal and bought a good-looking, chunky bay horse that had been raised in Oregon. He sent him out to me.

"He's gentle. Make a cow horse out of him," was the message I received.

Well, I got wised up pretty fast concerning this "gentle bay." He would go along quietly until urged into a lope. Then he'd begin a series of vicious-sounding snorts, as if warning me. If I persisted and touched him with spurs, he gave me the snorts, pawed the air, and broke into crazy pitching that rattled my teeth. He always bucked for all he was worth. He did a rough job consistently and could keep it up, and few men were ever able to ride him. But the trick that gave him his name was a dandy! If he couldn't throw his rider off, he became so furious that he'd squeal and switch his tail in under himself, turning loose his water at the same time. When his tail was well sopped, he'd smack his rider with it again and again, then make a last effort to pitch him off. I could think of no name more suitable for him than Panther Piss—plain Panther if ladies were present. But after his water broke he was all right and would attend to business. I trimmed his tail so he couldn't wet it, but I had to keep him in my string, too, for he was a horse no one wanted. He liked to work cattle from a roundup and became a very good one-man horse, giving way to his ornery nature only rarely.

But of all the horses I ever rode, I think Widow Maker was about the worst. He was a Colorado horse, too, and came to Dakota with the others. But he was from a different ranch and wore an Open A 4 on his left thigh. I spent weeks and weeks with this horse and he never improved at all. But there came a day in the future when we settled our differences for all time.

13. Headquarters at Benoist, 1905

When Dode came to Dakota, he changed quite a few things. He took the Matador office in Evarts away from the rooms above Phil Du Fran's saloon, to room above the Joe Arens saloon just across the street. It seemed that right from the start there was discord between these men. I know Dode found it amusing to turn as much business away from Du Fran as he could, but no one ever thought that one day a terrible tragedy would occur, involving both of these men.

It had been understood from the start that the Matador headquarters were only temporary. So, when I learned from Ambrose Benoist that his place could be leased for a headquarters, I told Brown about it and we talked with Ambrose again.

Ambrose had a wonderful river-bottom place. He had married Isabelle Whitney and had caused the Agency to change her allotment from a less desirable location to an ideal spot at the mouth of the Moreau River, across from the old Louie Benoist place. The Benoist family owned considerable land along the Moreau, all joining, and raised lots of stock. In the beginning, the first "Old Louie" Benoist, a Frenchman, had married an Indian girl. His son was the "Old Louie" Benoist of my time, a breed Indian who owned the place on the south bank of the Moreau, just across the river from Ambrose. Old Louie was brother to Narcisse, who lived just down the Missouri from him. Bill, another brother, lived up the Moreau from Old Louie, at the mouth of No Mouth Creek. These men were full brothers, but Ambrose was pure Frenchman. He was younger, because the first Old Louie had married a white woman after the Indian wife died, and Ambrose was her child.

Bill Benoist always gave the Matador trouble. He was a rather cantankerous breed, continually feuding with others, so much so that eventually he moved his whole belongings out to the Strip. His children had been allotted their land out there on this high, windswept region, far away from the river bottom. There, he attempted to build a ranch, but it was a troublesome attempt. His cattle kept returning to the river bottoms where they had been raised.

Bill was ever at odds with the Agency, too, over provisions of the leasing of the reservation to white cattlemen. He claimed it a shame for an Indian to have to pay a pasture fee on Indian domain. He owned about two thousand head of cattle, as well as bands of horses, so it was easy to see why he didn't want to pay pasture on all stock over one hundred head, as was required of everyone, although he accepted as his right the share of lease fee all of the Indians or breeds on the reservation received. He also contended that by living on the Strip, which was leased to the Milwaukee railroad, he was out of the reservation bounds and owed nothing at all, although he let his stock go anywhere they pleased.

When the Matador arrived, since Bill Benoist was partly in their range, or just off of it on the Strip, they found themselves embattled with him over his horses and cattle. And he feuded continually and forcefully. As fast as the Matador rounded up his stock and sent cowboys to return them to his range, doubtless losing no time and providing excellent roping practice en route for those so inclined, Benoist would turn the stock back into the reservation. He'd then dig up the hatchet and renew his war on the Agency. He would abide by none of the rules which bound the other Indian owners.

To offset the long, turbulent drives—sometimes twenty miles or so, which chousing and disturbance were bad for his stock—Benoist sent his cowboy, a colored man named Bunk White, to rep with us. White was to represent the W B Bar brand, and Bill intended him to stay right with the Matador wagon. Bunk would throw the cattle back onto the Strip in an easier way, after which they could come back again if they wanted to.

White was a very good cowboy and rider. There could have been no real aversion toward him among the men. I know I did not dislike or refuse to work with him, but for some reason, Con would not allow Bunk to work with the wagon. One morning, he told him to get his horses out of the *remuda* and go home, which Bunk did. This also infuriated Bill Benoist, so there was continual discord with this individual. As fast as his stock was driven from Matador range to the Strip, Benoist opened the gates and let them back again.

Bill Benoist was killed later, sometime in 1910. In addition to his cattle, he owned several hundred horses. One day he went horse hunting and at Bazil Dam he found a mare that he wanted. This dam was twelve miles east of the Dog Buttes, on the Strip. The mare had just got a drink and was standing on the breastworks above the dam when Bill threw a loop at her. It settled low on her neck, giving her a regular "work-horse pull" as she bolted away. Bill was riding an excellent roping horse he called Chief, but perhaps by being partially off balance on the breastworks, the mare jerked him down.

He fell on Bill, killing him instantly. Fred Seely was with him and saw the whole accident, but he could do nothing for Bill. He told me all about it some time afterwards. I stayed all night with Bill once, and when we went to bed, he put on a nightshirt and handed me one, too—the first time I ever saw a man wearing a nightshirt.

Seely married Bill Benoist's widow, and after a few months of marital life and the settling of her horse and cattle sales, he departed. No one knows where.

Brown and I laid the preliminaries for a meeting between Dode and Ambrose Benoist in Evarts. It took several rounds of hot liquid across the bar before the two worthy gents concluded a deal whereby Ambrose's place became the new headquarters. The Matador built a frame house there, with a bedroom and office for the manager, Dode MacKenzie. Ambrose kept his three-room log home where his family continued to live, and Mrs. Benoist cooked for the cowboys.

The Benoist place was eight miles down the Missouri from Evarts, and across on the west side. It was an excellent location. The Moreau River, which made the south side of Ambrose's, emptied into the Big Muddy there. As it hit the swift Missouri, the Moreau waters were checked so that the stream widened to three hundred feet of water, deep enough to float a big boat. It was full of fish, too, for many of the big ones left the Missouri and turned into this quiet zone. They traveled up the Moreau for miles. In winter, people cut holes in the ice until they reached water, then set baited hooks and lines, and caught many a fine mess of fish. Usually, the fishermen left their hooks overnight, gathering in the "take" in the morning. Pete Lear had a whole row of fishing holes. We cowboys, up long before he got around in the mornings, had ample opportunity to raid his lines. We used to hustle down and take off a fish or two for ourselves and rebait the hook, so that the lines were full again by the time Pete arrived.

With the establishment of the Matador headquarters at the Benoist place, Dode stayed around there a good deal of the time when he wasn't in Evarts making whoopee. Ambrose was a real character if one ever lived, and a convivial partner of Dode's for the entire time the headquarters remained there.

When winter began giving way to spring, Con took the broncs I had been riding and spread them around among his men, for it wasn't long until roundup time. I went back to Swift Bird for a short time and took the meanest horses with me. I rode them every day, helping with the riding as I had been doing before I was sent to break the new horses.

Riding daily up and down the Moreau, breaking broncs, I came to know every Indian and breed and heard all the news that traveled by moccasin telegraph. But one thing nagged me. I knew of an isolated and padlocked log house in the timber along the river. The more I thought of it, the more I wanted to look inside it—for a Matador man was always on the lookout for "beefeaters." The weather was cold enough at night so that a butchered and quartered beef in a dark little cabin like that would keep like it was in an icebox.

One day I rode up to it and started prying at the lock. In a short time, a young Frenchman appeared around the corner. He had been watching me from a distance and he came over to challenge me. He spoke naturally short anyway, and when he asked me what I wanted there, his voice fairly crackled.

"I want to see what's inside."

"None of your business what's in there."

We sparred for a while, both of us young and hot-headed, and we stood our ground. I wanted to look inside; the Frenchman didn't intend to open the door.

"If you don't unlock that door, I'll report this whole thing to the Agency," I said, and by the look of him, I knew I'd hit dead center. I knew he wanted to avoid that.

The Frenchman looked me in the eye for a while. Then he looked all around and back at me again. I urged him, "I'm not interested in what's in that house, unless it's beef," and that did it.

"All right. There's no beef in there, but I don't want you to open your mouth about what you see. If you do . . ." He just stood there looking at me in a way that I didn't need to have him finish the sentence. I knew what he meant.

"Unlock the door," I said. "If there's no beef in there, I'll have nothing to say."

He opened the door with a quick motion and we stepped inside. What a sight I beheld! Rich, brown beaver pelts by the score. Beautiful, silky furs, stretched and tacked over every wall and even the floor—a veritable pot of gold within the walls of this dingy old log house. And it was strictly against the law to trap beaver!

We didn't linger inside. The Frenchman locked the door again. I got on my horse and rode away. I didn't tell anyone about the furs. I had promised.

I was to know him for many years, and later, as a licensed beaver trapper, though he's an old man, he keeps beaver under control along the Missouri near where he lived then.

Wild animals were all around us on the big reservation range, but we seldom saw them unless we jumped a loafer or a coyote among the cattle. But many wildcat and lynx lived along the river, as well as beaver, mink, fox, and muskrat. Although it was long past fur-trading days, when the primary business of men in this vast wilderness of the Missouri and her tributaries was to bring in the prime pelts found out there, furs were still a source of cash which the natives didn't overlook. And that's how Smoky Dunn got into a terrible fracas one morning which left him scarred for life. It is a good example of how split-second action, without time for thought, can turn out. Smoky told me the story some time after it happened, and it stands out as quite a feat.

"Just once is enough, sometimes, to learn to let well enough alone," he said, grinning a little.

Smoky was a big, half-breed Indian-and-Irish son of Mike Dunn, noted Dakotan who had married a French and Cheyenne breed girl. She was a sister of Sarah, Scotty Philip's wife. They were sisters of Helen, wife of the Ogalala chief, Crazy Horse. Smoky hunted and trapped all along the Missouri where he grew up, and right there, without any warning at all, he got into the toughest predicament of his life.

Hurrying along the Missouri shore one morning just after sunup, going to see if he had any fish on the lines set in his fishing hole in the ice, Smoky passed near an old cottonwood tree toppled over into the water long ago. It was frozen into the river then, but part of the trunk still stuck above the ice. Stretched out on a limb, close under the protection of the bank, he spotted a full-grown wildcat. Stuffed from the night's hunt, the cat had jumped on the old log, tarried awhile, and had fallen asleep in the rising sun.

Smoky's gun was in the cabin, but here was a prime fur he couldn't let get away. On moccasin feet, he padded softly over the ice to reach the sleeping animal, but when his big hands grasped the night prowler by the back of his neck, out of reach of its teeth, Smoky knew he was in for a furious and unexpected battle. He had forgotten to reckon with cat claws.

"Why didn't you let him go?" I asked, for it was the natural thing to do, or so I thought; but Smoky didn't agree.

"Afraid he'd jump on me. He was the fiercest devil I ever saw. He looked soft and furry curled on the log, and I thought I'd take him alive. Soon as I grabbed him, I knew my mistake. He came alive—spitting, squalling, and clawing— and from then on, it was him or me." Smoky grinned a little.

"Once his fangs nearly slashed my jaw, and the deadly ferocity in those glassy eyes and wide-open mouth full of teeth, I don't want to face again, ever."

Snarling like a wounded panther, the wildcat twisted in Smoky's grip so that its powerful hind legs and long claws reached the man. Throwing every ounce of its muscular sixty pounds into the struggle, striving for a slash wherever possible, the cat came near to winning the fight, until Smoky, ignoring his pain, clamped the wildcat between his knees, clutched the thick throat tighter and hung on. With his bare hands, while blood spurted from his torn legs, Smoky choked the big cat to death.

"It was the only thing I could do." Smoky shook his head. "If he had gotten away and jumped on me, slashed up and bleeding like I was, I didn't know if I could fight him off. When he went limp, so did I. Blood squished out of my moccasins onto the snow. I had on heavy underwear and two pairs of overalls, but the cat had ripped them to ribbons. I wrapped my worst leg with my muffler and wound a piece of buckskin string around the other, to stop some of the bleeding until I could get back to the house." The wounds healed in time, but Smoky ever after carried great scars on his legs.

Matador men constantly watched for wolf signs among stock and we were sometimes rewarded for our efforts by destroying a den of loafers. All that winter, Jim Seals and I had noticed wolf signs on cattle, as well as dead stock here and there, and we knew that a pair of wolves were working in the Stove Creek region, but we never sighted either of them. One morning, quite by accident, we came across a fresh wolf trail on frosty grass. We followed it to where it led into a side-hill cavern hollowed out by snow water rushing downhill. Peering inside, we discovered that wolves had crept in there and tunneled a den of their own six feet further back into the hills.

"Likely, their pups were born there," Jim said.

Another cowboy, Tom Barnes, had joined us shortly before we found this den, but neither of these men could crawl through the outside opening. I was tall and thin, so I had to go in. I took my six-shooter, and, dragging the loop end of Tom's saddle rope with me, I wiggled along the narrow passage to where it widened out for a nest of eight pups. In the dim light from the several airholes above, I could see the bitch huddled under a little rocky shelf on the opposite side of the pups, just as far away from me as it was possible to get. She was growling a little and whimpering. It is a notable fact that for some reason—perhaps because it is really a wild dog—the wolf's courage and ferocity vanishes when man enters the den with it, but, nevertheless, I kept my gun handy.

She didn't fight while I fastened my rope in a double half-hitch on her hind legs, while directly above me, through the airholes in the roof, Jim Seals talked to me and kept track of my activities. Tom had tied the other end of the rope to his saddle horn and was waiting for orders from me. Trappers had told us that while a loafer wouldn't fight in the den, a more ferocious devil never lived when hauled into daylight. Jim advised me not to shoot inside the den because of the deafening report, so I decided to cut the wolf's throat as Tom dragged her past me in the narrow tunnel. I jerked the rope to signal Tom to haul her out, but had Jim to stop Tom when I shouted that the wolf was just under me. It was then I discovered that the ordinary jackknife will not go through the thick matted fur protecting the wolf's throat. I yelled for Tom to pull her on out by the heels—that she was very much alive. I scrambled out after her as fast as I could, to see what happened.

When the wolf saw daylight, she leaped high in the air, snarling and snapping. Had she caught the rope in her teeth, one snap would have freed her. The sight of the frantic wolf on the end of the rope stampeded Tom's horse off the hill, yanking the flouncing loafer along, too, giving Jim a hard target to shoot at. His first two shots missed, but the third one finished the wolf. Then I had to crawl inside again to get the pups, and when I wiggled out, lugging them along, I was well repaid. I was loaded with fleas the same as they were.

When dawn lighted the sky next morning, the dog wolf padded uneasily along the hillside above the den, sensing trouble. He circled to catch the wind and knew, without going closer, what had happened. Flinging his head back in a long, mournful howl, he climbed the pinnacle and dropped from sight over the rim.

We had routed a tough old loafer, his mate, and a den full of pups—and it was the first time I had crawled into a wolf den when a full-grown gray was in it.

14. Spring on the Range, 1906

Grass sprang up early that next spring and Con started his roundup wagons rolling. Men left winter camps, glad to get back to the fast action on the range. The first thing we did was to go to Evarts to receive a herd of two thousand cattle from Texas. Con wanted to put them on Beaver Creek, which was on the south side of the Moreau. This creek joined the river where old Dog Face lived.

When we got to the Moreau, it was up, so Con had us drive the herd across, but he didn't attempt to cross over with the wagon. The Moreau was only about half-side deep to a horse where we crossed that day. Once over there, Con left Dan Busby and me to settle the cattle and to camp and eat with the breed Indians living in that region for a few days. Dan left his bed with the roundup wagon, and we packed my bed over the stream on Dick. We intended to sleep in my bed what time we were away from the wagon. All we had to do was ride line on the cattle and skirmish for meals—to be paid for by the Matador.

After a few days, we decided that the new stock would stay

in the locality where Con wanted them, so we packed our bed on Dick again and started back to the north side of the river. Here, at the Moreau, I encountered the only horse I ever saw that couldn't swim—that would drown if he couldn't get back to shore. He was named Gus Winn, after the man who sold him to the Matador. It had rained again and the river was higher than when we had crossed the herd a few days before. We would have to swim it—but Gus wouldn't swim! Time after time, we got him into the water. He would sink and flounder back to shore. He would make no effort whatsoever to swim, and we were at a loss to know what to do with him.

Finally, we took the bed off of Dick and packed it on Gus. It had a waterproof tarp around it, and we roped it securely about the horse. I made a hackamore with my rope, put it on him and snubbed his head close up to my saddle horn, to keep it out of the water. Dan put his rope around Gus, too, and with the bed to keep him from sinking, our swimming horses were powerful enough to pull him along, so in that way we "floated" Gus across the bank-filled river. I have handled hundreds of horses, but never before or since did I see one act like Gus. Horses, like nearly all other animals, swim instinctively, but not Gus Winn.

It was a big country in which to seek our outfit, but we knew that Con would be gathering winter-drifted cattle from the east pasture and taking them back west where they would stay for at least another year. Following the route that Con usually took, we spotted the wagon and caught up to them about noon. I still had a lot of work to do, training the new horses, so Con told me to spend most of my time with them, which I did. But I went right along with the outfit and before long, I was doing considerable stock work as well. Some horses learned quicker than others, and if they were inclined to cow work, I even worked in the roundups on them. I changed mounts often so that all got some training every day or two.

Due to shipping cattle for the Indian owners each fall, and also because some of the breeds were buying stock, too, thereby exercising their reservation rights to run cattle on the Matador lease for the very reasonable price of a dollar a head per year, it became necessary to tally Indian stock every spring. By now, Con knew the Indians well enough that he could tell which brands to tally closely. He kept count of strays, too, and notified the owners. Since there were so many herds passing through the Matador, it was inevitable that quite a number escaped each time and remained in our range. New cattle were arriving often at Evarts, destined for our range, so before long, we were again on the Trail, going in to get another herd.

On the Trail, we met the Sword & Daggers with three thousand two-year-old heifers. Ernest Eidson was with them. They were the first of six thousand head the Daggers had contracted to buy from the Cheyenne Indian Agency. They were to be distributed to the heads of families for a cattle-raising project. Eidson, as Dagger manager, went to Texas to buy the heifers and was then delivering the first ones. The arrival of the balance was so timed that the Sword & Daggers could drive the first herd to the Agency and tally them out to the Indian Department men, and have time to get back to Evarts before the second bunch arrived.

We camped close to the Daggers that night, so Dan Busby, Roy Vivian, and I rode over to eat supper with them. Ernest had bought a new S. D. Myers saddle in Texas, and while he showed it to us he told me he had seen my mother and aunt and others I knew while he was at Sweetwater, Texas, so he told me a lot of news from home. The evening passed swiftly and it was late when we got back to our wagon.

At Evarts we found the Turkey Tracks waiting to receive cattle also, and Cap Mossman was in town. His men were filling idle hours at the local fun spots, in a merry way. Cap, himself, created a little excitement, too.

The evening was well along, and Mossman had retired to his room. But the night was just beginning for the others, excepting that one Track cowboy had run out of funds too soon to round out the night to his entire satisfaction. Since he knew just which room was Mossman's, in Joe Green's little two-story hotel, he figured that if he just went over under his window and called to the Captain that Mossman would readily supply him with more money. And to make it a right social call, the celebrating cowpuncher left the saloon and ambled over to the hotel, singing as sweetly as he knew how. When he was right under Mossman's window, he warbled: "Oooooooooooh-a-Captain? O-O-O-h-a-a, Cap! Tra-la, Tra-la, Drop me-e-e down a-bout f-o-r-t-y, Cap."

Cap Mossman was one of the greatest jokers that ever lived, and here was a chance too good to miss. Suddenly, he shoved the window up and stuck his head out. He had a .45 Colt six-shooter in his hand and he popped lead all around the serenader. He questioned him, singing it, too: "How-ow-ow would a-bout f-o-r-t-y f-i-v-e do you, Cowboy? Tra-la, Tra-la!"

Bullets thudding the ground all around him put the run in the cowboy's heels and he dug up a lot of dust wheeling out of there. After the shooting stopped, from afar out in the dark where he was safe, other men who rushed to the street, heard him shout: "O-o-o-o-h, Cowboys, I believe that ol' so-n-so was shootin' to kill!"

The word passed along that the gunfire came from the hotel, and the curious crowded into the hotel bar, seeking the cause. The much amused Cap Mossman dressed again and came downstairs. He didn't explain, but he bought drinks all around a few times, enjoyed the laughter for a while, and then went back to bed.

There was some delay en route and all of our cattle didn't

arrive at the same time, so Con camped the wagons across the river from Evarts and grazed the stock that had arrived on the Strip, while waiting for the rest of them. By then, the Daggers had reached the Agency with their heifer herd and news of an amusing sidelight to this transaction drifted up to Evarts.

These southern heifers were to be branded with an I D, denoting Indian Department, indicating they belonged to the Cheyenne River Indians, and a Diamond C. But it was not part of the Daggers' contract that they were to do the branding. This would be done later by the Indians and breeds, under Agency supervision, so all the Sword & Daggers had to do was to run the heifers into a corral and through a chute, tally them, and show that they were healthy animals, which didn't take long.

The Dagger men filled the corrals at the Agency with all the heifers they would hold, and kept the rest of them out on grass until the corrals were empty again. Then another bunch would be driven in.

Bill Smedley, fiery old Dagger wagon boss, anxious to get on with the work, prepared to tally the heifers through the chutes, when who should appear at the corrals but a top official from Washington, D. C., who had come all the way out west to inspect these heifers before the Indian Department accepted them. He made a pompous entrance into the corral and waited for the heifers to begin coming past him. When the first ones appeared, this official inspector stepped out in front of them to take a good look and to give his opinion. Naturally, the heifers, unused to meeting a man on foot, turned back, and could not be prodded into the chute. They simply would not take it. They milled and crowded back away from the big easterner standing before them shouting: "Drive the cows in! Drive them in!" at the same time waving his coat in his excitement. It had been his intention to have every last one of the six thousand heifers brought individually before him and held quietly while he personally inspected her. But the heifers would have none of him, and the Sword & Daggers had no intention of lingering with the job of delivering them to the Indian Department.

Smedley, well aware that the deal was still hanging fire until the Indian Department accepted the heifers, curbing his anger and desire to trim the "top hat's" toenails with his .38 automatic, rode over and asked the man from Washington to get away from in front of the heifers so they would pass through the chute for the tally. Whereupon, he was scathingly berated for an "inefficient cow servant," saying that it was nothing but utter cowboy stupidity that was delaying things, and that he, Mr. Top Official, had no intention of moving from his position. The heifers must be brought before him!

Unable to cope with the bigwig, and realizing that the Daggers might be left with six thousand heifers they didn't want, Smedley went out to where Eidson was with the herd and told him what happened. So Ernest went to the corral and found the official in an awful dither, still ordering the Sword & Dagger men to "drive the cows before me, slowly." They ignored him, and above his shouts, Art Bivins told him they would await orders from their boss. So that was the situation when Eidson rode into the corrals and tried again to put the heifers through the chute.

When he found the job as impossible as Smedley had said, he approached the irate official to explain that the heifers were wild, and were unused to men, "especially men walking and waving a black coat," and that if he would move back out of sight, he could watch them go through the chute, and could easily inspect them that way.

The Washington man, already top-heavy with offended ego, expressed his contempt for cowboys in general, and most sarcastically refused to budge from where he was. He boasted that his authority exceeded that of any man on the reservation—even that of the Indian Agent—and that he would do as he pleased.

This was more than Eidson could take. He swung down off his horse and made a beeline for the official, his fists doubled and his intention unmistakable. The official eyed him for a scant moment before he took to his heels. He cleared the fence in a mighty scramble, the scuff of cowboy chaps and jingling spurs close behind him as he went over. Had Eidson not been impeded by the cowboy riding gear he had not taken time to remove, he would have laid rough hands on the Washington man, whose actions showed how very unsuited he was for the job.

As the flying dignitary made for the Agency office, he heard Eidson call him every choice epithet known to range men, and he lost no time in ordering Indian policemen to "remove the scandalous Eidson from the reservation at once!"

Unwilling to clash with the Agency, Eidson crossed the Missouri with the police, and then he was out of Indian country. Mr. Webster, Sword & Dagger owner, was in the Forest City hotel, just across the river from the Agency. He was notified, and took a boat for the reservation at once.

As soon as the Washington official saw Webster, he demanded Eidson's permanent removal from the reservation. But Webster supported Eidson's stand, and again tried to explain the situation to the easterner, asserting that Eidson was his most valuable man, and he would not submit to losing him.

The stubborn official countered that he would personally see to it that the Sword & Dagger lease be canceled if his orders were not carried out.

Mr. Webster was a mild-mannered man who never used profanity, but he was far from being "soft." He met the threat with a point-blank statement that it would be a very serious matter to cancel a lease such as the Sword & Daggers held; that the Indian Department would find themselves in the midst of a costly litigation, in which the Daggers would have the backing of every big cattle operator on the reservation; that at least twenty-five men had been witness to the silly affair at the corral and would testify; that the official had been in the wrong from the very start; that he might find himself divested of his own job, since he had shown himself so utterly unqualified to act in the capacity he assumed. Mr. Webster sternly advised him that there was a code of the western rangeland from which the stranger could not hold himself immune.

Although the official obviously felt the truth of Webster's statements, he continued to argue, but eventually conceded that the deal might proceed if Eidson would apologize to him. Webster knew that Ernest would never extend his apology for what he had done. In his own mind, he might regret the whole affair, but he was not the kind to bend in apology when he knew he was right. And there matters stood until Webster agreed to talk to Eidson.

Eidson was adamant in his refusal to apologize. And, furthermore, he delegated Mr. Webster to inform the Washington highbrow that if he valued his hide, he had better stay over there on the reservation! That he, Eidson, would make use of every means to catch him after he left Indian country, whether by boat or train, and would thoroughly thrash him, cowboy fashion.

Mr. Webster went back and reported the results of his meeting with Eidson. The official listened, probably recalling the wild-eyed man, whose friends called him "Booger," chasing him out of the corral. He did not doubt what would have happened had not his own heels carried him out of danger. But, actually, it was the unprintable names that Eidson had called him which so upset his dignity and still stuck in his craw.

The Indian Agent realized the argument must end and business proceed, for he knew that the heifers as a whole were a very fine lot, well worth the price, and were just what the Agency wanted. So he and other men took a hand in the affair and convinced the official that his personal safety might well be in jeopardy, as well as the highly undesirable trouble with the big outfits leasing the Indian land which might result if things went further. So the Washington man decided to call it quits.

Accordingly, a boat was sent to bring Eidson back to the reservation. As soon as he was assured that Eidson had indeed crossed the Missouri again, and stood on reservation soil, the official hastened down to the ferry, crossed over the Big Muddy and departed the Indian country for good. He entrained for Washington without his apology, and without his giving his personal inspection to each heifer. But his hide was still whole and untrampled—which was probably compensation enough.

His departure was a big relief to everyone, even the Agency men. His presence there was none of their doings, but there was nothing they could do about it. After he was gone, the Agent sent out a man who understood what was to be done, and he checked the heifers for the Indian Department. The tally got under way, the deal turned out very satisfactorily, and Mr. Webster retained "his most valuable man."

Before all of the Matador cattle arrived, the Turkey Track trains came in. Cap Mossman had learned from his wagon boss that somehow more than the usual number of cattle from Matador range—most of them new cattle not yet accustomed to home range—had drifted into the Tracks through gates which had been left open.

So, after a talk with Con and Dode, Roy Vivian and I were sent along to rep with the Tracks and to bring back the strayed stock. We cut our mounts from the Matador *remuda,* packed our beds on a couple of them, and left Evarts with the Track wagon.

Between the Sword & Dagger and the Turkey Track ranges was a narrow strip of country extending from the Cheyenne River northward for several miles, but it didn't completely separate these ranges except where the Track's southwest line and Dagger's southeast line met. This land was leased by the Mississippi outfit, which was the Empire State Cattle Company with headquarters at Fort Pierre. Jeff Carr was the manager for years. They were known to the reservation men as the Mississippi outfit because they established their range on a big flatland known as the Mississippi Flat. They used the brands, DEL, LDT, and DLT, left side.

The Mississippi had range south of the Cheyenne River, too, and each year shipped in many cattle, the same as other outfits. A great many of them were three- and four-year-old longhorns, wearing the THS brand from the fabulous Don Luis Tarrazas ranches in Old Mexico. This brand was made all connected—the T and the H hooked onto it and across the bottom of the curve of the small *h* was the S, lying flat.

The Tarrazas longhorns were very good quality, big, solid-color cattle of considerable breeding—mostly duns and dark-red steers.

When the tale of great cattle kings is written, Don Luis Tarrazas, of Chihuahua, Mexico, will have a place near the top. He was a small, wiry, light-complexioned man whose bright blue eyes shown above a full beard and moustache. He didn't drink or smoke, and he supervised his entire ranching interests himself. He had competent men in charge at each ranch, and he made the rounds systematically. It took him a month to complete a visit to all of the ranches. His is a fabulous and almost unbelievable story, interwoven with Northern Mexico history. Tarrazas owned six and a half million acres of ranch land—four hundred thousand head of cattle, fourteen thousand horses, and countless sheep. He branded ninety thousand calves a year and all of this giant empire—twelve ranches—remained intact until the Villa revolution of 1910 broke it apart.

The Turkey Tracks shipped in many of the Tarrazas' steers, and T O's from Old Mexico, too, and in crossing Matador country, longhorns always escaped.

These stray steers, with their excellent horns, were considered "legal roping practice," especially if a man was training a roping horse. I was considered a good roper. I had always roped calves at branding time, and steers whenever we had any to brand. Otherwise, I roped anything I could find to snap my rope onto. I liked to rope, and I had natural ability, but a man doesn't become expert in anything unless he does a lot of it. The Matador didn't object to my roping under certain circumstances, for I was training horses all the time. To make a good roping horse, it requires long hours of practice and many "catches" before he can be depended on to know what is required of him. So I had my rope in my hand, flipping it over every rock or bush I passed, or just whirling and throwing it and re-coiling it constantly, which kept my aim accurate and my horses unafraid of a rope. Because of my love of roping, I made many fine roping horses in my time, and the THS Mexico steers provided a lot of training for them. Even when I wasn't roping them, it was fun to ride alongside of a running THS or T O. The faster he ran, the higher he raised his tail, until he would lay it right over in my lap. I'd grab it and, when his hind feet were off the ground, it took but a light jerk to upset him and send him rolling. This was a good method to keep them ready for a fast run when I wanted to rope one. It made it easier to "bust" them, for they hit the end of the rope harder. I trained my horses to keep the rope tight while I tied three of the steer's legs. "Roped and tied" was an accomplishment.

The Matador had bought a little bay horse from Pete Claymore. I called him Little Pete, and I thought he would make a good roping horse. He had the speed to catch most anything, and, in my opinion, all he needed was practice in tying onto something.

As Roy and I rode along with the Turkey Track men, we saw a lot of Mexicos, and four or five of us thought we'd do a little roping. I tightened the cinch on Little Pete and selected a leggy dun-yellow longhorn that could run like an antelope. I took after him and just as we hit a little downgrade over rocky ground, I sailed a loop after him and caught his horns. When the rope tightened as the steer hit the end of it, my horse began to buck, and before I knew what had happened, all three of us were down in one pile.

I rolled out of the heap with a broken leg, a badly mashed ankle, deep bruises, and a general shaking up. The nearest doctor was at Evarts, twenty-five miles away. The only ambulance was the bedwagon and it had no springs under it. Someone roped Little Pete, got my saddle, and turned the steer loose. They put my roundup bed in the wagon and helped me in. The Track wagon boss sent Roy with me, and we started for Evarts. Before long, my leg began to swell and pain terribly. About that time, we met a friend who had a quart of "medicine" with him, which I think was called Sunnybrook. He gave it to me, after taking one last swig to wish me luck. When we reached the Missouri, we were too late to catch the ferry, so had to wait two hours there for the boat to come back from the other shore. While we waited, Roy and I killed the Sunnybrook medicine.

Arriving at last at the Joe Green hotel, which also served as a hospital, we found that the doctor was on a drunk. By then, my leg was swelled big and black as a stovepipe. Eventually, Doc staggered in and looked me over, cheerful-like. He was in fine humor. He made a few passes over my ankle, shoved together what bones he could find through the swelling, and punched the rest of them in the general direction he figured they went. When the pain of his operations was nearly unendurable, the Doc got his bottle, took a couple of

swallows for comradeship and sympathy, and passed it over to me. I took a few to be sociable, as well as to fortify myself for more of his probing. The little sawbones finally shoved the broken ends around until all of them seemed to hit on something solid. He voiced the hope that they would be near enough to some other bone to knit onto it. He tied the whole works up tight, took a few more drinks, passed the bottle to me again, patted my shoulder in a buddylike way—and the job was done!

The bones knit well enough in the leg, but in the ankle, they evidently didn't hit the parts they were cracked off of, although they did a fair job of healing. I could walk again after that, but never without limping. I stayed in Evarts a few weeks, then went out to the Matador outfit. I rode on the bedwagon for some time, until I got so I could handle my leg pretty well again. Youth helps a lot in a case of that kind. When a fellow is young, he doesn't give a damn for a little pain, but he will "give" to the limp more and more as age catches up to him.

While I was in bed at the hotel and my outfit had gone back without me, one little Turkey Track cowboy, who had a habit of tarrying in town an extra day or two whenever he had the opportunity, came up to my room several times, usually to bring me a few snorts of the stuff he was pretty full of. He liked fun, and one morning we heard about how he broke a pretty strict cow outfit rule and got into trouble—in fact, he went visiting where he shouldn't have been, and wound up in the Missouri River. But he enlivened one evening for a while.

The cow outfits laid down a set of rules to their men, and one of the sternest concerned their horses—and women, the painted kind. These regulations forbade the men to ride company horses, no matter how much urge they had to wander down the back road to see The Girls in the House (which Evarts isolated away out toward the Missouri River shore).

They must leave their horses stabled in town. No taking them down there to tie to a handy tree, forgetting them for hours. To disregard this rule was a good way to get fired.

Out where the thumping piano and twinkling lights beckoned the idle males, like moths to a candle—and where they usually got singed—whirling crazily about, the boot-stomping visitors frolicked away idle hours, but it was all a part of frontier life and they went after it vigorously.

Since this was cattle country, it was to be expected that men from the open prairies would be there—and not one of them could resist boasting about the things they did. With female ears to listen, they detailed stories of lovable pet horses, spun harrowing tales of the wickedness of other horses. Naturally, a good rider was proud of his ability, and, aided by several jiggers of straight whisky, they dwelt on awesome accounts of bucking horses that knew every trick in a range outlaw's book. With all this exciting talk, The Girls were curious to see for themselves how these horsemen spurred a high-pitching bronc from ears to tail, making him do his worst, then riding him so easily that, according to some accounts, the rider could roll a cigarette with one hand, so secure was his seat upon the bronc's back! Ah, but it was a fine way to impress a female and elbow away some other contender for her favor.

And that is how it was when my cowboy friend disregarding regulations, sneaked his horse downriver by a circuitous route, purposely to show him to The Gals and to convince them he was a real bucker—which was what got him into a jam! He had continually lauded the tough bucking of the little black Turkey Track horse in his string—Nigger Heathen—and true enough, he would buck ferociously at little provocation; it took a good rider to stay on him. He was a good one to show off on—a handsome black, and full of salty action as ever a horse could be.

The cowboy appeared at the House near evening and the

women rushed out to see him. They praised and complimented him and Nigger Heathen, and expressed a great desire to see him buck. Before long, fortified by all this female attention—as well as a few more drinks—the young cowboy decided to treat The Gals to a little show. They didn't have much of a life, he reckoned, so he would give them a look at something different!

So with a flourish and a regular Comanche whoop, he leaned over and "thumbed" Nigger Heathen on both sides of his neck, from his shoulders to his ears. A dig like that—poking the thumbs into his neck and raking to his ears—was a definite insult to a cow pony, and Nigger Heathen dropped his head, stuck it between his knees and broke into downright rough bucking. He bawled and swapped ends, hitting the ground hard and stiff-legged, time after time, and once he broke loose, he couldn't be pulled up to end the exhibition.

Nigger Heathen took a course toward the cut bank of the Missouri, less than one hundred fifty feet away, where it was eight feet down to water running twenty-five feet deep. As he neared the edge, Nigger Heathen was pounding the gumbo in bow-backed jumps that bounced him a little higher each time. His last bounce carried him well over the river bank. He sank from sight and went to bedrock like a sack of sand! And with him went the Turkey Track cowboy!

When Nigger Heathen broke above the surface, his rider was still clinging to him haphazardly. But still with him. Nigger Heathen struck out swimming for Blue Blanket Island, lying offshore a few hundred yards. When they got out onto the sandbar, the wet cowboy took note of the swift water, the coming night that had already darkened the sky, and calculated his chances of swimming the horse downstream a half-mile to a break in the bank where they could climb out. He decided to unsaddle, leave the horse and his rigging on the Island until morning and try swimming to shore himself.

His hat had gone sailing downstream when he plunged into the water with Nigger Heathen, and without a hat, a cowboy is undressed indeed! He stripped off all the rest of his clothes except his underwear, tied his boots in his shirt, looped the sleeves around his neck and swam for the cutbank where he and his mount had dived off.

By then, every one of the girls had rushed to the river shore and frantically offered advice and aid. Using strips of bedsheets, The Girls lassoed him and fished him out of the water. Pleased and excited by their rescue, and comforting their hero en masse, they all but carried him into their bower. While his own clothes dried, they got the idea to dress him in silk petticoats and an evening gown, and introduce him as a new member of The House! Fancy high-heeled slippers just fit his small feet, and they topped their efforts with a well-done job of pinning false hair into place on his curly head. Before they finished with him, he made a very passable and well-painted Gal.

The evening had begun by then. The Girls wined and dined their new member. He was small and could easily be taken for one of them. This tickled the little hellion, and he fell right in with their fun. By the time the visitors arrived, the damp cowboy had dried out, outwardly, while inwardly, due to many little nips to warm his chilled person, he had grown wetter, until his delight with everyone reached the point where he greeted the arrivals as gaily and invitingly as any of the regular Girls did. He swished his skirts and flirted; he danced and flipped his hips, and for a time, so well did he fit into the clothes, and so well did he act his part, he enticed several amorous gents to go upstairs to be alone with "her." When they discovered they had been taken in, they helped hook others by spreading tales of the new Gal's charms. Then every man slanted an eye "her" way, and she became the "belle of the ball." All went hilariously well, and none suspected the fraud for quite a while. But eventually, the whisky impishness gave way to drowsiness, and The Girls put the little cowboy to bed.

The next day, he found a boatman to row him out to Blue Blanket Island, where he loaded his saddle, looped a lariat around Nigger Heathen's neck and led him along, swimming behind the boat. They got out of the river at the crossing downstream, near the stockyards.

Perhaps Nigger Heathen, when he made the high-dive into the Missouri, became one of the first water jumpers in the West, a trick that stunt horses do readily now, and it ended all right that time. But more often, the Missouri River did not give up that which came into her grasp.

Reportedly, there had been excitement at The House upon another occasion, when a cowboy shot up the place. It happened during the dancing one evening when a ranchman called a halt on going into the bar adjoining the dance floor to buy more drinks for himself or the girl who had attached herself to him. This sudden clampdown on the pocketbook irked the female. She called him a cheapskate, and it made him mad. He pushed her hands off his arm.

"Git away from me, or I'll scorch your tail feathers with a bullet."

The woman flipped her hips and snapped her fingers under his nose, "You stingy old son-of-an-ape," she hissed, "you wouldn't shoot anything but *bull!*"

That did it! The cowpuncher reached for the .38 automatic on his hip. When the somewhat tipsy gal caught a glimpse of that, she ran for the barroom. As her skirts swished through the door, he shot a row of bullet holes right up the casing, from floor to doorknob height.

The charmer disappeared like she really had been stung, and those who saw the incident laughed gleefully.

The man was a crack shot and knew where every bullet would strike when he pulled the trigger. He reloaded his gun with the nine bullets it held, shoved it back into his holster and started celebrating again.

15. Fall Roundup, 1906

Rain and wind and sunshine swept spring into early summer. My leg was getting well, and I began working with the other men and riding my gentlest horses. One morning, Con told me to cut my string from the *remuda,* for I was going to the Tracks once more. I caught up with their wagon just inside their fence and turned my horses with theirs.

We had worked on around the range to Stove Creek. Two strangers joined us there. They had been hired by the Turkey Track wagon boss, and neither one had a bed. As was customary, a new man with an outfit shared the bed with some other cowboy—generally a friend—until he could get his own bed from wherever he had left it. Both of the newcomers were clean-looking men, so when the wagon boss, Jess Knight, asked me if one of them could roll in with me for the night, I said he could. The other slept with old Peavine.

Three or four days later, both men admitted they were sick, and it turned out that they were already feverish with smallpox. Immediately, Jess sent them in a rig to what he designated as the "pesthouse," an old log cabin on Willow

Creek that the Tracks used for winter cow camp. It was above the forks of Willow Creek. They were given a supply of food and the doctor from the Agency came out to see them. They took care of each other. At least they were not alone. It was fifteen miles from the Cheyenne Agency, but the doctor made it out there to prescribe for them until he could release them.

It never occurred to me that I might catch the disease, but when we reached Charley Claymore Creek, in just the allotted time it takes to contract it, I came down with smallpox. The wagon boss told me to get my stuff together pronto and head for the pesthouse. I was as sick as I ever expect to be, but no one went along to see that I got there. I managed to load my bedroll on a pack horse and rode my good cow horse, Dick.

All along the whole miserable ten miles, in spite of the heavy coat I wore, I chilled to the bone, and my head swam with fever.

When I got to the pesthouse, the other men were leaving. The doctor had released them the day before. I was too weak to do anything more than hobble Dick, stake the other horse with a long rope, and drag my bed inside. I fell into it and lay there alone for days, burning with fever. I thought I was going to die, and I didn't care much if I did. I didn't have anything to eat or anyone to see whether I needed a drink of water. Neither of the men leaving as I came mentioned being sorry I had taken the pox, but one of them got a pail of water and left it in the house. There were a few cans of tomatoes there, and these and the water probably saved my life.

My pack horse could drink from the creek, and Dick was loose to go where he wished. There came several heavy rains which brought the creek up and kept it so high that the doctor couldn't get over to see me. He drove up a few times and shouted from the other side until I crawled out of bed to see what he wanted. He inquired how I was, and I could barely

shout an answer. I'd sag back into bed, wishing he was in hell or some place just as hot, for his visits made in that manner only hurt me more. He could have gotten a boat to get over to me, but evidently he concluded that if his shouts could bring me to the door, I wasn't dead enough to be buried, and that eventually I'd make it.

Not a soul came near me all the time I fought the fever, the sores, and the itching. Try as I would not to scratch, the itching at times was unbearable, and lest I could ever forget, I have a few pox marks to remind me of those days. Finally, the fever broke and I was hungry and weak. I knew I had to get somewhere, for even the tomatoes were about gone.

I wobbled out to my stake horse. He was as hungry as I was. He could get water and hadn't tangled up in the seventy-five-foot rope, but he had grubbed every spear of edible forage within the scope of his rope and as far out around as he could stretch his neck. I led him to the cabin and somehow pushed my bedroll up over his back and tied it on.

Old Dick was close by, still hobbled. I bridled him and finally lifted the saddle onto his back. I suppose it was the smell of the fever on my clothes and skin that made him keep touching me with his nose, making it seem like the gentle old horse was sympathizing with me and trying to help me get the saddle on. He acted like he knew I was in a bad way, and I thought at the moment that he was the only friend I had on earth.

When I finally puffed and sweated my way up onto his back and he moved away from that hole of a pesthouse, I just sat and swayed and hung onto the saddle horn for miles, until I met an Indian who told me where the Turkey Track wagon was. They had worked around to the head of Virgin Creek and I turned that way. They were about twenty miles from Willow Creek.

When I showed up on a hill near the wagon, Jess saw me

and rode out to meet me. "Where do you think you're going?"

"To your wagon, if I can make it," I told him, "I want something to eat."

"You can't come to the wagon. Go back to that pesthouse," he said, using a lot of cuss words. "You'll scatter that goddam smallpox all over the reservation. One thing sure, you won't stop at the Track wagon while I'm running it."

I didn't waste effort to tell him that the last time the doctor had come up and shouted over to me, he said that I would be over the pox enough not to give it to anyone as soon as I felt the fever leave and I was hungry. I rode on past Jess, telling him as loud as I could speak, "I'm going to get something to eat at the wagon, and I'll shoot any sonovabitch who molests me." I carried a six-shooter, the same as a lot of the men did. Jess rode along with me, cussing all the way. Thinking back on it now, I know he was excited and actually afraid that more of his men would break out with the fever. Since it is so highly contagious and so deadly, if it had ever hit an Indian camp it would spread like wildfire, and the Turkey Tracks would be barred from the reservation. The Indians were deathly afraid of it, too. When I got to the wagon, I slid down off of Dick and asked the cook for something to eat. I laid my gun close to me. But the cook was fine. He gave me a helping of stuff he thought I could eat, and wouldn't let me have but a little at a time. Jess didn't stick around to see if I'd shoot him. He probably knew I wouldn't. But he was worried and upset by my presence. I told the cook the doctor had released me and I wouldn't give the fever to anyone.

I stayed there with the wagon until I was able to make the ride back to the Matador. The Turkey Track men saddled my horse every day, and I trailed along with them from one campground to the next, but I spent most of my time in my bed. The Track men did my work and gathered all the strays

I was down there to get, but I couldn't take them home. As soon as I was able, I went home to the Matador and Con sent after the cattle.

Shortly after I went to the pesthouse, Peavine had thrown one of the "I quit" fits for which he was noted—and perhaps Jess helped him into his fit to get him out of his outfit. Anyway, he left the Tracks to go to the Matador to work for Con. After a few days there, he came down with smallpox too, but Con put him in a little tent off to himself and saw that he was fed and cared for. He recovered before I did. But we were both skeptical about sharing our beds with strange partners from then on, no matter how sad it was that they didn't have a bed, or how much it would accommodate a wagon boss. I can't recall whether the two men worked for the Tracks after they put in their session in the pesthouse or not, but I believe that Jess boosted them right on to town after they got back to his wagon.

Some months after that, I happened near the old pesthouse. I stopped long enough to stick a match to it, and rode away happy and content that no more would that hole of a camp be available to shove a sick man into, let him die if he couldn't make it.

It was always good to get back to Con's wagon and to Walter Krump's cooking. I guess I ate everything I could pile on my plate for a while. There was always plenty of beef, and big roasts or steaks, and Krump's biscuits and pies were a treat at any time. He always cooked plenty for second helpings, too. In fact, he often fed the remains of a meal to the Indians in the region where we were working. They generally hung around the wagon at mealtime in hopes they could get a chance to "clean up the kettles," and Con approved of Krump's feeding them. The Matador was never stingy with grub.

Before long, I was feeling nearly as good as ever. Fall shipping time was drawing close, so Con sent me to the Sword &

Daggers where I repped with them through the fall work.

I hadn't been with them long before a rider brought a letter to Ernest Eidson. It was from Sam Hooker, manager of the H A T outfit, west of the reservation line.

He informed the Sword & Dagger manager that the H A T's were gathering an immense herd, closing out, and were coming to Evarts to ship. They had cattle from both reservations, the letter said, and if the Sword & Dagger would send a man, the H A T's would work this herd for stock in their brand.

Ernest decided to go meet the H A T herd himself, and that I should go along to look for brands the Matador was interested in. We rode out into Perkins County, arriving just before the big drive got under way, so we helped them in any way we could as they came on toward Evarts. When we got opposite the Matador pastures, they held up the herd and we cut out the stock that belonged in our part of the Cheyenne River reservation—the Sword & Dagger, Matador, and the Indian brands. I began cutting cattle carrying the Three V's iron and found myself in the midst of a heated argument. The H A T manager contended that his outfit was entitled to the pasture bill on them, since these steers had been outside ever since the Three V's closed out.

Sam Hooker had some basis for his claim, since it was true that the Three V's roundups might have missed them. But after closing out west of the reservation, the Three V's had pastured their cattle with the Matador. I could tell by the age of the steers and the age of the Matador steers that were with them that all of these cattle had gotten out of Matador range and wandered back to Perkins County together. I stood my ground and told Hooker that they were Matador pasture stuff, and that I was entitled to cut them out and return them to Matador range. I won out and took the Three V's cattle for the Matador. Then Eidson and I rode back to his wagon, after we dropped the cattle where they belonged. I didn't know then that the drive we had just taken part in would be recorded historically as the last big roundup in Perkins County.

When we got back to the Dagger wagon, Narcisse Narcelle, one of the largest Indian cattle operators on the Cheyenne River Indian reservation whose range was in the Dagger lease, had stopped for the night. He was a great Indian humorist and he loved to tell stories around the campfire. It was then I heard him tell some anecdotes on his own people.

Narcisse talked pretty good English. He told about the first feast the white missionaries gave for the Indians, as a token of brotherhood between them.

A feast was a fine way to cement friendship, and this one was given for the very old Indians. The date was set, and pleased Indians arrived and everything was in order. The missionaries put the food on a long table that stood in a log house, pushed benches up beside it for them to sit on, and brought in the first group. When the red brothers were all standing around the table and a prayer had been said, the white people left the room so that their somewhat bashful guests could seat themselves and eat. Alone, the old Indians took a puzzled look at the table and the benches around it. Not being used to such, they bunched the food dishes to the center, stepped up on the benches and from there to the table top, where they seated themselves cross-legged around the grub and began to eat in their own way.

Another thing he liked to tell was about how the old Indians reacted when they went to eat at a white man's hotel in Forest City. By then, they knew better than to sit on the table, but had never seen meals served family style. Accordingly, when a bowl of food, whether it was meat, gravy, vegetables, or anything else, was passed to them, they would eat it all, believing it was their portion and that that was what they were supposed to do.

But the long-ago deal that tickled Narcisse the most was when the first wagons and harnesses were issued to the Indians. The whole Indian camp went to old Fort Bennett to get these wagons. None of them had ever used anything more complex than dog or pony travois, and they didn't know the first thing about wagons. They spent considerable time listening to the Indian Agent's instruction on how to care for and operate these new rigs, and after a while they hitched their gentlest ponies to them and drove around the Agency for a while, until it seemed that everything was safe for them to start out. They all left the Agency together.

Things went well enough until they came to the road going down into the Red Bull crossing—named for the old Indian living there—on the Cheyenne River. They had to travel down a long, narrow ridge that got steeper all the time as it angled to the bottom. It was a bad place for any kind of a rig to get down safely.

The one thing the Indians had failed to absorb was how to operate the hand brake on the wheels. By pulling this lever, they could hold the wagon back off of the heels of the teams on steep grades, for in places a team needed help to keep the wagons from running over them. And another thing, not being familiar with team driving, they didn't know how to make the horses—unschooled also in being hitched to wagons—hold them back on the grades. The trouble got so serious on the hog-back road that they stopped before they hit the steepest places and held a powwow. Suddenly, one old buck came up with an idea. *They would hobble the horses' front feet!* If the horses had to slow up and could not run, they would surely hold the wagons back. So there on the ridge, where the road really dropped down fast, that was just what they did. They put hobbles securely on each horse's front feet!

When they started their teams to go on down they got into the worst mixup possible. With their feet hobbled, the horses had no chance whatsoever of holding the wagons back off them. On the sharp incline, they got down, kicking and thrashing around on the ground as the wagons rolled up on top of them. It was the wildest jamboree the Indians had ever been in, and a lot of them had seen scalping raids and buffalo hunts.

They grabbed their knives and cut the new harness off of the horses, then boosted the wagons up, or pulled the horses out from under them, and let the wagons go where they would. Many of them rolled downgrade, veered into narrow gullies beside the road and turned bottom-side up. And there the whole glorious party halted, harness whacked to pieces, personal plunder scattered everywhere, shiny new wagons upended over gumbo cutbanks. The Indians were mystified and uncertain what to do until someone came along who knew about wagons and brakes and helped them out of their predicament. The teams were hitched to the wagons that were still on the road and the Indians were shown how to use the hand brake.

After considerable effort, the overturned wagons were brought up out of the gullies, while the squaws scrambled here and there gathering up their scattered plunder. Eventually, everyone reached the bottom of the hill and started on their way again. From then on, the whole lot of them hung to the brakes even on the slightest slope, so much so that the ponies practically had to pull the wagons downhill.

I worked through the Sword & Dagger range twice with them, then went home to Con's wagon. It was beginning to get pretty winterish and we knew it would not be long until we would go into winter camp. But just then the L7's sent Con word that there were Matador steers up there on the Standing Rock. So he sent me to bring them back.

It looked black and blustery away off in the northwest when I started for the L7's and the Standing Rock. A stinging wind was blowing, and it was after dark when I got there. By then everyone was in bed and the tent was crowded, so I rolled my bed out at the back of the tent, sheltered from the wind as much as possible. Bird Rose, L7 manager, came out after I was in bed and tossed harness on my tarp to keep it from whipping. Three inches of snow fell on me that night.

The Standing Rock Indian reservation joined the Cheyenne River reservation on the north, and was stocked by the Lake, Tomb Cattle Company, known as the L7's because of their brand. The Strip fence ran along the Standing Rock's south line. Another fence six miles farther south, running east and west, made the Trail lane, with gates opening out into the ranges bordering it. The east half of the Standing Rock didn't come under the lease, apparently, although the L7 pasture seemed to angle northeast and many L7 cattle drifted over into this Indian land. They were gathered and turned back by the Standing Rock Indian roundup wagon, which was run by Ben Lone Man.

Many fine streams traversed the L7 range on Standing Rock, the same way as they did on the Cheyennne River reservation. Timbered draws and river bottom rough land and cutbank windbreaks, high Buttes and the silvery-leafed thorny buffalo berry thickets provided winter protection for livestock. Of course, if a tough winter struck with drifting snow and no wind-swept-bare hills to provide some forage, stock met the same fate as those on other ranges. Horses usually wintered well. They grew heavy coats of hair, sought the leeward side of the hills, where the wind had whipped away part of the snow, and pawed down to plenty of grass. The continual action of their legs and ankles limbered up even old stiff horses until, by spring, they were supple.

Not all of the L7 range was rough country. There were vast stretches of level land, equally grassy, with only scattered

Indian garden patches, in all this virgin and unmolested range. Here the giant cattle-spread pastured fifty to sixty thousand stock. The L7's owned the N U N's, a cow- and calf-spread in Texas, which supplied part of the stock for L7 range, and they bought thousands more to fill their range. I have seen steers wearing my father's brand—the "crossed S" —from north of Red River, which now forms the Texas– Oklahoma line, fattening on L7 grass. Doubtless, these steers had been sold after his death, perhaps several times, before they finally made the long trip to the L7 range.

After the stormy night when I got to the L7, the weather cleared away and they went on gathering a herd. They had so many cattle to ship that they worked as long as the wagons could pull through the rain and snow. I think I learned more from the manager Bird Rose than anyone, excepting Con McMurry, in regard to handling beef to keep the fat on them and never run, or allow them to run, but it was hard for a young fellow to hold still and keep his patience, as Bird expected him to. He was one of the easiest men in a roundup that I ever knew. He rode a string of horses that carried their heads low and padded along as quiet as foxes. He wouldn't ride a blustery horse in a roundup, or allow a man to ride a high-headed horse. He wouldn't have a horse that wouldn't work without a lot of fuss. Snorting, throwing his head, or fighting the bit ruled a horse out in Bird's outfit.

Bird's cow horse, Frazier, the sorrel with one white stocking and white hairs scattered here and there in his coat, worked right up on his toes, stayed close to the steer indicated to him as the one to be cut. He had a catlike way of stepping to the right or left to keep the steer from turning back, or in any direction other than straight out to the cut. Horses like this rarely had to be guided; they knew what was wanted, and they went about it in their own way. They were natural cow horses.

If Bird encountered a touchy steer that showed signs of

being troublesome, he didn't molest him until he had quieted. Frazier always seemed to recognize what was wrong and behaved accordingly. He made me think of Pat, dock-tailed polo horse ridden by Con McMurry. Excepting for Pat's short tail, he looked like Frazier and had the same way of working stock.

Bird didn't always make a big roundup. Instead, he would jog through the range with his men, and if he came upon a bunch of steers at a watering place, full of grass and water and lying down resting, he didn't disturb them. He would drag through them, getting the ones he wanted, leaving the others where they were.

When Bird started this operation, he would ease up to the cattle and just sit around on his horse, near them. If one of them acted as if he would run, Bird often turned aside and rode in the opposite direction, not even looking back. After a while, he worked around and turned the flighty one back to the bunch. He took time to let stock get acquainted with him and see what he looked like. Strangely, while stock do not actually fear man, add a man to the back of a horse and it makes a difference. Wild cattle are inquisitive about a man on the ground. They circle and run around him, trot in nearer for a better look, and follow him, often too close for comfort, especially in the era when most of them carried a sturdy set of horns. The sight of a man plodding along on his own shanks could easily stampede a herd, yet I doubt if cattle of those days would hesitate if they really wanted to attack a man on foot.

When Bird sent his men on a wide circle for a roundup, he turned off one or two men in different parts of the range until he had encircled the region to be worked. As cattle drifted toward the center, routed from their haunts by cowboy shouts, he had us hold the roundup together for a while to let the cattle cool off before he started to work. He passed the time by riding among them, looking them over, and doing nothing further to excite them. If he saw a little bunch off to one side and all but two or three were prime for market, he'd shove them farther from the herd, motion a man to ride in and keep them there, and he'd have his cut start. He made no effort to cut out the cattle that weren't ready to go until the main job of getting a herd together was over. Then he would take time to clean up the herd and cut out the steers that could wait another three weeks to gain more poundage before they went. He always did this himself before he sent them down the Trail.

No matter which wagon gathered the cattle, his was the final word. It took him but a little time to examine a steer from his horse, to know whether he was prime or not. It was a lesson in patience to watch Bird fool along with an edgy steer that wanted to run and stampede all the rest. He simply sat his horse and waited until I'd think he was never going to move, but by then he could ride up to the steer and walk him out to the cut.

Many times as we rode along, Bird explained his method. He would point out the psychology of inducing a steer to believe a horse and rider were friendly. "Animals are a lot like human beings," he said. "If you go after them rough-shod, they react accordingly." But the patience which a human used made a vast difference to an animal and paid off well in the skill with which stock could be handled. Looking back over long years of experience, I can see how right he was.

Rose had gone to Texas to run the N U N's for several years, and Ed Lemmon, part owner of the L7's, had taken over management. I had worked awhile before with the L7 wagon as Matador rep while Ed Lemmon was boss. Ed is said to have "saddle handled" more cattle than any man in like position. He never used a buggy and team to cover his big range. He rode horseback and worked right with the roundups. His horses were fast, and so was he, and those of us young fellows who were a little on the "wild cowboy" order enjoyed working with Ed Lemmon's outfit. Everyone liked him. Once he was badly crippled when a horse fell with him, and forever afterward walked with a limp. The Indians called him Hoostay, which simply means "crippled," and they held him in high regard. Gradually everyone began calling him Hoostay, a name which stuck with him always.

Ed Lemmon slapped a roundup together fast. He rode out with his men and turned them off at points of a wide circle to drive stock from those regions toward the center where the roundup would collect. After a hurried meal and a change of mounts, we'd go to cutting out whatever it was that Lemmon wanted. As rep, I looked for the brands I was interested in. Sometimes, several men were in the roundup cutting out stock at the same time, while other boys held these cattle from running off. Later on, the cut were put with the day herd, cattle already gathered from previous round-ups.

Lemmon rode horses that were high-headed and thrashed around in a roundup more than most cowmen liked. They kept a roundup stirred up and ringy, but cowboys with a lot of the same kind of work to do, and a wide range to cover, didn't mind how ringy they got. Their business was to get the stock off the range in beef time, or take them out to grass when the spring shipments arrived in Evarts from the southern ranges. Ed Lemmon got the job done to the cowboy's satisfaction, at least, and he was an easy man to work with—much easier than Bird Rose. But it was from Bird Rose that I learned much about handling beef steers.

In 1906 when Bird closed out the N U N's, he had shipped everything to the L7 range in the north and come back to Dakota as manager again. Of the two chief owners of L7, Tomb and Lake, it was Tomb who had complete confidence in Bird. I have heard him say that Bird could put more fat on a steer and keep it on all the way to the shipping corrals than any man he knew. Lake always favored Lemmon to run the Dakota spread, while Tomb thought him too fast. Ed Lemmon turned to real estate after he left the L7's, and founded the thriving little town of Lemmon, South Dakota.

Winter had no intentions of delaying its arrival, and as October gave way to November, another big storm hit. The L7's had a herd half-gathered, but they turned them loose and the wagons went to headquarters for the winter. I had caught fifty Matador steers in the roundups and believed there were more on east, in the Indian range. The Standing Rock Indian wagon was still working farther down Grand River, so I decided to go to their wagon. Bird Rose sent a man to help take my throw-back and my string of saddle horses to Ben Lone Man's wagon. I turned my horses with theirs and put the steers into their herd. It was the same thing down there—the tent was full—so I slept outside. The storm turned worse during the night and the Indian night hawk, also the night guard, turned everything loose and came to the wagon.

Next morning, all of my horses were gone home except my night horse, Dick. They had pulled out for the mouth of the Moreau and the cattle had scattered. Ben let me have a bronc to ride and one of his men helped me get started. I packed my bed on Dick, saddled the bronc and made a little circle of my own. I found my steers and started for home. I had to drive them south into Matador range and turn them loose. The Indian turned back after I was well on my way. I wasn't worried about my saddle horses, for I knew they were ahead of me. And I could turn the bronc I was riding loose when I got home; he would go back to his range.

By noon, I came across some of my horses. They had stopped on a creek leading to the Moreau, but Happy Jack had taken his bunch on in. He was one of my winter horses and knew where he wanted to go. When the men saw him come in, they knew I was not far behind. I was glad to go into camp that winter. It had been a hard year for me, and I welcomed winter work, little suspecting what a calamity the following months would bring to the livestock world.

16. The Big Winter, 1906-1907

When the weather kept bringing snow and cold, Con came into headquarters with the wagons. He intended wintering there, and so did I, but as it turned out, I didn't spend much time at Ambrose's.

Since one winter's work is about like another, I was soon cutting water troughs in the ice, and riding among the stock. We didn't feed any hay. Cattle wintered themselves and so did horses. Although I thought that year had been a rough one for me, little did I suspect I was going into a winter which would go down in history.

Cattle were going into the winter in pretty fair shape, in spite of the early snowstorms. We were just settling down into steady routine when it happened and we met the vanguard of the ghastly winter of 1906–7 head-on!

Driven before a gale out of the northwest, a blinding, big-flake snowstorm pounced down without warning over the whole prairie, and within an hour everything was buried in white. As dark came on, the wind got higher and the snow turned powdery. It whirled and twisted and piled up, and the first fierce blizzard of one of the worst winters I ever saw struck the northern ranges. That was in November, and from then on until May, it was just one bad storm after another, week after week.

The death-dealing blizzards of the eighties, and the tough ones of the nineties crashed down upon the vast longhorn herds of those days, freezing all life from the ranges. After such disastrous losses, cattlemen in the north prepared somewhat for wintering cattle. Hay was stacked; weak stuff was gathered and fed, but still the majority of stock were expected to winter on what they could rustle along the creeks, river bottoms, and windswept hills. What stacked feed was available couldn't begin to feed the starving stock in a winter such as was upon us.

With the November blizzard, range hazards mounted as one storm beat on the heels of another all through December —blizzard after blizzard piling snow upon snow and drift upon drift. Four-wire fences were soon hidden. Feed was buried, and hungry cattle began walking, and bawling, miserable and empty.

Then came the Big Drift. We woke up one morning to find great numbers of cattle showing up in the sliding white ice-dust—cattle that was not the Matador's. Every day more and more appeared. They staggered in from far to the northwest of the Cannonball River in North Dakota, pushing into the forks of Grand River in South Dakota, waiting only for strength to go on. Leaving home range, they beat a wide path over divides, from one stream to another, lingering only between storms, hunting forage that was as deeply buried one place as another. Trekking along again with the next blizzard, they swept on by the hundreds over the ridges to the Moreau. Some crossed it; others trailed down it, heading ever southeastward with the wind—ghostly forms in the howling gale, heads lowered, hairy backs snow-driven and crusted, humped against the weather, their eyes but dark holes peering

out of the ice-pack on head and chin, most of them bellow-
ing forlornly as they stumbled on in the numbing cold.

The hungry hordes crossed the drifted-under fences and
level-full ravines, until eventually thousands crowded into
the Little Bend of the Missouri River, below Cheyenne River
Agency. This bend is not to be confused with Big Bend of
the Missouri, farther down. Cattle that came in lower down
missed this bend and landed on the Cheyenne—all of them
starving, eating brush, willow sticks, anything that stuck up
above the snow that buried everything for months. Countless
numbers crossed the frozen Missouri, still drifting, and yet
the reservation river bottoms were black with hollow-bellied
cattle.

All outfits sent men to trail along with the drifting cattle.
I was sent to follow the herds, too, to do what I could for
the great numbers of Matador cattle trekking on with the
strays. I went first to Swift Bird Camp, then to Jim Pearman's, in the Turkey Track range, and wound up still farther
away from home, at Charley Claymore's. The Pearman bottom below the mouth of Bull Creek and the Amadee Rouseau
river bottom were loaded with cattle. Little could be done
for the stock but try to get them out to the windswept spots
where grass showed up.

We built big V-shaped drags, hitched four horses to them,
and opened trails to the pinnacles. Every day, we fought the
hunger-weakened cattle out through these lanes to uncovered
grass, but most of them wouldn't stay. They huddled in
bunches as long as we stood guard on them, but in the end
almost beat us back to the starvation bottoms before the
freezing wind and sleet of another storm. Their legs and
hocks were sore and hairless from walking in crusted snow.
Hundreds got down and couldn't get up, and these we had
to kill if they didn't freeze to death first.

Men cut down the smaller trees along the streams so stock
could eat the bark and twigs in the tops. Temperatures

hovered below zero all through November; they reached twenty-five to thirty below in December, and dropped to forty and fifty below zero in January. Small trees froze solid. A man's axe bounced off the green frozen trunk, shaving off chips like cutting into thick ice. And big limbs split wide open.

Cattle ate anything they could find, from felled timber to all of the underbrush and lower tree branches that they could reach. Horses fared better. Staying on the ridges, pawing down to grass, eating snow for water, they grew long, shaggy coats and wintered fairly well. A few wise old steers stayed with the horse bands. Hooking the horse away after the grass was pawed clear, they managed to find enough to eat, defying the frozen death that most of their kind met.

Once I battled a bunch of Matador cattle back toward Swift Bird Creek, but they got away from me at Stove Creek, in another blizzard, and fought their way back to the death along the river. There was no hay to be had anywhere. The small ranchers across the Missouri had stacked some for their own small herds, but they saw it swallowed up by hungry cattle from distant parts, so desperate that they couldn't be driven away. Men who made a long, wide swing over the range, seeking some region where there might be less snow, reported that not a spear of grass could be seen for one hundred miles in any direction.

Matador and Turkey Track ranges, lying right in the path of the big trek, couldn't help but be hard hit. They might have made it through with less loss of their own but for the flood of strays coming in, their numbers increasing with every storm.

There was little anyone could do for the dying cattle excepting to put the helpless ones out of their misery with bullets. Indian cattle died, the same as the others. We gathered many cattle for the Indian owners and turned them into their corrals, but they could do nothing but turn them out again to hunt for food. Coyotes and gray wolves feasted all winter, and the next spring, they had the biggest litters of pups ever. It seemed like spring would never come, but the days wore on and the cold lessened.

I froze my feet that winter. I put off my boots for sheep-skin-lined moccasins under my overshoes. One day I got cold and dismounted to walk awhile. The exercise made my feet sweaty in the sheepskin, and the dampness caused my feet to freeze before I got back to Pearman's, where I was boarding. That night, my bare, numb feet clicked on the bunk-house floor like chunks of ice, and one heel burst open. Fred Seely and Bob Pearman helped me thaw them out in tubs of snow, but the crack in the frosted heel never completely closed again. I limped pretty much for quite a while.

In spite of it all, though, amusing things happened. While I was at Pearman's, old Jim had a few cows that he was trying to get through the winter alive by feeding them a little extra. One was a leggy old Texas cow. He turned her out to water one day; she was weak and easily irritated, and once she walked away from the barn she wouldn't go back. Jim asked me to ride out and bring her in, which I did. When she got back, she was "on the fight" and as she went in the barn and saw Jim there offering her soft feed in a bucket, she snuffed angrily, knocked him down and ran over him. Jim got to his feet, cussed her to hell-and-gone, and said that he never "saw *anyone or anything from Texas* that was worth a good god-dam!" And he stalked off to the house.

Some of Jim's kids were girls. Jim was a German and their mother was a breed. Evelyn, the youngest, was cute and blue-eyed. We cowboys boarding with the Pearmans gave the little girls a dime to keep our bunkhouse swept out and tidied up. Evelyn was the ambitious one. Every time one of us showed up, she would get there with her broom, and all the sweeping she did! Our bunkhouse got whisked out a dozen times a day—at a dime a whisk. Evelyn grew up and became a very beautiful woman. I knew her and her husband, Bunk Vandever, for many years afterward.

Chinook winds came at last. Snow melted away, revealing the frightful livestock tragedy on the range that winter. As water began to run, the creeks brought in their load of dead. All winter long, when men had skinned carcasses, they hauled the remains as far as possible out onto the Missouri river ice. Every Indian who wanted to make a few dollars was skinning off hides. Cattle lay so thick in the river bottoms where they had huddled together that a man could fairly step from one dead critter to another for a quarter of a mile at a time. This was true for miles along the Missouri—a pitiful, unforgettable sight.

Finally, the ice in the Missouri broke up and moved out. One had only to stand on the shore of the big stream as it fought its way out of its winter burden of ice and whatever had perished there, to gain some idea of the frozen horror the northern ranges had endured. Dead bodies lodged along the creeks where they entered the Big Muddy, until higher water helped to dislodge them and carry them on oceanward. The streams were full of floating death.

On the reservation, it was months later before a man would ride anywhere near Swift Bird and other river bottoms where stock had died in droves, because of the horrible stench. Natives who lived too close to these places moved out temporarily if they could.

After there was nothing more I could do for the drifted cattle, I went back to the Matador. Spring would be mighty sweet that year, after the white hell of the winter. Roundup work would soon get under way, and we all were anxious to see what the winter had done to our outfit, as well as to the other outfits in that big country. I was glad to be going home.

There was one lawsuit of note that built up out of the

hard winter of 1906–7, but it didn't break into the open until a couple of years afterward. Fred La Plant sued Cap Mossman to recover cattle losses he sustained "because of Mossman's mismanagement," he contended.

Some time after Mossman opened up his Dakota range in 1904, he leased the Fred La Plant ranch on the head of Virgin Creek, just south of the Matador–Turkey Track fence. He agreed to treat and to care for La Plant's cattle as he did his own. Nevertheless, to make sure that his Half Moon cattle got a fair deal, La Plant, operator of a store at the Agency, employed Isaac Arpan, his foreman for years, to watch them. During the frightful hard winter, Mossman's men gathered many Half Moon cattle and turned them into the La Plant corrals, so Isaac could feed them if possible. But having no hay, and none being available, Isaac turned the stock out again to forage for food. And like thousands of others that winter, they died. Arpan himself was a heavy loser.

But La Plant believed that Mossman owed him damages, so he sued for $9600, and Mossman fought the suit—the largest civil case ever held in Dewey County, South Dakota, up to then. In fighting the case, Mossman wanted to prove by La Plant's own foreman how impossible it was to save the La Plant stock; that every livestock owner in the country lost cattle, and many of them lost all they owned. The elements were too forceful to beat. But no one could find Isaac! And unless he was found, he couldn't have a subpoena served on him to bring him into court. Possibly the La Plant side felt that Isaac's testimony couldn't help their case.

In spite of Mossman's witnesses swearing to their utter helplessness to save the La Plant stock, it was plain that Cap needed his foreman, and when officers failed to find him after several attempts, Mossman went after him in his own way. Without asking me, he had me deputized to go get Isaac Arpan.

"You know every hole and hideout on the whole reservation," Cap told me. "Go get Isaac, if you have to follow him down a wolf hole." So I started that afternoon.

I loaded my saddle in the buggy, hitched a fast pair of my own horses to it, and drove down into Indian country. I stayed all night with a friend who had married a breed girl. He lived on the Moreau, and he knew where Isaac was.

"Isaac's running the Indian roundup wagon," he told me. "You'll never catch him at the wagon. He doesn't even sleep there. He's not going to court if he can help it, and no one will tell an officer where to find him. He's mighty careful to keep out of sight. The Indian wagon is on Cottonwood Creek."

Next morning, I saddled one of my buggy horses and rode toward the Indian cattle roundup. I found the wagon without trouble. The cook and the horse wrangler were at camp. I let them believe I was looking for cattle to buy, and during the talk I learned that Isaac was riding a big buckskin horse. But they had no idea where he was. However, I had learned all I needed to know. I jogged out into the region where they were working that day.

Before long, I spotted a buckskin horse on a high pinnacle out on the head of Cottonwood, and I knew I had found Isaac. I knew his horses, knew he rode good ones, but I was riding a good one, too. I knew I could catch him if, when he saw me riding toward him, he became suspicious and took off.

But I didn't hurry. I let my horse set his own pace. There was no activity atop the hill as I came closer, and finally I could see the horse was saddled. Before long, I climbed the pinnacle, and there was Isaac stretched out on the ground in the shade of his horse, sound asleep! He had started his men out to round up the country, and while he waited, he selected a high spot for a good lookout, made himself comfortable for the several hours' wait. His horse moved as I rode up beside him, which aroused Isaac. When he rolled over and sat up, I was holding the subpoena in my hand.

Isaac took one look and roared: "Goddam!" I began to read the summons aloud. When I finished, Isaac swore again and pulled on his boots. He dug his heels into the ground in an agitated way and said, "Ike, I'll give you four or five horses—good ones, too—if you will go away and say you didn't see me."

"I can't do that, Isaac."

"But how can I go against my good friend, Fred?" he said sadly.

"You will have to tell the truth, Isaac," I told him. "I don't like to go against Fred, either, or to come to get you, but this is a dispute between two men before a jury. You have to tell the truth and let the jury decide."

Isaac was still hunched up on the ground in the shade of his horse when I left him, but he came to court.

His testimony proved to be the very thing that Cap Mossman needed. Under skillful questioning of the reluctant witness, Mossman's lawyer, Glen Martin, established by La Plant's own foreman the utter impossibility to relieve the bitter cruelty of that winter, or to avoid the appalling stock losses.

The result was that Cap Mossman and Fred La Plant settled their differences out of court, reportedly by each paying his own costs, and La Plant dropped the suit.

Spring weather came on with rain and melting snow; streams ran bank-full for weeks. Con rode out over the range to estimate the winter's damage to fences, and the number and brands of cattle in the Matador range.

He found them by the hundreds. Grass came on pretty fast, as it usually does when winter moisture is so plentiful.

I went back to headquarters, where my first job was to line up the broncs for roundup time. They had all been turned out the fall before, and as snow left the ridges they got plenty to eat. They were salty enough by the time I got them in.

I hadn't seen much of the Matador men all winter—hadn't seen Dode at all. I had heard of him, though, for he kept things lively wherever he was. He spent the most of the winter in Evarts, where he met and hired a young fellow named Candee to be his secretary. Candee could sing and play the guitar, and they became pals. About the only time the secretary left Dode was when Murdo was due and Dode knew when to expect him. Then he would hustle Candee into cowboy clothes and send him out to Con. The cowboys called him "Candy" and never missed a chance to pull a trick on him, on the rare occasions when they had him under their thumbs.

One amusing incident happened later that spring after the roundup started, when Candy had to hurry out to Con's wagon for a few days. Oh, but it was a dandy prank, but it all backfired and Candy emerged hero of the day.

Dode got a kick out of rigging Candy out in cowboy trappings that leaned a good deal toward dudishness. His boots were shop-made; good shirts and pants, topped off by one of Dode's Stetson hats; and from somewhere Candee got a pair of chaps made of woolly white angora. They nearly hid a pair of Dode's silver-mounted spurs buckled neatly onto his fancy boots—and a pretty picture he made, too!

The very sight of him inspired the ambitious tricksters to do their worst, and when they singled out a little red-roan Down F, guaranteed to raise hell for no reason at all, they fully expected to send Candy to roost on a cloud for a day or two. To show their good intentions, they gathered round solicitously, giving advice calculated to get him thrown higher than a kite. And all the while, they helped him get the horse saddled just right.

"Get on him and try to knock his head off with your quirt," they said. "That's the first thing you do. That's the way to get the run on him—get your bluff in first!"

They listened gleefully as Candy puffed his chest, professing to be quite a rider. He jerked up his chaps and tightened his belt, pulled down his hat and ringingly announced: "Let me get aboard that locoed steed! I'll subdue him in short order!"

Eagle-eyed and happy, the old hands stepped back to watch the fun, ready to roll with laughter when the dude went sailing high and far. Imagine their surprise when Candy, following their advice to the letter, advanced and boldly mounted the red-roan. The horse rolled his eyes back, blowed up his belly, and while he was in the very act of dropping his head to buck, Candy swung his heavy quirt and hit him a terrific pop under the eye and over the nose, the lash curling down under his jaw! At the same instant, still following instructions, Candy socked his spurs into the horse's ribs just as hard as he could. And that was the very second that the dude should have joined the clouds!

Instead, the astonished red-roan flung up his head, stuck his tail straight out, blowed off, and raced out across the prairie with nary a buck in him! Candy yanked him around, set him up and set him down, whirled him this way and that. He spurred him plenty, and before we changed mounts again, he had ridden him to a lather. From that morning on, Candy claimed the horse and rode him in just that manner, and he never did buck. Not once. And Candy fully believed he was riding a bronc that the other men were afraid of! He boasted constantly of his ability to handle tough horses, little suspecting that the affable cowboys agreeing with him longed to kick his pants in their disappointment. But another day was coming, and next time they would be more careful about schooling Candy too well before he made the ride!

Dode's most spectacular transaction that winter caused everyone to chuckle and shake their heads—and a number of natives got some extra grub.

As always when he was drinking, Dode was in an expansive mood. He must have been extra reckless one day that spring when a meat salesman came to Evarts and got his attention.

After an evening of dickering and discussion, Dode was convinced that there would be something of a shortage of beef for the cowboys after such a hard winter. From his cozy nook in the hotel, he had heard the winds and the blizzards beating the life out of the range—but with the Matador checkbook at his fingertips, he could and would provide meat for the cowboys, regardless!

Before dawn, he had bought a half a carload of pork products from the salesman! Hams, bacon, weiners, lard, canned meat of all kinds, pickled pigs feet—just anything the salesman could think of to round out the order, and what an order! Never before had any man sold such a collection of pork products to a going beef concern!

Dode whipped out his checkbook, paid cash on the barrelhead, and went to bed! The salesman departed before Dode sobered up. In fact, Dode didn't think about his purchases until he got a message that the shipment was about to arrive in Evarts. Dode blinked his eyes over that deal, and stayed sober enough until he could figure out what to do with it all. Then it arrived. There it was, down on the railroad siding waiting to be unloaded.

If ever a man needed an efficient secretary it was then— and doubtless, here was a time when Candy earned his pay, helping dispose of the big pork shipment, although it was probably Dode who figured out a plan. As it turned out, the young Scot emerged from the crisis with flying colors; and not a bit of pork was wasted, either.

Dode had coped with bigger troubles than this, and here he turned the whole thing into a grand gesture of love and friendship for his red brothers. He would make them a magnificent gift!

After storing more hams and bacon than the whole outfit would use in a year, Dode sent his messenger over to the reservation, inviting the Indians to Evarts to receive a present! And they came, afoot and on horseback, in old rigs, and for a week Dode and his secretary were busy handing out pork! Every squaw on the reservation hustled down to the pork car, and hustled away again with a slab of bacon or a big ham under her shawl. Possibly, she had two, if she looked hungry or had a pack of little kids with her.

As for Dode, he had the time of his life. He could fix the expense account so it would read just and fair to a faraway general bookkeeper. Dode was generous, in spite of his faults, and he never did things by halves.

Evarts was never low on excitement of some sort. If nothing else, a cowboy full of fiery cheer was liable to burst into flame any minute. One little Irish cowboy had ridden in to celebrate the Saint Patrick's day, as all good Irishmen should. In making his jolly way about town greeting other wearers of the green, he came across a Russian who had not only pinned a shamrock to his hat, but had tied a big green bow to each suspender.

The sight of the happy Russian walking along behind all that green stuff was too much for the Irishman, fortified as he was by numerous trips to the bars. He flew into the farmer, stripped him of every bit of his Irish colors, jerked out his pistol and popped a few bullets around the non-Irishman's feet. The man hopped about like a rabbit with a hotfoot, in an effort to dance an Irish jig, which the Turkey Track man insisted he must do as penance for his so presuming on an Irishman's rights.

Other men bore down on the outrageous little hellion and took him away, green ribbons still clutched tightly in one fist. The Russian disappeared in the opposite direction, glad to be done with the Irish and their green ribbons.

17. The Big Roundups

Con started his roundup wagons just as soon as possible that spring, for the Matador pastures were black with cattle that didn't belong there. We had some of the biggest roundups I ever saw. One in particular was held on a big flat just north of the Little Moreau, not far from where it joins the Moreau. We had cleared the whole northwest corner of Matador range in one big drive, for we had at least sixty reps with us that spring.

They came from miles around; some were from North Dakota, some from Wyoming or Montana. Others came from out west in Perkins County, representing many brands.

Con had dozens of messages to be on the lookout for brands from ranchers who had perhaps lost every single critter. The L7's alone gathered twenty-five hundred cattle from our range. Some reps couldn't find a single steer. Others found a hundred head and figured themselves lucky.

Con camped the wagon on the Little Moreau and started such a big circle that fifteen thousand cattle collected on the roundup ground. This herd was far too large to work all in one piece, so Con had it cut into four parts. Twenty-five men were cutting cattle from these herds, and more than fifty men held together the different cuts and the roundup. They started cuts to the center and to the sides. Men working in the roundup knew where the L7 cut, or the Flying V, or the H O cut was, so they turned a steer that way as they came across him.

It was spectacular work. If several brands were going west, for instance, all cattle of those brands were run into the same cut, and reps took them out of the way. They would be separated later on the journey back to home range.

Actually, in spite of these giant roundups held in Matador range, reps found few cattle in proportion to those drifted away and still missing, unless from such really big outfits as the L7's. The northern ranges had passed through a winter that shook the cattle empire to its very core, and had cut the whole foundation from under some of the smaller operators. That year was to see several outfits close their operations and turn their leases to others. Among them were the L7's and the Sword & Daggers. The C7's took over part of the L7 range, and the ZT, belonging to Walker and Field, took the rest. These cattlemen operated there for a few years longer before they, too, began to close out or to move farther on. The town of Walker, South Dakota, was named after I. W. Walker.

We put in long hours in the saddle, and made roundup after roundup. Breakfast at dawn, riding circle to throw a roundup together; working the herd after the noon meal; stopping range work to go to Evarts to bring out new cattle; branding, dipping, or something, continually. We were pelted with rainstorms; hail pounded us a lot; wind beat the hills and dried the range. But we had long, pleasant days, too, and the hours flew by. We were a well-fed crew, well mounted, and liked our work. We liked the looks of the pretty breed girls, too, and made whoopee whenever we got a chance to stop in town a while, or go to a dance on the reservation.

Con always camped the wagon out on the Strip a ways when we had to go to Evarts for cattle. There was not so much temptation for the boys to wander off if the town was out of sight. However, one day in June, while waiting for cattle, three of us—Dan Busby, Roy Vivian, and I—slipped off to Evarts for a few hours. Con knew we were going, but he expected us to be back to the wagon before dark. Our intentions were good, but we lingered a little too long, until a real old soaker of a rain swooped down out of nowhere, and we were caught far from home without our slickers.

Our oilskins had seen a lot of use anyway, so when the rain kept on pounding and we knew we had to leave town regardless, we decided to buy new slickers. Having decided, we popped out of the saloon door and in six jumps made it to a dry goods store run by a chubby little woman. She met us with a smile—and "yes," she just "happened to have three slickers left!"

From the minute we asked about slickers, she cast a calculating eye on us—and on a few extra dollars which she might garner on this little "slicker" deal. The dear old matron promptly began extolling the scarcity of slickers in all that region; she dwelt long on the need for a slicker in such frightful weather. The rain was still pouring down her shop windows. While we shifted from one foot to another, she got down to really touching descriptions of men who had caught cold and died of the terrible lung fever. In fact, the good woman seemed so concerned about us that we thought maybe she'd invite us all over to a fried chicken supper, and to snuggle into warm feather beds for the night, so greatly did she seem to worry about our health.

We glanced sideways at each other, for such motherly interest was beginning to pull our heartstrings—and then one of us got a chance to cut in and ask the price of the slickers.

The tender-hearted old dear had shot the price up from the usual three dollars when we entered the store to five dollars apiece. We told her we didn't have five dollars apiece with us. But she wouldn't budge from her price, even when we dug up a little over twelve dollars between us. Plainly, she believed that we could produce more if we wanted to, and we probably could have, too.

We shot inquiring glances at each other. Should we three young cowboys who happened to stray into town at the wrong time be plucked by an old hen like her?

We didn't have long to decide, for the boat would make its last crossing for the day without us, come hell or high water, if we weren't there on time. We put our money back in our pockets, set our hats tighter, and amidst a renewal of her dire predictions of horrible death we might face by getting soaked to the hide, we let her keep her slickers and backed out of her presence.

I was riding an L G Bar—Louie Garreau—white-eyed bronc and he was mad at the weather, and at me. Our horses were tied right in front of the lady merchant's store. In my haste to mount, I somehow irritated my horse, so that he bucked and splashed mud all over the store front and spattered the windows, too. The last I heard, as I got him started out of town, was some mighty ungracious words from the lady herself about "no-good heathen-hellions and their equally no-good heathen-horses."

We made the boat and got to camp, wet as drowned cottontails, but with a good warm feeling inside us that we hadn't been taken by the lady merchant.

This dear soul had her trouble, too, later. She had a fine mare which she kept well cared for and sometimes drove her to a buggy, or rode her. She also had a big, husky son who was an easterner, but everyone liked him.

About this time, Dode thought it would be good for the cowboys to put on a little rodeo one Sunday, strictly for local entertainment. This friendly get-together was to be staged at the edge of town. The slicker lady thought it would be a wonderful experience for her son to ride the fine mare and mingle with the cowboys during the celebration.

He was a very heavy fellow, wore a derby hat and a large, loose, checkered suit and big stout shoes. He was not a bad sort at all, but the sight of him squeezed into his mother's saddle, which was way too small for him, was too much for some of the pranksters—especially one named Rufe, who "desired, Suh, to see some fun, Suh!" He was the same mouthy one who nearly caused Con to make us stand night guard on a herd one rainy night. And he conspired to make the gentle old mare cut up in a scandalous way totally new to her.

The woman was so proud of her son and the mare that she had walked all the way out to the celebration just to see him riding around. By then, the evil Rufe had maneuvered around close enough to pour a small bottle of "high-life" somewhere on the mare's posterior, while his fellow scoundrels kept her rider busy looking elsewhere. Rufe disappeared, and the riders rode on.

Suddenly, the mare went plumb berserk! She reared, then swapped ends; she heisted her hind parts and kicked up as high as she could. She leaped away out and with her head between her legs, she bucked with all her might as the big man scratched about for anything at all that he could hang onto. But no use. Up, up, he went, his coattails flapping. He sailed into a swan dive from high overhead. Somehow his derby beat him to the ground, and he landed squarely on it. It folded up with a crunch. One shoe had also forsaken him. So had the mare. Also his friendly companions, and for good reason!

His mother arrived at the very moment the mare exploded, so she was on hand to pick him up. I didn't hear her, but it was rumored that she said some mighty uncouth things for a lady. Also, she posted a reward of one hundred dollars for the name of the culprit who had high-lifed her pet.

I knew some of the boys who dangled with the idea of collecting that reward, but they heard, also, that Rufe had a reward out, too: "I'll blast the hind end off the man who collects that reward, Suh!" Since he was quite handy with his six-shooter, no one ever collected the reward.

Not only had other cattle drifted through the reservation during the winter, but they had taken many cattle along with them as they traveled onward over the frozen hills and streams. And now, from the region south of the Cheyenne, where many had stopped, came a loud clamor for the reservation outfits to "come get their cattle."

The farmers and smaller ranchers were organizing a great roundup of their own, to rid their region of the hordes of stray cattle eating their crops and hay meadows. South of the reservation bounds, across the Cheyenne, was a region known as Honyocker, or homesteader country. The settlers there raised grain—wheat, barley, corn—and livestock. There were schoolhouses, stores, and small road ranches where one could stop for the night if necessary. Dance halls were used for churches, funerals, and all sorts of public meetings.

At one of these gatherings, the honyockers hatched up the idea of a "pool" roundup wagon, with all the farmers joining in, to clear the strays from land they considered was their private range. They called their operation the Plum Creek Pool Roundup, and they wanted the reservation outfits to send men to help take away all the cattle the farmers didn't claim.

The Matador sent me to join other reservation reps working with this pool. I was to cut out and bring back not only Matador stock, but all cattle carrying brands belonging in the Matador lease.

Along with four or five other men, I got there about the

time Big Jim Kennedy did. He was repping for some of the Indian cattlemen on Herbert, Rattlesnake, Cottonwood, and other creeks in the Sword & Dagger range. We discovered the Plum Creek Pool was made up of assorted cowboys. Some of the young fellows were pretty fair hands, but others were one-spur farmers who could barely sit on a slow-moving, gentle mare.

They had rigged their outfit with a chuck wagon, tent, stove, wagon boss, horse wranglers, and night hawk. Their mounts were mostly mares, and they sure got our saddle horses to raising hell with each other. Before I had been with the pool a week, most of my string had either been kicked or had their backs chewed up, nosing around some filly that flirted with more than one gelding at a time.

The chuck with this roundup was home-grown, good-solid-fat-pork and spuds, so we settled down to a regular diet of fried pork, fried spuds, fried flapjacks, and rocky biscuits with syrup—all of it far different than we had grown accustomed to. The cook was a jolly fat farmer, more than a little greasy, and growing worse by the hour. But the Plum Creek Pool got going and we gathered lots of reservation stock.

But before we started home with the throw-back, the Pool wagon ran short on grub and pulled into a store to load supplies. All of the reps went along, too, and with their own funds bought canned goods they had been used to eating and sent it along with the load.

Off of the reservation, all of the stores were licensed to sell whisky. So while loading the Plum Creek wagon, all of the men took a few drinks around, and several bottles were carried along to camp to wet their whistles for a few hours longer. By the time we reached camp, rollicky Jim Kennedy had swallowed a lot of "snake medicine." In fact, the whole Plum Creek Pool had livened up considerably. Like kids on a holiday, they had a lot of fun and pulled jokes on others.

While the Pool cowboys were loading grub, each his share

of the same old fare, salt pork, molasses, and rice, Jim could see well enough that we were in for more of the same kind of eats. So after we bought our contributions, he slipped around into the dry goods department and bought a big snow-white cook's apron and chef's hat, such as the reservation roundup cooks wore, and put it in with the reps' purchases. He also bought a can opener.

At camp again, Jim was pretty well fortified with the snake juice, and he buddied right up to the partly tipsy cook, volunteering to help him with the cooking. The two frisky partners started a merry fire in the sheet-iron stove, while the rest of the outfit set up the tent.

"Now," Jim says to his jolly pal, "first we gotta fix you up like a real cook. We gotta have a first-rate cap and apron on a cook with the Plum Creek Pool." So he unwraps the package and takes out the apron, flips the neck string over the cook's head, and ties the rest of it snug around his big middle. He shook out the cap and set it at a cocky angle on the man's head. Jim stepped back, admiring his work and complimenting the cook on his fine looks, much to the sly amusement of the other reps who knew Jim pretty well and were not misled by this new friendliness. The cook bowed low and thanked him for his compliments.

"Now, Cookie," Jim turned him around to the chuck box while he reached for several cans of corn, peas, and tomatoes. He dug around and found his can opener and held it up for the cook to see. "See this little do-hickey? It's called a can opener. This Pool outfit never saw one of them before, but it's a handy little dandy. You jab the point into the tin, like this—" and Jim proceeded to open several cans of tomatoes. He held out one can for the cook to see how pretty and red they were, then set it back handy with the others, and opened a few more, and several cans of peas and corn, too. Then he put a kettle on the stove and dumped the corn into it, talking and eyeing his buddy.

"Now, you greasy bastard," Jim said, "I've showed you how a *decent cook looks*. Now I'll show you that you can cook a lot of things besides sowbelly for cowboys, if you're not too damned lazy." Jim stirred the kettle and added salt. "This is corn," he said. "Cowboys like it now and then, in place of so much sow bosom. You fix it with a little salt and pepper and cook it a few minutes. 'Tain't hard work at all."

Jim got another pan and fixed peas, talking all the time about how to prepare them. Then he harked back to the tomatoes, and all the while the cook in his new apron stood there listening attentively.

"This stuff," Jim picked up the can of tomatoes, "is what us reps call *tomatoes*. You open a half a dozen cans for a crew of this size. They make good cowboy chuck, raw—or you can add a little sugar, salt, bacon grease, pepper, and maybe a few crackers, and they taste pretty nifty, cooked."

Then, with the cook's attention focused full on him, standing spraddle-legged three feet away, Jim upended the tomatoes square on top of the white cap. He grabbed another can, and another, splashing a half-dozen cans over the cook, thoroughly wetting him down from head to toe before anyone could stop him. The bright fruit mingled with the man's whiskers, it went down his collar, and streamed over the white apron. It filled the pockets of the apron and puddled up on the ground, a grand and glorious red-and-white mixture molded to the big frame in wet splotches.

The lesson was cut short when the other reps hopped in and grabbed Jim, hustling him away before he could protest. The Plum Creek Pool outfit, surprised and indignant, cleaned up their man and the tent. Supper was a slim affair that night, but Jim wasn't present for it. He went to bed.

Next morning, the whisky was all gone. Jim and the cook laughed off any grievance. The cook washed his apron and cap, dried them on a sage bush and put them on. He wore them all the time, and did a pretty good job of cooking.

We found the stray cattle and went home. I didn't see Jim Kennedy again for years. We met again far out west across the mountains, where we both worked for the same outfit.

Before I went to the Plum Creek Pool Roundup, I gave some of my rough string, including Rollers and Danger, to cowboys I thought could handle them, which was the usual procedure. Both horses were mean, but they had been through a tough winter, and while they were thin and shaggy I rode them considerably to gentle them. Horses of this sort needed regular riding to keep them gentle. If they weren't ridden, a little rest and green grass soon put them right back where they were—mean as could be. While I was gone, somehow these horses got unruly again, so I got them back first thing. They were more trouble than they were worth, and I couldn't blame a man for avoiding such mounts. They should have been cut out and sold, but here they were, waiting for me.

One morning I saddled Danger. We were moving camp and also intended riding circle for a roundup that day. I thought a good, long trip like that would take some of the buck out of him. He kept me watching him continually. If he struck at me with a forefoot, he meant business. He didn't kick for fun, either, but I managed to be ready when the other men were.

The afternoon before, we had killed a beef downhill a ways from the wagons and left the paunch—stomach—laying there, since we would be leaving that place the next morning. The weather was very warm, causing gas from the fermenting grass to form inside the paunch, until by daylight it had swelled up big and tight as a drum.

Danger was even more grouchy than usual and he didn't waste time raising hell. He dropped his head and bucked, and he headed right down the slope toward the blowed-up paunch. He saw it, too, and bucked right toward it. He thrust his head right up to it, and deliberately struck it a wicked blow with a front foot. His hoof broke through and the paunch exploded with a loud bang, and the green "filling" flew everywhere. It spattered all over Danger's head and chest, and all over me. It plastered my saddle, my face, and even under my hat brim—slimy, green, and stinking as ever a thing could be!

The report scared some of the temper out of Danger, but even so he whirled and kicked hell out of what was left of the paunch before he took off and ran like an antelope.

The sight of me getting all of that green stuff on me and the pure cussedness of the horse gave the cowboys a good laugh. Even Peavine, the crankiest old cowpuncher ever to fork a horse, laughed like a kid every time he thought of it.

Rollers was the evil partner of Danger. He was a gray horse, eleven hundred pounds of touchy dynamite. When his temper was up, he showed the white of his eyes a lot and bucked at the least excuse. We had worked on around the range and camped the wagon at the mouth of No Mouth Creek, which flows into the Moreau, when I decided I'd better ride Rollers before he got any saltier. I knew this bronc would buck as soon as I mounted, and I needed a man to keep him away from the tent and wagon.

Ambrose Benoist was repping with us, and he offered to haze Rollers out of camp toward the big flat. Dinner was just over and, as was his custom, Krump was allowing some Indians to feast on what remained after the cowboys finished eating. There were at least a dozen of the old blanket bucks squatting around on the ground inside the tent gobbling up the grub in the kettles and pans.

The roundup tent was rigged with a rope ridgepole, using but one wooden pole at the back of the tent, over which the ridgepole rope was run. The front end of the tent was fastened to an iron pole on the back of the wagon above the mess box, so the stove and cooking department were under cover. Picket pins anchored guy ropes and side walls to the ground.

When I swung up on Rollers, he didn't wait! He made the fierce noise in his nose and gave me all he had. As things happened, everyone suspicioned that fun-loving Ambrose hankered for excitement that day. Certainly, from atop the high-pitching Rollers, it looked to me like Ambrose did more to point the horse toward the tent than away from it. Fresh, fat, and ready, Rollers bucked harder than usual and landed right straddle the guy rope holding the ridge rope tight. The pegs pulled up under our weight and the tent swayed. The canvas sagged to the middle and Rollers thrashed right up on top of the tent. When Krump heard thudding hoofs right at his back door, he stepped up on a wagon wheel, but the flattened tent was bumpy with Indians scrambling around under it.

Rollers swapped ends about three times in the center of the tent. I heard kettles crunch and a howl or two before he roared on across. As we went, I glanced back and saw black braids and beads and heard war whoops coming from under the tent walls on all sides. They were poking out from under, Injuns making their getaway! Miraculously, Rollers didn't land on but two of them. One old buck got his hand in the way and Rollers mashed his knuckles to a painful red lump. He tramped another buck's toes nearly off through his moccasin. I guess he was the one I heard howl.

When he left the tent, Rollers headed for the big flat, running hard. He dropped his head and kicked high and wicked, then ran again, stopping to pitch in a reckless way until he got his fill of the spurs.

At camp, the tent was sure a scrambled mess. Walker doctored the beat-up bucks, gave them tobacco and a hunk of beef, which squared things with them. He put up the tent again, threw out a few smashed kettles and tidied things up. Krump took such things in his stride. He had our next

meal ready for us, same as usual, and didn't get mad at me for the ruckus.

I thought I was going to stay with Con's wagon during shipping that fall, but I was mistaken. When we got to Evarts to receive a late shipment of pasture cattle and the Turkey Tracks were in to get a herd of R O heifers, Con decided I'd better go with them and work through their range while they gathered their first beef herd. If I found Matador steers, I was just to throw them back into the pasture and then come home. It was on this trip that the Turkey Track men trained up their new cook—an unforgettable incident.

Before the Tracks left Evarts, their cook, Cimmaron, quit. He was a big man, inclined to be tough, but he fed the men well enough, even if he did get pretty greasy, personally. Sometimes one of the cowboys would tease him about being so careless by tossing a can of sand onto the wagon seat just before Cimmaron heaved himself up, lines in hand, ready to move camp. He'd roar profanity as he brushed it off, for he well knew the guilty one was indicating he would slide off the seat and break his neck if it wasn't sanded.

Cimmaron was replaced by a hobo sort of fellow, the only available man at the time. He turned out to be a poor cook. He was lazy, belligerent, and the cowboys didn't dare question as to when mealtime would come. He never washed a towel—probably he didn't know that it was his job to keep dish towels and face towels clean. Before long, the cowboys began to yell plenty about the slothful cook who grew dirtier and lazier by the hour. But he worked around to Beaver Creek before things came to a head.

It was while they pitched camp that the Track men looked their cook over and got the idea that this was a perfect time for him to take a bath. Right out there in the creek. There was plenty of nice, clear water in the long pools which were six to eight feet deep. The helpful cowpunchers carried the idea to the cook, making it clear that if he didn't do something about it, they would.

The cook threatened loudly that his person *had better not be molested,* if they knew what was good for them. The wagon boss took issue with the cook, advising him not to talk so tough. The cook sassed back in a lively manner, and that was the cue for the men to rush in. They picked him up bodily and carried him to a thirty-foot-long water hole up the creek and dumped him in. Every time he crawled out, they threw him in again. Finally, someone yanked off his shirt when he scrambled out for about the tenth time. They all agreed he had been soaked long enough to loosen the dirt, that soap and sapolio—a white powder used to scour pots and pans—and a good scrubbing should come next. While someone went for those articles, the others used their pocket knives to trim his hair off in chunks. They pulled off his pants and old shoes, and when the soap and sapolio arrived, they went to work in dead earnest. They scoured him until he was a sunset red from head to heel. They donated him a whole clean outfit—pants, shirt, boots—and threw his old ones away. By then, he was plumb gentle!

It was too far away from any place for him to quit and walk away from the outfit. He was afraid of the range cattle, afraid of the Indians, and afraid of the wolves, so he had to stay with the Turkey Tracks and cook. The men showed him how things should go and saw to it that he didn't shirk any more. The cook stayed clean, but by the time the Tracks got their herd together and were back in Evarts again, he had had enough and was ready to leave. And they were glad to see him go.

The men with the reservation outfits had certain unwritten rules and regulations among themselves that governed their own deportment in camp with other men. The laws of common decency were well enforced. Just because men lived in the open, slept on the ground, and more often than otherwise used the good earth for a table, a rock or mound of dirt for a chair, a bush for a clothesline to spread washing to dry, and the like, there was no reason why they must drop all habits of civilized man.

Cowboys made a worthy effort to be manly, to act in accordance with what was right, no matter their surroundings —mud, wind, rain, heat, or fine summer sunshine. There was little rough talk, other than simple swearing which seemed more a part of that way of life than disrespect and offensiveness. Obscenity was frowned upon. Any indecent act was met with stern disapproval. Improper talk about women or lewd jokes had little part in the regular everyday busy life these men lived. And the man who persisted in overstepping these rules was punished, not by arrest or by going to jail, but by the cowboys' law which governed such breaches of decency and order.

If a man didn't believe his ideas and deportment could be changed, it took but one or two trips to a good-sized bedroll over which he found himself stretched so that the seat of his britches were good and tight. A pair of heavy leather chaps held by the belt and wielded by a big-fisted cowpuncher in a way which brought the bottom of the leggings smartly down across the offender's posterior a dozen times usually corrected any such false ideas. To be offensive enough to be "chapped" was a painful experience that no one relished.

We were in the midst of an unusually busy season. Several outfits were closing out and the Matador wanted to get all of their stock from these ranges, so as soon as I got back home, Con sent me to the L7 again. Bird Rose had sent a message to Dode MacKenzie requesting a rep come to work with the L7's; quite a few Matador steers were in their range. We were camped at Tony Akers Corners, about fifteen miles from Evarts, when Dode drove out to the wagon. He had left the letter in Evarts, but told Con that Bird said the L7 wagon would be in the southeast corner of their range to start their beef roundup, and for a rep to meet them there.

Con was skeptical about the L7's starting to work in the southeast, or Fire Steel, corner. It didn't sound logical. He questioned Dode considerably as to whether he might be mistaken. Dode had been having a few too many drinks across the bar, and although he should have brought the letter to Con, he stood his ground, insisting that he knew what the letter said. He was the Dakota manager, so Con shut up.

After a while, Con told me to cut my ten saddle horses from the *remuda,* pack my bed horse and take off for the L7's. I never forgot that mixup, and I thought I would starve to death on that trip!

I was to gather all Matador, H O, 73, Turkey Track, and Sword & Dagger cattle as well as any stock belonging to Indians, of which there were several hundred brands—in short, anything I came across that belonged south in the Cheyenne River reservation I was to cut and hold. From time to time, these cattle would be taken off my hands, as well as the L7's, by cowboys from the owner's outfit and returned to their ranges. In this way, it wasn't necessary for so many cowboys to rep with the L7's, but these other outfits, when they sent a rep to some distant range, performed like service for the Matador and all their neighboring cattlemen, which promoted friendship among them.

I left the Matador wagon early the next morning. It was all of fifty miles out to the Fire Steel Corner. When I got to where the L7's were supposed to be, it was past mid-afternoon, and there was no sign of them. My horses were tired, so I let them graze and rode on six or seven miles to another campground. There wasn't as much as a hoofprint there. I turned back toward another old campground. When I reached it, all was as silent as the first one had been, and there was nothing left for me to do but ride back to where my horses were.

It was night by then, and I was hungry, for my scant breakfast had vanished long ago. I caught my old night horse, Dick, and took my bedroll off his back, hobbled some of the other horses, staked Dick and went to bed.

A cowboy told the time of day by the sun, and the time of night by the stars. Chief among his "timepieces" was the North Star. Next was the Big Dipper. Now here is something which always interested me—Ursa Major, the Big Dipper.

Of the seven stars in the Big Dipper, the most important ones are the two known as Pointers, since they always point to the North Star as they revolve around it. Duhbe, "Greatest Bear," is at the upper right, while the lower one of the pointers is known as Mirack, the loin or lower back of the bear. Who in the world figured that all out?

Anyway, I had plenty of time that night to watch these seven stars and speculate as to why some men called them "Great Bear." And thinking of bear, a good piece of roasted bear meat would have made my stomach feel better.

Next morning, I rode forty miles to the L7 ranch below the forks of North and South Grand River, but on the way, I scouted all of the old campgrounds. I knew before I reached the ranch that the L7's were not in that end of the range at all. Had I but known it, they were then about one hundred miles northwest, diagonally across the range from Fire Steel Corner. They had already made a big circle outside of their own range to catch any stray cattle that might have drifted out there, and were starting work along the Cannonball. But it was some hours before I learned that.

Since I knew the location of the L7 ranch on Grand River, I had no trouble finding it. By then, I was getting really hungry. No one was at the ranch except Mrs. Bird Rose and her little girl. I remembered Mrs. Rose very well, and I had been at the N U N ranch in Texas the night the little girl was born.

I told Mrs. Rose that I had left the Matador wagon the day before and of the ride I had made trying to find the L7 wagon in the southeast corner.

"You must have read the letter wrong," she said and went to Bird's desk to get a copy of it. Sure enough, Con had been right, and Dode had his directions all mixed.

I'd gone without food for thirty-six hours then, and I was ready to eat a raw bear, fur, claws, and all. Mrs. Rose fixed me a light lunch and would allow me to eat only that amount, but a few hours later, she set out a more substantial meal, and by the time I rolled my bed out on the kitchen floor that night, I was as full and contented as ever. I felt a lot different than I had the night before out on Fire Steel Creek, where there was nothing but grass and cattle, coyotes and wolves, hawks and wind, and the stars above me.

Mrs. Rose advised me to stay at the ranch until Bird came home next day, which I did. When he saw me, he remarked that he knew I had not reached the L7 wagon as I should have, and wondered what delayed me. We didn't leave the ranch until the following morning, going directly to the wagon then. Bird had been on a scouting ride through the range, sizing up where the most cattle were running, and other conditions.

I worked up there on the Standing Rock for several weeks before I went back to the Matador with the Drag V steers I had gathered. Bird closed out the L7's that year. They were running three wagons and kept on the jump from daylight until after dark. After all of the winter losses, and without any of the usual incoming cattle the fall before or that spring, the L7's reportedly shipped forty-two thousand cattle.

When shipping was done, the L7 range cleared and turned over to the C7's, I talked to Bird Rose for the last time as he was taking a train out of Evarts. He was one of the best cowmen of the northern ranges.

18. Brand Man

Fall weather came on and the days turned chilly. Although the sun shone brightly, it had a faraway feel, and it headed steadily southward. Old Sol had to go to the end of his orbit before he could swing back toward us again.

I came home from the L7's with seventy-five steers, and then worked with Con's wagon, gathering a beef herd. We met the Sword & Daggers taking a herd across Matador range to ship. Ernest Eidson came to our wagon and discussed range problems with Con. The Daggers were closing out that fall, too, and wanted to be sure they didn't leave cattle in neighboring pastures. Cap Mossman, representing Bloom Cattle Company, was taking over their lease for the Diamond A.

Mossman had dealt for the Sword & Dagger lease and agreed to buy the top one hundred saddle horses for one hundred dollars apiece, and let the cowboys select them. The rest went in the sale for a lower price. He bought the Sword & Dagger wagons and teams, and hired their cowboys.

In order that the range might be stocked early, he had already shipped in several trainloads of little, wild New Mexico yearlings that spring and turned them loose on Sword & Dagger range.

Con decided to send me with Eidson, as I was considered an expert "brand man" by then. I believe I can truthfully say that when I worked a herd for brands I was representing, I left none behind me. I knew every brand and ear mark, and the owner's name, not only on the reservation, but far out to the west and south. Experience is a splendid teacher, but a genuine interest and liking for the work is also a big help.

So I went to the Sword & Daggers for the rest of that fall and saw the last of their herds leave Dakota. Some were shipped from Philip, some from Evarts, and a herd or two went out from Wakpala.

It was the first year that west-of-the-Missouri-River cattlemen could ship from Wakpala, north of Grand River, for with completion of the bridge spanning the Big Muddy, the rails had crossed to the reservation country for the first time. The construction wasn't entirely complete, but it was safe enough for the long trains of livestock to move slowly over the naked trestle. Although most of the shipping still went out from Evarts, crossing over the pontoon bridge built by the Milwaukee Railroad, every fall some herds went to Wakpala to avoid the delay caused when too many herds were due in Evarts at the same time. Crowding was poor business, so the range foremen always kept informed as to when other outfits would be shipping, and from what place.

Johnny Bloom, tall and good-natured nephew of Frank Bloom, was Diamond A manager. He worked with the Sword & Dagger wagon, too, looking after their interests. Since Sword & Daggers were clearing their range, they gathered everything that was fat, and here, for the first time since they had come to Dakota in 1904, we caught some big Matador steers in a roundup. They were the wildest cattle I ever saw. They had come from the Croton River breaks in Texas, where they had escaped from every beef roundup. When the

Dakota lease was opened, cowboys hunted them down, one or two at a time, necked them together, or to a gentle steer, and after exhausting efforts got them to corrals and shipped them to Dakota.

The old steers found each other again in the new pasture and stayed together, as of old, gradually working back into the roughest part of the range, the Goose Creek breaks, almost as rough as those in the Texas country, and once more they easily evaded going to market.

During the cold white fury of the preceding winter, they drifted over to the Sword & Dagger range. We caught them in a drive through one of their haunts, either on Rattlesnake, or on one of the Cottonwoods. Bill Smedley, Sword & Dagger wagon boss, was a crack shot with a revolver. With the old steers in the herd and headed for market, Smedley gave orders that they not be allowed to get away. That if one broke back and a man couldn't rope him, then to shoot a horn off, or anything which would turn him back to the herd.

The first steer to break for it was close to Smedley, and he went after it with all he had. He couldn't turn him, and after the steer had ripped a horn at Smedley's horse, the old cowboy quit fooling with him. His temper aroused, he spurred right up alongside, aimed his gun, shot a little low, and the bullet punctured the horn a short ways from the skull. It evidently shattered the core and the horn dropped down, dangling beside the steer's head. The wild bovine character forgot all about running. He whirled and whirled, round and round, with the horn nearly dragging the ground.

Other cowboys came to help Smedley and they brought the steer back to the herd, but a few nights later he escaped in the dark hours and was never rounded up again. About six others escaped being shipped, but what happened to them I never knew.

The Sword & Dagger settled down to fast work, for they

had a lot of cattle to ship. To complicate the job, the Diamond A yearlings, which were scattered all through the Sword & Dagger range, gave us considerable trouble by getting into a herd. They would burst from a roundup and run out to the cut. Pretty soon, there they came back, perfect nuisances, I thought, as I sat on Greyhound, my good rope horse, between the roundup and the cut. I had a tally book in my hand, and as each steer was cut out, the brand was called and I made the tally.

Ernest Eidson was working in the roundup. His horse, Blue, got tired, and he came out to get me to cut beef awhile. But I told him to take my horse and I'd keep on with the tally.

One of the yearlings made a run from the herd just then, and I headed him back for about the third time. Ernest remarked that they all needed forefooting a few times to give them something else to think about. Johnny Bloom was with us to see that the reckless Sword & Dagger cowboys didn't do much of that—and then it happened!

A crazy little yearling jumped out of the roundup right beside me, and raced over to the cut. Before I knew it, I had forefooted him—caught him by one leg and broke it.

You could hear it pop clear across the roundup. Ernest laughed, so did Johnny Bloom—not because the yearling was crippled, but because of my embarrassment. I had no intention of doing anything but "busting" him, to stop his chasing back and forth.

They called me "Ike the Roper" the rest of the afternoon.

The first herd we gathered after I got to the Sword & Daggers was shipped from Philip, South Dakota.

We had begun rounding up on Cottonwood Creek and worked through the Dagger range to the Cheyenne, forded the river at Red Bull Crossing and turned toward the little town. After shipping out, we went back to the range, but

before we gathered another herd I was to become involved in an incident that could well have had serious results. I learned then that sometimes it is mighty easy to suspect a man, and if some good judgment isn't used much harm can be done.

Bill Smedley was shipping steers he owned with the Sword & Dagger herd, and he decided to go along to Chicago to see them sold. Besides being a salty old wagon boss, Bill was a right lively old gambler, too. He loved the game of Monte. He always had a deck of cards with him and often he played Monte for pastime when things were slack. It was mostly for fun, but at times when some of the cowpunchers would get together and try to break Bill, it would be a hot game—and he usually won.

We had to wait for cars at Philip, and some of Bill's acquaintances came out to the wagon, bringing plenty of money and whisky. Before long, there was a fast Monte game going, with Bill doing the dealing. A lot of money changed hands that night, and Bill wound up choking the top of his buckskin moneybag to keep all his winnings inside. Bill called this bag his Monte bank, and all the cowpunchers had seen it many times, and it was no secret that he kept it among the blankets of his bed. Bill, Ernest, and I slept in the same tepee. Ernest slept with me, and across from us was Bill and his Monte bank. No one ever thought of things being stolen in those days, with a good cow outfit. *The other fellow's stuff was his, and no meddling with it!*

When Bill left for Chicago, he told me to keep track of his bedroll and to sun it when a hot day came along. He said he would catch us on the Cheyenne River when he got back. Eidson stayed with the wagon and the outfit went right on working.

One day, I had a little time to spare, so I unrolled both Bill's bed and mine and let the sun shine on them. I put the Monte bank to one side while I did this. Everyone knew about Bill's winnings. None of us thought twice about it when I rolled the aired bed, moneybag and all, and put it back on the bed wagon, where it stayed all the while he was gone.

We camped on the Cheyenne just below Pedro, where we spent a few days repairing fences along the river. Bill caught us there, stopped awhile, and then went on to camp. That night he opened up his Monte game as usual, but he seemed peevish because he was so short of cash to make change with the players. Since all of us knew about his moneybag, I asked him: "Where's your Monte bank?"

He gave me a sharp look, and a sharper answer. "You should know where it is, you sunned my bed while I was gone."

The way he said that sure set me back on my heels, and for a while I didn't say anything, but I sure felt jumpy. The more I thought about it, the more irritated I was, until I shot a question at him.

"What do you mean about that moneybag, Bill?"

He looked me square in the eye, "My Monte bank's gone."

The other men had suspected something was wrong, but no one knew the bag was missing. Now they all knew the money was gone and the finger pointed straight out at me.

I knew as well as anyone that Bill was a tough hombre when riled, and a thing like this could make him mean. I recalled I had scarcely glanced at Bill's bedroll since I had sunned it as a favor to him, and I sure didn't like the insinuation that I might have taken the money. I got up from the game, and in the dead silence around the blanket, Ernest Eidson told Bill that he *"might as well accuse me [Eidson] of taking the bag, too,"* because he, and everyone else, for that matter, knew where it was. He said that he had helped me sun the bed and that the buckskin bag was sure put back into it. Eidson was a man with whom it was equally unsafe to meddle when he was aroused. What he said across the Monte blanket, and the look of him, slowed up anything further just then.

I was all for rolling my bed, taking my horses, and going home to my own outfit. I told Eidson I intended to get out in the morning but he said, "No, just hold onto your britches awhile. You didn't take the money any more than I did, but someone sure as hell did, and we'll find out who. It won't hurt you to shoulder the blame for the moment."

I squirmed and seethed, but decided to stay on and see what happened. Next morning, Bill and Eidson rode away together, after the boys were busy on the fence work. I didn't guess it at the time, but the two of them were making medicine and trying to figure out, since it had to be someone with the outfit, who the guilty man might be. The night before, Eidson had eyed the men around the Monte game just as sharply as Bill had eyed me. While every eye was on Bill and me, Eidson was searching their faces, and he believed he had spotted the guilty man.

Eidson and Smedley just "happened" to go by a little store in a nearby town. They both knew that a young fellow who had just started working for the Sword & Dagger owed a good-sized bill to the storekeeper. When they discovered the boy had recently paid up in full, that clinched the case as far as Bill was concerned.

They both bought a few things, and then suddenly Bill remembered that he "needed a lot of change for his Monte games." He gave the store man a fifty-dollar bill and asked for all the quarters, half-dollars, nickles, and dimes that he could spare.

Bill had handled the Monte bank money so many times he fairly knew the feel of it, and the boys who were losing, or perhaps winning now and then, had scratched little marks on the coins to see if they'd ever get them back. Or they marked a lucky handful of coins, hoping to be lucky again.

BRAND MAN 267

Some had a brand or an initial on them. One slick dime even had my own name scratched on it.

When the two men got out on the creek again, they rolled the change out and looked it over. The little country store did a small business, and it had been a short time since the money disappeared. Their guess was right! In that heap of coins was just about every piece of marked money that had been in the original sackful!

When Bill got back to the men, he rode up to the scoundrel, got off his horse, pulled his .38 automatic from its scabbard, and without saying a word knocked the young fellow down with it. When he got up, he knocked him down again. Then he told him in short, profane words that he stole the money sack and that he would have but a few short minutes to get his stuff together and get out of the outfit. Bill promised to kill him if he didn't dig the money up, and threatened the same if he ever caught him on the Sword & Dagger lease again. And all the while, he held him by the nape of the neck, his pistol in his hand, ready to whack him again if he as much as looked like denying it!

The young man admitted taking the money, declaring that neither the storekeeper nor anyone else had anything to do with it, and if Bill would let him go he'd return it. While he held him prisoner, Bill told him that he had nearly caused an innocent man to get the treatment he was getting, and that probably someone would have died over it.

By sundown, the man was gone. Most of the cowpunchers witnessed the incident, but one of them who didn't saw the fellow leaving, saw his swollen and blackened face. Astonished, he asked, "What happened to you?" He got a short answer, "I got into trouble with Bill."

That was the way the early-day cattlemen dealt with a thief—no court, no fooling. Men were their own judge and jury, and justice, right or wrong, was meted out swiftly and forcefully. In this case, the culprit was certainly punished according to what the judge believed. Bill was severe, but such treatment usually made an honest man out of a crook.

And after that, Bill always treated me most considerately, showing in many wordless ways that he was sorry he had come so near blaming me. He told me that the way I looked at him across the Monte blanket uprooted his suspicion of me. But I have always believed that the affair might never have ended that way, were it not for my friend Ernest Eidson.

This incident made me think of something that occurred shortly before my father died. He was buying and branding steers near our ranch in Texas when a strange thing happened that, if he hadn't seen it, would have thrown suspicion on someone.

While working, he hung his vest on the corral. In one of the pockets was seventeen hundred dollars in greenbacks. In those days, cattlemen carried money instead of checkbooks. A yearling wandered by, nosed over the vest, spied the bit of green and licked it out of the pocket. My Dad looked around just in time to see the last of the roll going down the yearling's throat. They caught the steer, and Dad rammed his hand inside his throat and recovered part of the money, but they had to kill the yearling to get the rest of it.

That fall, the Sword & Daggers shipped the biggest herd ever to leave reservation leases—three thousand head. This herd was tallied as it was gathered, and the number of cattle in each brand recorded. That they counted out exactly when loaded at Wakpala speaks well for the efficiency of the Dagger cowboys.

Many reps came to the Sword & Daggers, partly because they were closing out, and partly because of the hard winter before. Men were still looking for stock that had drifted with the blizzards.

Beginning on the Cheyenne, about 125 miles from the shipping point, gathering everything that was fleshy, regardless of age, we worked northwest across the Dagger range, almost to the Eagle Butte, which was just outside their fence in the Turkey Track range. When the herd was ready to go, it was sure a big one to move all in one piece. The usual herd of about twelve hundred head made four hundred cattle to a trainload. We grazed the cattle along slowly, perhaps ten miles a day, reaching the Wakpala stockyards without mishap.

But the drive was not without incident. Before we left the Sword & Dagger range, we had a fracas with a buffalo bull, branded Circle D, which belonged to the breed Indian, Pete Du Pris. During a last big buffalo hunt on Grand River in 1880, he had roped five buffalo calves and hauled them home to the Cheyenne. He branded them and turned them loose with his cattle. Eventually, they made a large herd, and when Du Pris died, Scotty Philip bought the entire herd from the estate and took them to his own ranch near Pierre. But there were a few old renegade bulls left in the Sword & Dagger range, and we had considerable buffalo trouble all the time.

The huge, bewhiskered monarchs would go to a watering place for a drink, then stand around it for hours. If they happened to be in the path of a beef herd, there was certain to be a disturbance, perhaps even a stampede, unless the cattle were kept away from the water until the surly buffalo moved on. Steers were afraid of them, and the buffalo seemed to know it. They delighted in marching across the prairie toward a beef herd, even if they had to angle a little to get the steers directly in their path. Without turning to right or to left, they waded right through, scattering the whole works. A scrambled herd was just the cowboy's hard luck!

Saddle horses and Indian teams were as fearful of the buffalo as were cattle; in fact, everything on the range gave ground to these big creatures. One bull became more and more sullen the older he got, and finally he acquired a great liking for gates—just any gate—and once he took his stand be-

side one he would stay there for hours. If anything approached him, he presented a belligerent, vicious mood that
caused animals and men to shy around him.

As the big herd approached what was called the Sword &
Dagger gate, which opened into the Turkey Track range,
Joe Stanley, piloting the roundup wagons, came upon this
mean buffalo bull holding forth there in his most pugilistic
manner. If there ever was a tough-looking stack of hide and
hair, it's a buffalo bull on the fight! He appeared so dangerous that Stanley turned back down the four-wire fence, going
to another gate, rather than cut the wires to get by the buffalo peacefully.

There were so many reps with the Sword & Daggers at that
time, besides their regular men, that not all of them were
needed to drive the herd. Those of us who would go on night
guard, seven or eight men, were jogging along up in front
with Ernest Eidson, expecting to sleep awhile after the noon
meal, in anticipation of the night job. When we saw Stanley
loping along the fence, coming back, with the two roundup
wagons trailing and their teams in a lope, too, all of us galloped toward him to see what was wrong.

Stanley saw us and turned our way.

"What's the matter?" Ernest asked.

Stan cussed a little and declared that the buffalo bull had
the other gate and that he was really on the fight, that it
seemed best to go around him. "That buffalo is mean and
won't budge a foot."

Ernest rode over and opened the cowboy box on the chuck
wagon, reached in and got his .38 Colt automatic. "He'll
move over when I get there," he said; "we've tip-toed around
those sonsabitches too long." He spurred the slim bay horse,
Hatchet, right out to the lead, waved at the wagon drivers,
and they swung their teams around to follow him. We all
went along to see the fun. Hatchet was afraid of the buffalo,
too, but he carried Ernest right up to him.

When this sour-souled buffalo bull saw the horseman loping right toward him without the hesitation he expected, he
gave forth with a mighty roar in his chin whiskers. And then,
as he prepared for all-out war, he not only pawed the virgin
prairie and lowered his spike-horned head to give ugly little
upward rips, indicating the death toss, but he got down on
his knees and gouged the side of his head and one horn into
the ground; he rolled his frame far up onto his neck, first one
side, then the other; he put a lot of weight on his neck; he
roared and blowed off and snuffed dirt from his nostrils; and
to show his utter contempt for the oncoming enemy, he
swung his hind end around toward Ernest. As he gouged the
prairie with his foreparts, he must necessarily stick his posterior right up in the air. It was while in this position of deep
scorn and insult that the first blast of the .38 caught him
somewhere in the region that was heisted highest.

He must have sustained a rough shock in spite of his thick
hide, for he jerked his horn out of the ground and looked
around. The next blast got him up off his knees. With the
third, he curled his short tail up over his back and turned
on a blast of his own. He dashed away from there in a fast,
lumbering gallop. With every crack of the .38, he blowed
dust and mucus from his nose, and tightened his speed. A regular alkali dust storm followed his flying heels as he charged
out over the flat, topped a hill, and went from sight. The
roundup wagons came on through the gate, the *remuda* and
the big herd also passed through with no interruption—and
the big buffalo with the Circle D on his hide was considerably
less belligerent from then on.

As we passed the spot where the town of Eagle Butte now
stands and turned toward the Moreau, intending to water
the steers there and then bed them in the big horseshoe bend
of that river, just below the mouth of Green Grass Creek,
we met a group of United States soldiers. They told us they
were guarding a band of Ute Indians on that very spot. They

talked with Ernest awhile and asked him to turn his herd aside so that they would by-pass the Ute camp.

It seemed that they had moved the Utes in from the West, intending to cut off the Green Grass region of the Sioux reservation to make a separate reservation for them. The officer in charge said that this band of Utes were particularly restless and troublesome and were then in an ugly mood, far from satisfied with the new arrangement. "Anything," he told us, "could happen, with possible gunfire, which might stampede the herd." It was a risk the Daggers didn't want to take, so we swung off our usual trail and crossed the Moreau where later the bridge spanned the river on the Timber Lake–Eagle Butte highway.

A few of us rode up to take a look at the Utes. They were sure-enough a rough-looking band, but gave no trouble that I ever heard of. They seemed as curious about us as we were about them. The Indian Department didn't settle them there at Green Grass after all, and it was reported that they were eventually taken back West, to where they came from.

19. Trouble at the Matador

As we drove the big Sword & Dagger herd to Wakpala on the Standing Rock reservation, we had to cross the Strip. The L7's, with so many cattle to ship that fall, were going to both Evarts and Wakpala, whichever place could provide stock cars when needed. Here we met Oliver Rose riding out to meet an L7 herd.

I knew Oliver very well. When he rode over and said, "Did you know you were fired?" I thought he was joking, so I grinned and answered, "No, I didn't. Who fired me?" But I could see by his face that there was more to it than that, and his next words nearly knocked me off my horse.

"Murdo MacKenzie came to Evarts and fired the whole Matador outfit!" Oliver said.

I was so dumbfounded I just sat there looking at him. I couldn't think of anything I had done to be fired for, so I said, "I guess I'll just keep on working until someone tells me to turn in my horses and get my check."

Had anyone but Oliver brought the news, I would have

called him a liar, but I knew Oliver wouldn't pass along idle talk. I asked him what about Dode and Con.

"Dode is gone," he said. "Con and Dode and all of their men were drunk. They have been staying drunk all fall and somehow Murdo got wind of it. He came into Evarts unexpectedly and found the Matador outfit in bad shape. He cleaned house then and there. Con is gone, too. Joe Lackey and Jim Burr are in Evarts. Jim is acting in Dode's place, and Lackey is range foreman and wagon boss."

James R. Burr was bookkeeper and Joe Lackey was wagon boss from Alamocitas ranch in Texas.

Roy Vivian was repping with the Turkey Tracks, so I figured he wasn't in on the deal, any more than I was. But I believed that Dode had actually been the cause of it all. He set the pace and Con had been foolish enough to go along with the drinking. Liquor was Con's only fault, and now it had gotten him fired. I was sure a troubled cowboy that night.

It seemed as if everything that I had faith in had toppled. The Matador had been home to me almost since I left my folks to work for the cattle outfits—and now Con and all the boys I had worked with would be gone, or so I thought then.

As it turned out, I wasn't fired. Several of the old hands were still Matador men. Murdo had fired only those who had been, in his opinion, the really irresponsible men.

But it wasn't until later, after I went home to Texas, that I learned from Frank Mitchell just how it all happened. Mitchell had received a letter from a responsible man in Evarts, Hugh Chittick, advising him of the miserable situation in the Matador outfit—shipping neglected, men carousing and loafing around, too much drinking were the main complaints, with something of a report on other things which had occurred, and which were Matador affairs.

When Mitchell got the letter, he was so agitated, and knew that Murdo would really be hit hard, that for several hours he withheld the letter from him. But finally he decided that he must give it to him, which he did, turning away so that he might not witness how deeply this fine old Scot was hurt. As far as Murdo was concerned, Dode was perfect. He either didn't know or wouldn't believe that his beloved son wasn't all he had hoped—that he was irresponsible and a drunkard. Dode was capable when he let drink alone, and perhaps that is what Murdo clung to.

As he read the letter from Dakota, he wept great, salty tears wrung from the very heart of a great man. But even so, he didn't weaken. He didn't hesitate in making his decision. He hurriedly packed his grip and ordered a fleet ranch team to take him to the fastest train to Dakota.

"Jim Burr and Joe Lackey are to follow me to Dakota immediately, Frank," Murdo said to Mitchell as he headed north and sped down on Evarts without the warning telegram he usually sent in advance of his arrival.

He found things in Dakota even worse than he expected. Not only was Dode drunk, but he was sick. Murdo bundled him off to Hot Springs, Arkansas, without delay for the doctoring he needed. But he didn't remove Dode from his position, even though he had failed him. He still tried to cover up his son's weakness, and he contrived to have the main responsibilities handled by Jim Burr. To have done anything different would have been impossible for Murdo, loyal old Scot that he was, yet he could not entirely hide his disappointment and grief.

After Dode left, Murdo fired his men, one by one, as he came upon them. When he found Con, it is said that the two of them, who had known each other so long, sat down on the hotel steps and Murdo paid Con off. Both had tears in their eyes. Liquor and nothing else had been the cause of it all.

Con left Evarts. He swore off liquor which had led him by the nose for so long, and some years later he was back at his old job in Dakota—wagon boss and range foreman—closing out the Matadors.

When Jim Burr and Joe Lackey arrived in Evarts, they began reorganizing. Joe hired another crew of cowboys and took over the range work. Jim became assistant manager and did all of the bookkeeping. He attended to Matador affairs and wrote all the checks. Although Dode came back to Dakota from time to time, and to all appearances was still Matador manager and did sign the checks, it was actually Jim Burr who controlled the Matador finances. At times our checks were delayed for a week or two until Dode got in to sign them. He spent his time around the ranch or in town, wherever he pleased, for it wouldn't be like his father to deprive him of all duties. Regardless of all Dode's shortcomings, he was well liked. His generosity and sympathy rode high above his personal faults.

It had been a policy with the Matador that when any of the men stayed in the north three years, they were entitled to a trip home, if they desired. Dode had promise me, months before, that I could go home for Christmas after the fall roundups were over, and I was looking forward to it.

Roy Vivian had quit the Matador and had gone to the Sword & Daggers because he didn't like Joe Lackey. He went out with the last Sword & Dagger herd, on the first leg of his journey back to Texas to work for Frank Mitchell as wagon boss at Alamocitas.

When I went back to the Matador headquarters with my horses, it seemed strange not to see Con there. Even Walker Krump had gone south by then, as he did every year after the roundups were over. I began to think of starting for Texas, too, although I intended coming back to Dakota.

Joe Lackey had been wagon boss at Alamocitas, and here in Dakota he took over easily in Con's place and things went along smoothly, for Joe was capable and experienced.

Somehow, Dode had kept Charley Brown from getting fired during his father's housecleaning job.

Although I was coming back after my visit with the home folks, Jim Burr and Lackey tried to talk me out of leaving. But I had looked forward to the trip and wanted to go. Dode got into it and said that he had promised me that I could go after fall work. So that helped, and eventually I turned my horses out, rolled my bed, sacked my saddle, and went to Evarts to take the train.

Little did I think then that I would never see Dode again, that tragedy would strike the Matadors in Dakota more than once before I came back, or that when I did return it would be from far north of here. So, I departed on my holiday with a light heart.

Christmas in Texas! I'd half forgotten what a mild winter was like, without deep snow and below-zero temperatures. I was homesick for Dakota, deep snow and all. Dakota was home to me now, so after the holidays I prepared to start north.

Before I left, I got a letter from Murdo MacKenzie telling me that Frank Mitchell wanted to see me at the Alamocitas ranch.

When I got there, I found that Roy Vivian had been hurt. He had roped a bull that jerked his horse down, and Mitchell wanted Roy to go home to rest and get well. Frank would have it no other way than that I run the Matador roundup wagon in Roy's place. I didn't want to stay in Texas, but Roy needed considerable time to recover, and I couldn't run out when I was needed.

I took the wagon until the Pig Pen outfit on the Texas–New-Mexico line began gathering three thousand big steers from their range southwest of Alamocitas. Mitchell sent me over there to rep with that work and Ira Stoughbaugh took over the Matador wagon.

I wasn't with the Pig Pens very long until Ernest Spears came to take my place. He told me to leave my horses, but to take my personal belongings and go back to Alamocitas. Much mystified, I saddled up and pulled out.

Murdo was there when I arrived, and before long, I knew he was sending me to Canada with three trainloads of cattle —3061 head. I was to run the wagon in Canada, where Dave Somerville was manager. Murdo made me promise to stay at least two seasons. I was a little skeptical about Canada, but I'd heard of the big lease up there already stocked with thousands of cattle, so I headed for Canada. Theodore Green and two men went along to help with the cattle. Green was a good hand and intended to work for the Matadors in Canada, too.

The cattle destined for Canada were coming from the Matador's Lower Ranch in Motley County, and would entrain from Estelline, Texas. I went there with a letter from Murdo to John MacBain, his brother-in-law, who was assistant general manager of the Matador empire in the United States.

The cattle trains left Estelline a few hours apart, and I went with the lead. MacKenzie and MacBain caught up with us in Sioux City, and as each trainload came in we worked the weak and thin cattle into separate corrals. When we finished with all three trains, we had one train of thin stock. These were held in Sioux City and fed for three days.

After the required time to rest and feed the cattle, we again loaded the first train. The next stop would be Velva, North Dakota. I went with the lead again, and Green was to come with the second train. MacKenzie and MacBain left us there and went on to the Dakota ranch.

We were on the road for eleven days and had a downpour every day but one. I got a new slicker at Estelline, and by the time I got to Canada the paint was beginning to slip.

At Velva we unloaded again. The stockyards were poor,

far too small to hold a thousand cattle, and were knee-deep in mud, so I turned everything outside. They were eager to hit the ground. They grazed, watered, and rested as much as the soggy earth would let them, while I hired every horse and man the livery stable could supply as well as every kid who owned a horse and saddle, to keep cattle on the ground controlled by the railroad.

As the time came to move on, we began penning and loading. John MacBain caught up with me there. He put his belongings in the caboose and helped with the loading. He was not afraid to get a little dirty. If there was work to do, he would help. As we were pulling out, heading for Portal, the gateway to Canada, the second train from Sioux City was just coming into Velva.

As the train picked up speed, I went to the corner of the caboose, where there was a place to wash up. I cleaned the mud from my face and hands and reached for a towel hanging there. The brakeman stepped up, snatched it away, and said, "That's not for *you!* That belongs to *us.*"

I didn't answer, but started fumbling in my hip pocket for my handkerchief. MacBain, who was sitting nearby, had heard what the brakeman said. He jumped to his feet, opened his grip and pulled out a big, white towel. "Here, Ernest, use this. This is *our* towel!" (None of the Scotsmen, MacKenzie, MacBain, or Somerville, called me by my nickname, Ike.)

The trainman glared at us, but he was too thick-headed to heed a warning. He sat down and glowered but said nothing further until I asked him, since this was the last run before reaching Canada, to punch my contract, which would make it good as a ticket if I needed it for the return trip.

It was customary to use a regular punch on these papers, but the trainmen had been refusing to do it for the Matador cowboys, and this one didn't intend to, either. He fairly barked his refusal. MacBain stood up and asked him to punch the pass, but the brakeman was just as short with Johnny as he was with me.

"What the hell business is it of yours?" he demanded. *"Who do you think you are—*giving *me* orders?"

Then Johnny MacBain went to work on him! The words rolled off his tongue like quicksilver off a platter, and although he burred his *r*'s in deep Scots accent, he was plainly understood.

"I'm John MacBain, general bookkeeper and assistant general manager of the Matador Land & Cattle Company, Dundee, Scotland! Who are *you? Give me your name!"* Johnny reached inside his coat and brought out a small book and pencil. "Give me your name, I say!" he repeated, as the brakeman stood there dumbfounded.

MacBain continued, "You railroaders up on this end of the line have a habit of running it over our men. I'll see to it that it doesn't happen after this!"

The brakeman squirmed. The Matadors were big shippers whose business was valued by the railroads, and he knew he was as good as fired if MacBain reported this incident. He was utterly surprised that this top man of a big cattle company was riding in the dirty little caboose like a common cowboy. In a way, it was comical to see such an overbearing individual put in his place. He begged John not to report him —that he had a family and needed his job. With all his bluster gone, he was indeed a sad-looking creature.

MacBain was adamant, though, and let him squirm. He demanded that he punch the contract and when the fellow protested that one reason he didn't was because he had no punch with which to do it, MacBain gave him a pencil and told him to punch it with that.

"If you have neither punch nor pencil, use a nail or anything else that will make a hole!" he demanded.

The man gladly complied and asked again that he not be reported. Eventually, Johnny let him off the hook and told him he would skip it this time, but warned him never to be discourteous to a Matador man again. The brakeman promised to cooperate henceforth, and the Matador cowboys had less trouble on the run from Velva to Portal after that.

At Portal, we had to have our belongings inspected, as well as the shipping papers for the stock, and that's when we met another "wise one."

Frank Mitchell told us to take along a big supply of tobacco, an item which was hard to get as well as expensive, in Canada. So I had a two-year supply of Bull Durham rolled in my bed. At that time, there were hay racks built all along the inside of the cattle cars, and I had put my bedroll in one of them, safe above trampling hoofs. I had to get it out and unroll it for the inspector.

This official had been confiscating anything he wanted from the cowboys as they went through with cattle, and right away, he pounced on my tobacco. "Can't take that across the line," he growled.

Once again, John MacBain came to my rescue. "Why not?" he demanded. "His tobacco is for personal use." Johnny stood eye to eye with Mr. Inspector, and after a right salty speech, won again—and I rolled my tobacco back in my bedroll, tied it up good and tight, and dropped it back in the hayrack.

John went on with the cattle to Waldeck, Canada, but he sent me back to Velva on a fast train to take over in Green's place while Green went back to meet the train of weak stock coming in from Sioux City. It was still raining and as nasty as ever.

I loaded out again at Velva, and MacBain had backtracked to meet us at Portal. When we got there, he went on with the cattle, while I again turned back to help Green with the train of thin ones. They were certainly a pitiful-looking sight. Several were dead in the cars. We got everything out on the ground at Velva, but some were too weak to get more than a few steps away from the train. However, feed and rest helped them considerably, and they were in much better shape when reloaded. When they got to Waldeck, we held them on good grass until they gained strength to travel to the ranch on the Saskatchewan, where they soon looked different.

It is notable that all livestock, once acclimated to the cold weather, mature to bigger animals on the northern pastures. I remember my surprise when I saw a fine-looking horse at the ranch. He looked so familiar I thought I knew him. Sure enough, I had broken him in Texas, and because he was so sorry and scrubby-looking I named him Last Chance. He still had the name, but he had developed and filled out to twice his former size.

The Matador Canadian range of more than a half-million acres was situated in a bend on the north side of the mighty Saskatchewan. This river, one-half to a full mile wide and flowing eight miles an hour, formed part of the boundary. Because of severe climate, the Matador shipped nothing but two-year-old steers to Canada to be double-wintered there and sold as four-year-old beef.

The steers for fall shipment were summer-ranged in the 108 section fenced beef pasture lying closest to the ranch headquarters eight miles northeast and downriver from Saskatchewan Landing.

There were no bridges over this stream. Cattle had to swim it, and here was considered the best place to cross herds. Although the river widened out to a mile across, it split into two channels. Along the north bank the stream ran fairly shallow for three hundred yards to the deep, swift first channel; gradually, then, it leveled off to a wide sandbar where, according to the season, water was but five to eight feet deep. Then it dropped again into the wider, swifter channel that ended in a stretch of shallow water along the south shore.

When the weather turned warm, grass grew amazingly fast. Besides their fenced beef pasture, the Matador had outside range extending seventy miles to the north. We kept the roundup wagon camped out there all of the time until beef work started, and we rode the outside line of this unfenced range to keep cattle turned back. There was just one big lake or marsh after another out there, and mosquitoes hatched by the million. Cattle walked into the wind, to protect themselves from the stinging hordes, and many times I've come across a wide trail through the lush, stirrup-high grass, and followed ten or fifteen—even twenty-five—miles after stock that were facing the wind, before I caught and turned them back.

Of all the yarns about giant mosquitoes and the vicious attacks credited to them, I doubt if any can top the actual story of these pests in Canada. They hid in the grass by day, and every evening the vicious tormentors took to their wings.

Horses suffered most, and we had to build smoke-smudges to partly relieve their misery. The horse wrangler mowed heavy slough grass, raked it, and hauled it to the smudge corral to make the smoke needed to rout the insects. The smudge had to be enclosed, for the horses were so crazed by the mosquitoes they would actually step into the fire in an effort to free themselves.

To make the smudge, a big fire was built in the corral. After it was going good, green grass was heaped on it, choking it down to great billowing smoke-clouds. When the first smoke rose from the corral, horses saw it and came loping in, knowing that it would drive the biting millions off them. Some of the horses were so covered with mosquitoes, their stingers driven down to blood and their bodies gorged, that in brushing against other horses, they crushed them in masses, leaving big bloody spots on their hair. A white or light-colored dun was a strange looking horse with all the smashed insects and blood plastered on him. If they rolled to rid themselves of pests, the blood was muddied and matted on their bodies. South Dakota had a lot of mosquitoes, especially in rainy seasons, but nothing like Canada.

We were glad when beef shipping time approached, for then we rounded up all the stock from the range which wasn't under fence and put them in the north end of the beef pasture, from which the big steers had been moved, to the pasture next to the river. The big steers going to market would have to swim the Saskatchewan before they made the sixty-mile trek to the shipping point at Waldeck.

When we cut the first two hundred fifty steers from the thousand head and drove them down to the Saskatchewan, we crowded them right out into the water. I took the lead on Water Dog to point the first steers toward swimming water and the farther shore. Once they were well lined out, men in boats kept them going, and when the leaders began to swim they kept right on. Water Dog liked to work with cattle in water, and he would become so interested in what he was doing that he paid little attention to his rider. In fact, he loved to swim, and that day he performed a swimming feat that holds the horse record as far as I am concerned.

I hadn't noticed how far we were from shore until suddenly everything hit the deep water of the first channel. Dave Somerville, who was in one of the boats, seeing Water Dog drop into the channel, fearing he would attempt the dangerous swim with me, shouted: "Turn back!"

In the excitement of swift water, crowding steers, an unruly horse anxious to make the trip, and trying to hear what Dave said, I pulled the reins which will (and did) sink a horse. A horse pulled and sunk in that way is very apt to be rolled over and over by the swift water and drowned—often both man and horse drowned.

But not Water Dog. He came to the surface twenty feet away but I came up among the steers, fortunately near the edge. I wrapped an arm around a big steer's neck and hung to his horn with the other hand. The spooked steer lunged around among the others, ducked both of us several times without losing me, then he lit out swimming for all he was worth. All around us, the river was solid with steer horns and heads.

The canoemen tried repeatedly to reach me, but every time a boat got close, the steers would hit the light craft, knocking it back, and the fast current carried it downstream before one finally edged close enough for me to let my steer go and swim to it.

A steer just naturally swims faster than most horses, as a usual thing—but not Water Dog! He beat the steers across and climbed the shore.

Boatmen led him back and a few hours later I was again pointing two hundred steers into the stream, and again riding the same horse. Water Dog would not be turned from what he was doing and once more he dropped off into the first channel.

The watching boatmen saw it happen, and that time paddled right up beside us. I slipped off the horse when he wouldn't turn back, and swam beside him on the downstream side, holding to him until the boat got close, then went to it. But Water Dog swam powerfully on and would have taken me safely across. As it was, he led the steers again, and boatmen brought him back to the north shore once more, which made his fourth trip that day!

Good river horses were seldom used except to swim herds —other than to keep them in stout condition—so Water Dog was supposed to stay at the ranch when his work was finished. But when he saw the saddle horse *remuda* loping down to the river to go across (the roundup wagons crossed by barge) Water Dog quit the horses in the pasture and galloped down to the *remuda*. He splashed through the shallow water, ignored the boatmen, took the lead of the other horses, and led the way for his fifth "Saskatchewan swim" that day!

We didn't send him back any more. Water Dog had shown that he knew what to do about crossing herds in swift water; he'd lead the way, riderless if necessary. So we let him make the trip with the *remuda* to the shipping point at Waldeck, Canada.

Water Dog wasn't a very likable horse in lots of ways. He was a leggy, flea-bitten gray and was mean to kick until he got in water above his hocks. Then he didn't care what a man did. He'd blow up his belly and swim. You could hang to his tail, swim beside him, or grab hold of him any old way —it didn't matter. He'd take you along and never look back, but you'd better watch out when he came to shallow water! Regardless of that, as a river horse, he was one of the best.

When the last herd was on board cars at Waldeck, going to Winnipeg to take the boat, Mr. Spears offered to pay me to go across to England with them to see that they were well cared for. It would have been a grand trip, and I still wonder how those big, wild steers acted, tied to a manger and hand-fed, you might say. It must have taken stout timbers to hold them, and I'd like to have watched while each of them had a halter put on his head. I surely wanted to go with them, but Somerville didn't want me to go, so I turned back to the ranch and we began preparations for winter work.

I had thought Dakota was cold, but it was nothing in comparison to the real cold of Canada. The Matadors put up tons and tons of hay for winter feeding. Several men were employed to haul hay to cattle that were going into the winter in rather poor shape. We had a busy fall, fixing barns for saddle horses and making the house snug at Bone Pile Camp.

One day, Dave Somerville got a telegram which brought the tragic news that Dode MacKenzie had been killed in Le Beau, South Dakota. It is the only time I can remember being extremely shocked. I couldn't believe it. It seemed incredible that anyone wanted to kill Dode. We were both young when our trails parted in Dakota—and now I would never see him again.

Dave began hastily finishing his book work for the year just ending. He left signed checks for wages and other things, gave me the keys to the desk and to his office so I could give the men their checks and attend to what needed doing until he returned. He packed his grips and drove Dan and Bennie to Swift Current, where he left them in the livery barn. Then he took the train to go to Dode's funeral. After that, he made a trip to Scotland and I didn't see him again until February.

It was near the end of the big cattle empires on the northern ranges that Dode MacKenzie, son of Murdo, was shot to death in Le Beau, South Dakota. It was one of the saddest and most wantonly cruel shootings of those wild cattle-kingdom days—one that many of us old cowboys believe sounded the deep-toned death knell for the frontier shipping point of Le Beau, on the east bluffs above the Missouri. Dode was shot in the Phil Du Fran saloon. It was a chilly December morning in 1909 and Le Beau was in a festive mood for the Christmas holidays when Dode, manager of the Matador Land and Cattle Company, was killed by a fellow he had befriended many times.

Le Beau was one of the oldest trading posts in central South Dakota, started by the black-bearded Frenchman, Antoine Le Beau, in 1875. For a time, due to railroads bypassing Le Beau, the town died out. Years later, a branch line of the M & St. L ran a spur out to it and the town built up again. Old buildings took on new life and new enterprises, and at one time the town boasted sixty buildings. Historians point to the revived Le Beau as one of the largest shipping points for cattle from west of the Missouri, once it got a railroad connection. The livestock industry was the backbone of both old and new Le Beau.

There were various stories of the shooting of David G.

(Dode) MacKenzie. The killer claimed self-defense as his reason. Walter MacDonald, who stood next to Dode and saw Bud Stephens shoot him full of lead, told me about it. He said that Dode had not even hinted harm to Bud.

It is true that Dode wore a gun. Everyone wore a gun in those days if he wanted to, but Dode made no attempt to use it, even after he was shot. Whatever he may have said to the man was of a rough, rollicky nature such as was Dode's custom with all, for he was a friendly man. His one weakness was drink, but even then, he wasn't mean.

Bud Stephen must never have lived to see the day he could forget the look on the face of the man he had always called friend, as he lifted both hands to his chest where the first bullet tore into him. Yet Bud Stephens pumped two more bullets into Dode's back as he staggered out of the saloon. He stumbled to the street, collapsed, and died in Ambrose Benoist's arms. Doctor's opinion was that he might have survived the first shot, but that the second and third, which tore into his back, finished him, showing Bud's grim determination to deal him death.

With the trial and someone's heavy purse behind him, for certainly Bud Stephens had no money, he was cleared. There were few who agreed with the verdict. Everyone knew that Bud's claim of fear of Dode was false. And the pale hand of retribution even then began spreading the shroud, as ghostly wings hovered above the lusty, hard-bitten river town, decreeing its doom.

A few months after Dode died in her streets, the first lethal blow fell upon Le Beau. Fire started on Main Street and raced through most of her business section—a loss estimated at two hundred thousand dollars.

Half-heartedly, as though now fully aware that the day of reckoning was near, the town struggled to survive. By then, whether they foresaw the encroachment of the homesteader with his plows and barbed-wire fences spelling the end of the big cattle spreads on the reservation, or whether their lease could not be renewed profitably, no one knows, the Matador began pulling out of the Dakota range. Certainly no Matador herd ever again entrained from Le Beau stockyards. No Matador cowboy ever again trod her streets in the same friendliness as before. All of us knew the deep personal grief our chief, Murdo MacKenzie, had suffered over his beloved David—Dode—good cowboy and always one of us, regardless of his position as Murdo's son. And we stayed away from Le Beau!

What was left of Le Beau after the first fire was wiped out by a second fire a few months later, and after that she ceased to exist—only in caved-in cellars, crumbling sidewalks, and broken brick, all of it weed-grown and lonely. Even the railroad tracks were pulled up. Nothing remains.

The phantoms of memory have had it since then—except for the little wild rodents scurrying here and there. Each spring, rain and gentle breezes beckon native flowers and grasses to life, as in the past. Summer heat browns the hills and dries the streams. Wintry blasts and heavy snowstorms rage over the old ghost town with the same ferocity. Between the solid shores, the great muddy Missouri rolls on past the high banks at the mouth of Swan Creek, the same as it did centuries before Le Beau ever existed.

Dode MacKenzie was buried in Trinidad, Colorado. I was still in Canada when I saw Murdo for the first time after Dode's death. He was a heartbroken man. He came toward me saying, "How are you, Er-r-nest—" rolling his *r*'s in his deep Scots way. While we shook hands, Murdo's eyes filled with tears, both of us remembering Dode and the affection we held for him. We spoke no word of the tragedy, yet each of us knew what was in the heart of the other. My own eyes misted as Murdo turned aside to hide his emotion, for he couldn't talk. And I got on my horse to ride out and corral the saddle horses.

20. Back to Dakota

I began looking forward to going back to Dakota just as soon as beef shipping was over, and one day I got a letter from Jim Burr, Dakota manager since Dode MacKenzie's death. He knew I was leaving Canada that fall and asked me to come back and take my old string of horses. It sounded good to me, so I told him I would. Theodore Green left Canada the same time I did, but he went on back to Texas.

When I reached Dakota, after being away only three summers, it seemed strange to see the towns springing up west of the Missouri, and homesteaders building shacks, barns, fences, and plowing up land where shortly before it had taken a permit from the Indian Department to cross the Missouri to Indian country. White people were swarming all over the old reservation range, and it could mean but one thing: the big outfits must go. Here was the first step to turn the last of the Indian's buffalo grass to the farmer and his plow—the end of the era of big herds and wide grasslands in the north. It wasn't a farmer's land; it belonged to cattle

land, but there it was—the move which cradled the beginning
of the dust bowl in later years.

Someday, some of us would see the old Missouri held in
check by a giant dam—Oahe Dam—see its dark waters spreading over old landmarks, river crossings, roundup grounds.
Old Indian places, churches, cemeteries—all these would be
gone forever. Once again the big river would hold all that
came within her grasp—but perhaps bringing a vastly richer
way of life to this ages-old land of the buffalo grass.

In his letter to me, Jim Burr spoke of a contemplated
change of range boss and said I was in line for it. Joe Lackey,
who was range boss when I went to Canada, had been sick
since before Dode was killed. The first attack he had came
after getting extremely hot fighting a prairie fire. He was sitting on his horse watching the fire and resting when suddenly
he toppled to the ground in a sort of fit. The Matador sent
him everywhere for doctoring but he grew steadily worse.
Finally, they took him home to Texas and put him in a hospital there, close to his people. It was Matador policy to take
care of their employees, and to pay their salary during illness.

When I returned to the Matador in South Dakota, I found
that they had changed headquarters again, to the Alec
Landreaux place, farther away from Evarts than Ambrose's
place, where our second headquarters was.

One day, a livery rig from Evarts drove into the yard and
who should step out of it, happy as a lark, but Joe Lackey.
He wasn't the big, rugged man I had known, but he seemed
well enough, and so happy to be back. He unloaded a fine
new saddle, blankets, chaps. He had several hats, pants, and
new boots; gloves, coats, and a good bedroll. He had saved
his paychecks during his illness, so he had enough money
to make one more effort at cowboy life, until suddenly his
old trouble attacked him again. The exertion had been too
much, and he was stricken severely. We put him to bed, and

Jim sent out to the wagon for Dick Holder, one of the cowboys, to come in and help care for Joe.

Alec Landreaux was a squaw man, and his home was nearby. The Matador had taken over his big two-story log structure and built him a nice little home, since his family was nearly all grown and married. Alec had suffered from an old injury for years. When he was young, he had been cutting down a tree. It didn't fall immediately, so he hit it once more, which caused it to bounce off the stump, and the jagged end landed squarely on Alec's toes.

Finally, after all these years, he had to have his leg amputated at the knee, and at the time Joe became ill there was a trained nurse with Alec continually. Jim Burr made arrangements for her to come over once a day and oversee Joe's care until his folks could come for him.

In Texas, they had been searching everywhere for Joe until his brother thought of wiring Jim Burr, and found out that, sure enough, Joe had come home to Dakota. When the brother arrived, he said gently, "You'll have to come back to the hospital, Joe." Joe broke down and cried like a baby. He begged to remain in Dakota, but, in the end, he knew he must go back to Texas. I pulled his new boots on his feet for him, and if there was ever a brokenhearted cowboy who realized he could no longer carry on, it was Joe. He had taken one last fling at cowboy life, but I think he knew when he left us that his days were numbered. He died shortly after he got back to Texas.

About then, the Matador sent for Con McMurry, Ernest Eidson, and of course, I was already there. We were to come to some decision as to a new range boss. None of us thought that Con was available, but when he actually came, we were glad to see him. Ernest and I had a little talk and backed out of any part of it. We believed that both Murdo and Jim were sorry that Con had been away from the Matador so long and would be most happy to put him back in his old place.

This suited both of us, and we informed Jim about it. So Con came back to his old job and stayed with the Matador until the end. I went back to riding broncs, and Eidson went to another job he had been offered.

Winter came on and I stayed at the Landreaux place. I rode pretty salty horses and looked after stock, water holes, and wolf work. One day I rode out to get a fat cow in to butcher. I had to bring her right down a lane and was having good luck getting her in without heating her up any, when we met Jim Burr and his dog, Boomer. They were standing under a little tree, waiting to see the cow penned.

The cow took one look and bolted. She almost ran over me, and hard as I tried to head her, she got away. She would be too heated up to kill then, so I rode on down the lane to the corral. On the way, I passed Jim. He asked me why I didn't pen the cow. I was mad. "No one could pen a wild cow with a damn Scotchman and a bulldog standing right in the way," I said.

Jim went on toward the house, but he suddenly stopped and called to me. "Ike," he said, "I do not mind being called a *damned Scotchman,* but I'll have you know that *Boomer is not a bulldog.* He's a pedigreed *Scotch terrier!"* With that, Jim turned away. "Come, Boomer," he said, and the two of them walked to the house in a most dignified manner, leaving me thoroughly squelched by the witty Jim Burr.

Alec Landreaux' wife, Moli Ciqa (Little Mollie), had been raised in a buffalo-hide tepee by her grandparents, Swift Cloud and his squaw. She remembered the days of the buffalo and the deer and antelope that long ago ran everywhere on the prairies and river bottoms. Little Mollie was a member of the Sioux tribe and was born south of Pierre. She married the young Canadian Frenchman, Alec Landreaux, Indian custom in 1875. Later they were remarried at Ft. Pierre in 1879 by Rev. G. D. Crocker, post chaplain. She lived to be a hundred and two, and left nearly one hundred descendants. She had ten grandsons and one grandaughter in the armed forces in World War II.

Moli Ciqa was one hundred years old and blind when I saw her last, but she remembered me. I couldn't forget her, either, for whenever I had a beef to butcher at the Landreaux place, she got sharp knives and came to help. She was an expert.

It makes little difference how many broncs a man has topped off, or with what degree of success he has ridden some of the meanest; if he keeps at it long enough, he is certain to meet one that will outsmart, out-figure, out-struggle, out-outlaw, and out-best him any way he goes. And nothing more arouses a man's anger than to get on a bronc he cannot ride, or if he does win a temporary victory, he can do little else but keep an eye on his mount, doing slack and unsatisfactory work because of an unruly horse. If a horse bucks now and then to rid his system of accumulated orneriness, he can be tolerated, but one that paws, kicks, bites, bucks for pure obstinate pleasure and intent to do harm, never earns the grass he eats.

Widow Maker was my nemesis! He was one of those really snaky horses riders love to tell about. He was a dark bay Colorado horse, branded Open A 4, connected, left thigh.

Widow Maker bucked ferociously and with all he had. He was one horse I could not ride. His hide was as loose as a steer's and would roll with his action. You'd think the saddle was coming off, sure! He never did throw me off completely, but only because some other rider was handy to pull his head up, just in the nick of time to keep him from pitching me overboard and high-tailing it for tall timber with my saddle. Everyone with the outfit who was considered a tight rider had tried him, but the story was the same—down he came. And Widow Maker ran off with the saddle.

I was the last man to get him. If I ever did manage to stay on board and got headed out to do some work, about all I could do was to pamper and watch him the whole time, for he seldom overlooked a chance to pitch a man over his head.

Only once did he do me a favor and not buck when by all rights I expected it. It was one mean, cold morning. It had been rainy and muddy, then turned colder and snowed a lot. Our ropes were crusted with mud and snow. I threw a loop out into the *remuda,* intending it for another horse, and who should stick his head in the loop but Widow Maker! For some unaccountable reason, I had no trouble with him. He didn't offer to buck at all—but the next time I rode him, he made up for it and kept me sitting on edge all day!

It was during the first spring days of the year I returned from Canada that Widow Maker and I parted for all time. I had ridden out to gather in the saddle horses from the range. They had all been turned out to rustle grass and rest through the winter. It was nearly April, roundup time was near, and the weather was nasty. I found a mixed bunch of Indian and Matador horses, and Widow Maker was among them.

When I rode up, Widow Maker tossed his head, raised his tail, curled it, waved it around over his hips, snorting and prancing all around me. He was the hatefulest sight in horseflesh I ever saw, and I knew I was going to have to put up with him, for no one else could, or would, even try. I thought how utterly useless as a saddle horse he was! He wouldn't even do for a circle horse, and some of the craziest horses I'd known made good, long-winded circle horses.

I rode around him and tried to take him in, but he swung away from me. I thought I'd cut him out and leave him out there, but he wouldn't do that, either. He swept in ahead of the horses I was driving, to lead them off in a different direction, and I rode hard to "bend" them.

After a while, I quit running the bunch and they slowed down. I slipped around them, while off to one side Widow

Maker pranced and coaxed the others to follow him. He snorted to the high dome of Heaven forty times—putting fear into the others.

I eyed him awhile and made a decision. I eased my gun out, edged slowly around as close to him as I could get, and shot him! He dropped without a sign or the bat of an eyelash! Widow Maker's troubles with me were over—and so were mine with him! I left him lying there on the prairie and went to camp with the rest of the horses. The last I saw of him, his dark bay hide blended with the clump of wild plum bushes he had been standing near when I shot him.

When the snow left that spring, I had quite a few new horses for the cowboys and one day I drove them out to the roundup wagon for Con to distribute as he saw fit.

One was a black horse from the Pig Pen ranch in Colorado. He was a hot-headed horse and inclined to buck. Dick Holder got him and had ridden him some. But one morning something happened just after Dick mounted him to go on circle that day. They were but a few hundred feet from the wagon when the black bronc blew up, bucked like a scalded hound, threw Dick full length on the sod, and got away with the saddle and bridle, leaving Dick afoot. One or two men made a run after the horse, intending to head him back toward Dick, but he only put on more speed. Thinking he might stop if left alone, these men let him go, rather than keep after him until he ran clear out of the country. But the Pig Pen black didn't stop running as long as anyone could see him—just held to a swift lope, getting a little faster, it seemed, until he disappeared from sight.

There was never any report of anyone seeing this horse, even though the whole region was alerted to watch for him. There was general supposition that the dragging reins had finally become entangled in brush and had stopped him, that someone had stripped the Frazier saddle from his back, pulled off his bridle, and let him go free.

We all watched every celebration where people gathered, hoping that the saddle would show up, and once the search appeared ended when an Indian's horse was discovered at one of these places wearing a Frazier saddle. It was the same make and number, same slick leather, metal horn, metal tabs on the skirt corners, but Dick knew when he saw it that it wasn't his rig because once, when a horse bucked him off, his spur had dug across the seat of his saddle, leaving a deep spur track.

The mystery remained unsolved until late that fall when a horse and saddle were found tangled in driftwood on a sandbar in the Missouri, approximately thirty-five miles from the point where the Pig Pen black was believed to have hit the river.

A man knowing horses could easily reconstruct the picture. A hot-blooded horse, mad, scared, and fanning the breeze wide open, will often run himself to death. By the time he had run fourteen miles to the Missouri, he became crazed, and apparently didn't see or notice his surroundings, exhausted and unaware of danger.

At the time, the Missouri was running bank-full in the June rise, and when the still-traveling, winded horse reached the river, not really seeing it, he plunged in. The silt-loaded waters tumbled him over and over until he drowned, carrying him on downstream, where he finally lodged among tree limbs buried in a sand bar, where he remained under water until the river reached low levels late in the season.

That fall when he was found, the sheriff was notified. Investigation identified the horse as the Matador Pig Pen black, and the saddle and bridle which he was still wearing belonged to Dick Holder. All of the riding gear had been under water so long that when exposed to sun and air, the leather cracked. Dick went to see it, but sold the whole outfit—saddle,

bridle, and blankets—to a farm kid for twenty-five dollars.

Once more the big stream grasped and held that which came its way, and its dark waters hurried on, the Pig Pen black incident barely a ripple in its long history.

After I had my broncs going pretty good, I went to the roundup wagon to work. We had gathered a herd of two thousand heifers and were holding them on Bear Neckless Creek. The Matador had decided to spay this young she-stock, but it was something new, then, as far as range work went, and not many men could do the veterinary work. Fred Barthold was the closest spayer, and he lived away west on Thunder Butte Creek, a tributary of the upper Moreau. His fee was twenty-five cents a head, and the Matador wanted him to do the work.

Because mail was slow, Jim Burr wanted me to ride out there horseback with a letter for Fred, telling him the heifers were ready and where to find the herd.

At four A.M. on Memorial Day, I left the Matador ranch six miles east of Promise, riding Champagnee, a big, blaze-faced, stocking-legged brown horse named for the Sioux word meaning wagon. He was a long-winded, easy riding mount, ready for anything. He was the kind that could be saddled to make a heartbreaking journey without warning, and never did he fail. Champagnee was shod all around and grain-fed, one of the winter horses, and had been ridden at the ranch after spring came.

Taking the Indian wagon road that wound westward along the Moreau, I reached Green Grass Creek before noon, just above where the Timber Lake–Eagle Butte highway bridge later crossed the Moreau River. I watered Champagnee and let him graze a while before starting on. We reached the end of the ride about five P.M., a distance that Barthold estimated to be ninety miles as the crow flies, but all of a hundred or more counting the winding twists of the river road.

At his ranch, I was told that Fred had gone out to his other ranch, fifteen miles farther on. I rode one of his horses on out there and found him. He commented briefly: "Two thousand head is a pretty large order." When we got back to his ranch, it made a good 130 miles for me that day.

Barthold had plenty of saddle horses, but all of them were fat and soft from idleness, making them unfit for a ride of that distance, so I decided to ride Champagnee on the return trip.

By three A.M. next day we had ridden seventy-five miles and were back inside Matador pasture, where we stayed all night at one of their west-side cow camps.

Champagnee had traveled 185 miles or more since dawn the day before. He was tired, but far from exhausted. I left him on pasture to rest, and the next day I rode another Matador horse.

We left the line camp early and headed for the Matador wagon on Bear Neckless. The work of spaying began about noon, with no chute or corrals. The heifers were roped and thrown, with their left side up. Ropes on the two front feet and the right hind foot, snubbed to the saddle horns, held each heifer in a stretched-out position, but leaving the left leg free. Barthold made the spaying incision just in front of the hip bone, angling down a little toward the flank.

As soon as he finished with a heifer, she was turned loose on the range. Cowboys had another one stretched out for the operation. There was no delay. Barthold went from one heifer to another, doing swift, competent work.

Spaying paid off when both steers and heifers were run in the same range. These heifers got very fat, and being rounder and smoother finished than steers, brought a steer price on the market when four-year-olds.

It was shortly after my trip out to Barthold's that I talked to that old master trickster, Charley Brown. He was staying in one of the line camps, keeping cattle inside Matador fences, and he told me of a big, sullen squaw of another reservation who owned hundreds of horses. Her man was French. When he died, she employed a little white man who had worked for him, and promptly named him Ce-sli Ci-ga-la, Sioux words used contemptuously, meaning "little defecate."

She hated white people, but was wise enough to know the white man savvied the business end of her ranch operations. She objected to her children adopting white-man ways and once, so they said, she was greatly angered when her daughters bought fine furniture for their new ranch home. She refused to leave her tepee for the "white-man house" excepting to stalk in one day with an axe. Before she left, she had chopped, hacked, and beat every piece of the new furniture.

At times, she had Ce-sli Ci-ga-la drive her rig and take her where she wanted to go. But if she became angered en route, she would get out of the wagon and lay on the ground until she got over her mad spell, while all the man could do was wait for her. The Indian woman possessed a huge frame. She was both tall and wide. When she flopped down on the prairie, she made a heap about the size of a buffalo—and she was just about as short-tempered!

Old Charley Brown told me that one day when he was in their region he spotted them on a high ridge, the Indian woman down on the ground, the man sitting on the wagon, waiting. Charley rode over to see what was wrong. The squaw saw him coming, pulled her shawl up over her head, and stayed where she was.

"What's wrong? She sick?" Charley indicated the heap on the ground.

"Nah! She's just sulled [mad]."

Charley looked her over and says: "It might be a good thing to get rid of a sullen critter like that."

The other man grunted.

"I'll shoot her," Charley said, "I'll blow her up, if you say the word."

Ce-sli Ci-ga-la grunted again and looked at Charley. "Guess it might be a good idea."

"I'll shoot her," Charley promised, "if you won't ever tell I did it. Wolves and coyotes will eat her in a few days and pack her bones off. No one will ever find her. No one will know what became of her." Well he knew the Indian woman understood him.

"Won't tell," the man in the wagon promised.

Charley pulled out his gun, spun the cylinder, clicked the hammer up and down on an empty chamber. "Just got three bullets," he said, "but that ought to do it." He shifted in his saddle. "I'll count to three. Never like to shoot too fast. One—" There came stirrings under the shawl and the Indian woman looked out.

"Two—" She rolled up on her hands and knees. She was taking no chances with a despised white man!

"Three—" She was on her feet and getting into the rig, and that was that! Ce-sli Ci-ga-la drove off and Charley Brown went on his way.

21. Homesteader

As summer came on, now and then one of the Matador horses would be missing. Since these horses were not all handled daily, but allowed to run on the range until needed, it was some time before we knew for sure that they were gone from Matador country.

A Bar, a brown horse; Whitney, a big bay that Joe Lackey was riding when he had his first attack of illness; Charley Tigner, a horse Dode was so fond of; Roy, a gray that had a big amber splotch on one shoulder which looked like someone had spit tobacco juice on him; several Straight 50 horses the Matador raised; Little Hanover, so named because he looked like Con's horse, Big Hanover—all of these and many more were missing.

The Matador was very particular about horses. If it was but one, not even a really good one, either, that was missing, they went all out to find him. And these horses were some of the best.

Before long, word came in that Matador horses had been seen away out in the Montana country. Murdo and Jim decided that I was to go out there and work with the big horse outfits. It seemed the best way to see all horses belonging to many owners. I had broken the most of the Matador *remuda*, so it was logical that I should be the one to hunt them. Jim Burr gave me a letter authorizing me to act for the Matador in any way I deemed best to recover the horses, if I found them. I rolled my bed, sacked my saddle, and took a train for Miles City, Montana. I didn't wait around long before I was hired by one of the biggest horse owners out there, Johnny Ramer.

Out in the then unpopulated Pumpkin, Sand, Mizpah, and Hercules creeks and Powder River country in Montana was a vast grassland known as "wild horse country." It extended far beyond this region mentioned, a perfect setup for a horse range.

In that scope of wild pasture were many big ranchers who owned cattle in addition to thousands of horses. Colt branding and gelding the two-year-old studs was a big job every summer when the horse roundup got under way. These horsemen ran a roundup wagon the same as cow outfits did; they rounded up a region and held the horses together the same as in cattle work, while reps and others cut for strays, for young studs to castrate, and for colts to brand. Usually the horses were corralled while branding and gelding was done. Big horse corrals were a part of the open range equipment, and thousands of horses were taken care of every year.

John Ramer's headquarters were on Sand Creek. His brand was an A, reverse 7, connected, on the left jaw. His wife branded the same, only on the right jaw. Ramer ran three thousand Percherons in addition to several hundred thoroughbreds.

After I got somewhat acquainted, Ramer sent me and one of the men who took care of his studs to the Cross S to work with the horse roundup. Bill Anderson was the Cross S manager, and Hank Dykes was range boss of this English-owned outfit. They had mostly Shire horses and thoroughbreds, which make a good cross, if one doesn't mind the hair on their legs.

The Cross S horse runners rode good mounts. It was while running horses in their rough Hercules Creek country that I got the "wild" tacked onto my nickname Ike, and it stayed with me all the while I was in Montana.

I had an A7 horse in my string. He threw other men off as regularly as they got on him, so they gave him to me to ride. He was a big, long-legged gray with splotches of red hair on him. He was sired by Ramer's imported thorough-bred stud, Proper, and he could run like hell! I took him along to the Cross S horse work.

One morning, the man who came with me from Ramer's, pretending he was afraid the horse would get away from the Cross S wrangler and go home, insisted that I ride him. When the horse *remuda* was corralled about sunup, the man roped the gray for me, and since he was top man with the Ramer spread, I didn't argue. I knew I could ride him, even if Ramer's rep didn't think so.

It had rained during the night—a poor time to ride a mean horse—but one of the horse runners eared him down while I saddled and got on him. Meanwhile, this friendly fellow stood near, telling me I couldn't ride the gray.

When I hit the saddle, the horse turned on and bucked pretty rough. He slipped down once, but I'd had enough to know that I could ride him easy.

"Don't brag," the Ramer horseman said. In fact, he smarted off considerable about my riding and seemed to hold some grudge against me. He was all for seeing me get bucked off and probably break my neck, so he insisted, "Let him out of this wet corral; he'll show you a few tricks!" When they opened the gate and the gray saw daylight, out we went, and

as we swept through I knew I intended to give him as much competition as he gave me.

Hank Dykes, a big man from Texas, who was one of the men hearing all the remarks, yelled at me as we cleared the gate: "Hope you work that hoss over plenty! Ramer hasn't a man that can ride him!"

The gray wasn't slow about giving me all he had in him. He couldn't budge me, and I spurred him from neck to hips, so much so that Ramer's man howled about my spur tracks on the gray bronc.

It was then that he and Hank Dykes got into it. They had a hot argument about it, and Dykes said, "Shut up! You've tried to promote trouble and a nasty accident here this morning, and I've had enough of it." I didn't hear all of the talk, but the man cut his string of horses and went back to Ramer's ranch.

As I had figured, if one could ride the gray, he would be a plumb good one to run horses on, for he fairly cut a hole in the wind! He was powerful, long-winded, and he liked to run.

One morning we jumped fifty horses near Hercules Pass. If they beat a rider to the pass, they would be gone to the badland country, where it was nearly impossible to get them out. I was riding the gray thoroughbred and stood a chance to head them if I let him go, so I gave him his head. We were fairly skimming the ground when right in front of us loomed a badland cutbank gulch, twenty feet across and fifteen feet to the bottom! The horse band, knowing the country, had cut around it by crossing lower down.

I had no intention of trying to jump the gulch, but the gray did. He took the bit and never slacked up. He raised in the air in the longest jump I ever experienced or had ever seen up to then! I thought my time had come for sure, but he cleared it with room to spare, and drove on to head the wild ones in the pass.

I turned the bunch three times in the pass before Dykes got to me. He cut in, took them from me when I whirled them once more, and turned them toward the other horse runners riding in from all sides. Eventually, and after a lot of hard riding, the band was corralled and the outlaw, bunch-quitter leaders that gave so much trouble swinging away from the main band and would not be penned, teaching others this aggravating trick, were roped and "kneed," especially one old mare, the nemesis of the horse roundup. A cord is cut in the leg, below the knee, which prevents the animal from running with the old swiftness.

When Bill Anderson, Cross S manager, watching through his field glasses from a pinnacle afar off, saw my horse make the long jump over the cutbank gulch, and saw the gray and me bending the wild ones in the pass, he commented to the man with him, "Look at that 'Wild Ike' ride!" The "wild" was added to Ike that day, and stuck.

After the horse work on the Cross S Range, Dykes sent a man along, and I took the Ramer horses I had gathered back to his ranch. I found no trace of Matador horses in the Cross S country, nor in Ramer's, so I quit and went to the L O's where I got a job breaking broncs, and batched with a kid at their horse camp on Bobcat Creek. He had a string of broncs to ride, too—and he also had a mandolin! He spent so much time with it he was pretty slow with the colts. When I had a bunch ready for the boss, his were only half-ready. It irritated me when he picked that mandolin instead of keeping up his share of camp chores.

Usually, in the heat of day, after the noon meal, I'd try to snatch a few winks of sleep before the afternoon riding. By then, the kid, who had napped while I cooked and washed dishes, was ready for his music lesson, and it would be "plink —ting-a-ling, plunk—tang-a-lang" until, coupled with fly annoyance, I'd give up and go to work.

One day when I had to skip my nap, a bright, happy

thought came to me. *I'd buy the mandolin!* I sat up on my bunk, rubbed my eyes, looked as pleased as I possibly could, and asked if I could try to play it. The kid handed over the little music box, and I plink—ting-a-linged, plunk—tang-a-langed, and then gave her a few fast jerks of my own idea of music, rattling all the strings at one time, good and loud!

"Right purty," I said.

"Yep! Maybe you could learn to play it someday," he said, but he looked skeptical.

"Would you sell the mandolin?" I asked.

He lifted his brows speculatively and thought awhile. "Guess I might," he said, and I knew he figured on playing it too, with me as the new owner.

"What'll you take for it?"

"Oh-h-h, 'bout three dollars will do. I can buy another when I get to Miles City."

I dug around in my pockets and fished out three dollars, which my camp partner took and put deep in his pockets.

I got up, reached for my hat, and went out the door plink —ting-a-linging, all the way to some big posts, a part of the old hitch rack that had once stood in front of the camp. I wrapped the little mandolin around one of them until it was a mangled, splintered wreck!

Man, was the young fellow fighting mad about that! We nearly had a battle over it. He declared that had he even suspected such treachery, he would never have sold the mandolin. But during our hostilities, we came to an understanding— that he was to help around camp, fifty-fifty. He found more time for his colts and things got better all the time. He was a good kid, and long years afterward I had a letter from him.

He apparently thought he was writing to someone, perhaps related to me, for he assumed I had been dead for forty years. He spoke of my riding. Referring to it, he said: "The things Ike could do with horses were positively uncanny." I often wonder if he still plays the mandolin, or if the affair out on Bobcat spoiled his ambition.

After a while, I worked with the L O horse roundup and got to see thousands of horses belonging to many big horse outfits in that region. At last, I began to find Matador horses. I didn't say anything about it when I spotted one. I could scarcely keep from whooping when I saw Tignor, A Bar, and Little Hanover show up. I felt pretty sure that they would all be caught in these roundups. I noticed that they were cut into the stray bunch, and then later they were put in the *remuda*.

There was a rule that stray horses were not to be ridden, that they were to be held in the stray pasture and the owners notified. I waited until I knew that the Matador horses had all been gathered before I made any move that would let others know I was looking for them. Who brought the horses out there, I never knew. Nor did I hear anyone claim them. Some of them were turned in the saddle *remuda*, and I believe that eventually someone would have ridden them.

But I was ready to go home, now, so one morning when the horses were corralled and others were catching mounts, I roped Tignor and put my saddle on him.

When the wagon boss, "Bones" Drinkerd, saw me saddling Tignor, he protested and informed me I was to turn him loose.

"Not this horse," I said, and got on him. It was like finding an old friend. Charley Tignor had come to me in a string of broncs from the Lewis place in Texas, three miles west of Alamocitas, early in 1904. He was not a Straight 50 horse, as I have heard men claim. He came from Colorado and was branded Pig Pen.

After he was gentled, Dode MacKenzie had taken him. He was a natural cow horse, but Dode didn't ride him much. Others rode him after I went to South Dakota, and later, when Dode came to Dakota, he brought Tignor and A Bar along. I rode Tignor again in Dakota and worked him in the roundups.

So that morning at the L O corrals, I wasn't about to give him up. I told Bones that I was a Matador man and had come out to find Matador horses that were missing, that I knew all of them were in the stray pasture or *remuda,* and that I wanted them.

The wagon boss said, "You will have to show your authority for that." So I went to my bedroll and got Jim Burr's letter. After that, there wasn't any more argument. Bones commented that he had suspected I was a Matador man when he saw a letter that came to me from Dakota. It was from Jim, who had forgotten to use a plain envelope instead of one with Matador Land and Cattle Company heading.

We cut the Matador horses from the stray pasture. I packed my bed on one of them and headed for Dakota. I kept Tignor and A Bar in my string when I got back.

After I returned from Montana, I went to Con's wagon. The Matadors were shipping beef then, and I rode Tignor and A Bar to cut fat stock from our roundups. Con had always let me do a lot of that work, and it was a pleasure to get off a bronc and ride a good cutting horse in a roundup. Joe Lackey had ridden Tignor while I was in Canada, so he wasn't rusty by any means. Lackey was a good man in a roundup, and his horses had to be, too. Dode always liked to watch Tignor work cattle, and I think Murdo was glad to see me riding him again when he came to our beef herd at Dog Buttes, as we were going in to ship from Trail City.

This was the last time I was to see Murdo. He was going to Brazil to head the giant concern, the Brazil Land, Cattle and Packing Company. The very size of the venture attracted MacKenzie, finally, after the men financing it had been after him for months. John MacBain, long MacKenzie's assistant manager and general bookkeeper, would take over management of the Matador. Jim Burr was going with MacKenzie as his bookkeeper and assistant. Other men who had worked for the Matador for years were going along, too, to become managers of the numerous divisions in the huge Brazil range.

When Murdo came out to the beef herd at Dog Buttes that fall day, he called me aside and asked me to go with him to Brazil. He said that each man could take two horses from the Matador *remuda*—and right there I told him I wanted to take Charley Tignor and A Bar, for I was sure I was going with him. So that was agreed on.

When our last shipment of beef went to Chicago that fall, Charley Tignor and A Bar went with them. From Chicago they were shipped to Alamocitas ranch, after which they went to Galveston, Texas, to take the boat. Murdo bought six hundred purebred Hereford heifers from the Matador, and six hundred more from the King ranch, in Texas, for the Brazil outfit. He believed that since these heifers were already used to hot country, they would suffer less while becoming acclimated in Brazil. Tignor and A Bar went with these cattle.

After MacKenzie left Dakota, I began to think seriously about going to Brazil. Perhaps it was the stories we heard of the big snakes in that country, lying in wait on a tree limb, ready to pounce down on anything going along underneath. Perhaps it was the war clouds already looming over Europe—or maybe it was just that I liked Dakota and hesitated to leave the United States. Anyway, I delayed going, and afterwards I was glad, excepting that Tignor and A Bar had gone on. I knew I'd miss them, but the Matador had other good ones that I rode whenever I wanted to. Con was still with the Dakota spread, and some of the other old hands were still around.

As it turned out, the First World War broke out in Europe and dealt a hard blow to the Brazil enterprise. It didn't reach the scope MacKenzie had envisioned for it. Some of the

Matador men came back to the States after a few years, and Murdo returned, also.

When Jim Burr left Dakota to go to Brazil, new Matador management took over on the reservation. New men came to Dakota from Texas, and a lot of changes took place. Things didn't go along as smoothly as they had, partly because the new men didn't understand the winters Dakota had, and the importance of keeping stock in the protected regions along the rivers. Above all, they wanted to do things their way, even if they did run into difficulties.

The riders were particularly sure of themselves, especially one comical, cocky little puncher who just couldn't believe he could be thrown. He wanted a certain horse, named Mildred, to ride. I had broken him, and Jim Burr named him for a girl he knew. I knew Mildred would be too salty for this little guy and told him so, but he insisted he could ride anything I could—until he mounted this sorrel. Mildred threw him high as a kite, three times in a row, and that ended the argument.

The horse Rollers was still in the *remuda,* mean as ever. Charlie Frazier, a young fellow I knew, came to the Matador to work, and we were standing near the rope corral when the wrangler penned the *remuda.* Charlie asked me about the horses. Knowing that he might possibly get Rollers in his string—for Frazier was a good rider—I pointed him out and said, "Be careful about him. He pitches high and throws himself."

I hadn't said anything about Charlie being unable to ride Rollers, but one of the new bosses who was standing a few feet away, cut me off short, "Charlie can ride that horse if *you* can!"

No one said anything further, but I had warned Charlie, and later, I was glad I did.

Sure enough, Rollers was roped for Charlie—perhaps to

show me. Rollers made no fuss about being saddled—he never did. But when Charlie mounted, Rollers made the rolling racket in his nostrils and blowed up. He pitched higher and higher, and Charlie was riding him fine, but from the very peak of a high jump, Rollers fell—hard and deliberately. And Charlie's leg snapped. Within twenty minutes after my warning, Rollers had given him a broken leg.

That was the last time Rollers was ridden, and I was glad of it. Both he and Danger were broke to harness, and though they had to be watched for kicking, they made a stout team and did lots of work.

Rather rapidly now, the Matador began closing their leases. The winter of 1911–12 was a tough one in Dakota and stock didn't do well. When beef roundup time approached, the Canadian ranch needed men, so several of us were sent there to help. Then the outfit in Canada moved to Fort Belknap Indian reservation in Montana, and I came back to Dakota. It wasn't long until the South Dakota spread was moved to Fort Belknap.

About this time, John MacBain died, and Murdo MacKenzie, free of his Brazil venture, became head of the Matador again. News trickled through to us that Murdo, keenly disappointed because so many of the old Matador cowboys in Dakota were gone, discharged the one he held responsible for "scattering the Matador outfit to the four winds."

Later on, the Fort Belknap lease expired and the Matador went to Pine Ridge reservation, in South Dakota.

When the big cattle outfits pulled out, the homesteader crowded their heels. He filled the old range with little homes, fields, and small herds of a different kind of cattle. Gone were the wild steers and cowboys. The fences along both sides of the Strip were sold to homesteaders who tore them down to enclose their places.

Many of those I knew and worked with on the old cattle ranges of the north have gone to the Happy Hunting Grounds, along with Moli Ciqa. The old cow town of Evarts is but a memory now, buried in a grainfield. A lake not far away has been named for it. That is all. The half-century has changed many old landmarks and places.

My old pacing night horse, Dick, remained behind when the Matador pulled out. I rode him so much, and we went through so many experiences with him beside me or under my saddle that he, to me, was almost human. He was ever a horse of character.

Dick was afraid of ice, especially with all the grinding, crunching noise it makes breaking up. Sometimes I'd ride him along the Moreau river bottom just above the forks where it joins the Missouri, in plain hearing of the moving ice. Suddenly I'd turn him right down the trail toward the crossing, as if I intended to go on over, just to see him cut up. He was so nervous it was pitiful, and how he ever came to drown in an airhole will always mystify me.

It happened long after Dick's days with me. He had been given to Ambrose Benoist's little girls to ride.

One winter, sharp-shod, Dick walked out on the Missouri ice to an airhole that looked like a little lake. He apparently didn't sense the danger, was probably thirsty and went to get a drink. The ice gave way under him, he dropped into the airhole and was drowned, which ended the life of one of the most useful old cowhorses a cowboy ever rode.

I didn't leave Dakota with the Matador. My thoughts turned to a ranch of my own. I bought land on the Little Moreau, in the former Matador range. It included the old beaver dam, where we had turned the first herd of Matador yearlings loose on the new lease in 1904. The whole west-river country was settling up by then, and out on the old

Trail, I discovered a black-haired, gray-eyed girl who held my interest—and still does. I married Clara Condon, and we moved to the Little Moreau, where we ranched and raised a girl and two boys.

My kids were privileged to learn to ride on a Sword & Dagger cowhorse that Cap Mossman claimed as his private mount when he came to his Dakota range—Papoose, a gruya with black points. Though he came from tough Spanish stock, he was extremely gentle with his young riders. He lived to be twenty-six years old.

With the smothering dust and drouth of the thirties, I drifted on west, like the old gray wolf, following the cattle trail. I kept the herds in sight. Not the vast herds I grew up with, on the wide, fenceless ranges I once knew, but as measured today, they were big cattle concerns, and I never strayed far from them.

The steers I watch over now are good Herefords, behind wire fences. The broncs I ride are gentle, but active. I still enjoy stock work. With grandkids to listen to my yarns, I expect to keep a good cowhorse under me and a saddle rope in my hand until I, too, reach the Great Roundup.